National health policy and the underserved
ETHNIC MINORITIES, WOMEN, AND THE ELDERLY

D0908907

Issues and problems in health care

Paul R. Torrens, M.D., M.P.H., Series editor

School of Public Health,
University of California,
Los Angeles

National health policy and the underserved

ETHNIC MINORITIES, WOMEN, AND THE ELDERLY

Jerry L. Weaver, Ph.D.

Department of Political Science,
University of California,
Los Angeles, California

Saint Louis

The C. V. Mosby Company

1976

Copyright © 1976 by The C. V. Mosby Company

Printed in the United States of America

Distributed in Great Britain by Henry Kimpton, London

Library of Congress Cataloging in Publication Data

Weaver, Jerry L
    National health policy and the underserved:
ethnic minorities, women, and the elderly.

    (Issues and problems in health care)
    Bibliography: p.
    1. Medical policy—United States. 2. Minorities—
Medical care—United States. 3. Women's health
services—United States. 4. Aged—Medical care—
United States. I. Title.
RA395.A3W4   362.1   76-6955
ISBN 0-8016-5360-6

TS/M/M 9 8 7 6 5 4 3 2 1

For Dora

Preface

On being handed the following work in manuscript form, a colleague of mine scanned the title page and the table of contents, looked up over his eyeglasses, and inquired, "But what are you, a political scientist, doing writing about *health?*" I wish that I had had the presence of mind to reply that in the provision and utilization of personal health services are many of the classic foci of my discipline: interest groups, politicians, mass versus elite confrontations, the competition of rival ideologies, partisan appeals for electoral support, and, most essentially, the struggle to win control over government decision making. From the physician's examining room to congressional committee rooms, health care reveals the drama of human beings attempting to use *power.* And the discipline of political science rests squarely on the study of power.

Rather than a conscious effort to bring the tools and perceptions of the political scientist into a little explored region of social concern, this book emerged from a series of chance occurrences, challenges, and a slowly awakening, but rapidly growing fascination with the politics of health.

The chance occurrence arose when a representative of a branch of the Student Health Organization (a group of medical students, interns, and other health workers concerned with redirecting medicine into a broader commitment to community health, the health problems of the disadvantaged, and similar progressive concerns) sought someone to "find out what the Mexican Americans in Orange County know about places to get help." I had lived and conducted survey research in Guatemala, so that both methodologically and culturally the project appealed to me.

The challenge occurred in 1973 when I became involved with a small band of political scientists in the Committee on Health Politics. Under the friendly and skillful prodding of its chairman, Ralph A. Straetz of New York University, the case study of Orange County Chicanos had been the vehicle for thinking about health care as an aspect of political mobilization. Discussions with other Committee members pointed me to health care administration, the legislative struggle for Medicare, formulation of cancer research policy, the contest over national health insurance, and other dimensions of health politics. Several of these topics came together with the establishment of a course entitled The Politics of Health.

This course produced a number of challenges. Asian, Black, and women students asked for examples and data from their communities to compliment an admittedly overrich helping of the Chicano main dish. Without their questions and willingness to search through medical journals, talk with physicians and hospital administrators, and spend their days interviewing and nights coding, punching cards, and interpreting printouts, there would have been no book.

The fascination grew as it became increasingly clear to me that in the arena of national health policy making, in the operation of health care delivery industry, and in the provider/consumer relationship, we witness a ritualized struggle for dominance and advantage among industries, classes, age cohorts, men and women, and ethnic and racial communities. Here, too, is evidenced the stark inequality, injustice, and exploitation inherent in any complex hierarchically organized enterprise. Viewed another way, the provision and utilization of health services offer an opportunity to test the proposition that a multiracial, multiclass, capitalist society can provide a system of social justice through a dynamic interchange between public authority and private capital. Health is such a major personal concern in addition to being a massive economic sector that political decisions related to it are not socially trivial or commercially insignificant. Thus, national health policy provides a singular opportunity to observe the responses of the political elite to the needs and preferences of the masses.

The book itself is directed to four distinct considerations. One is to provide information for individuals concerned with the health care needs and behavior of the underserved: an extensive literature and sizable body of survey data reporting on the Black, Chicano, elderly, Japanese, Pilipino, and female communities are reviewed. This review is not intended to be comprehensive; there are health problems in each community that have been ignored. Rather, the aim is to suggest the range of needs, not to document them fully. A second task is elaboration of the similarities as well as differences among the six target communities. All too often the needs of a particular community or segment in the national population are brought before policy makers and politicians, but no meaningful action is taken. Or we find spokespersons for one community who are attempting to advance their claim by arguing its special or unique importance compared with other claimants, only to be rebuffed by the political partisans of other communities. It is my hope that by comparing a series of disadvantaged, underserved communities, reformers, educators, and policy makers may see the overwhelming magnitude of problems and the common roots of apparently different health needs and preferences among millions of Americans. A third aim is to encourage other social scientists to turn attention on the relationships among populations, economic and political institutions, and the formulation, implementation, and consequences of government actions in the provision of personal health services. The field is wide open for both empirical documentation and the development of heuristic, research, and normative theories. Collaborative projects that team economists, epidemiologists, social psychologists, and cultural anthropologists would be especially useful—and might quickly relegate to a back shelf the results of my poaching in their preserves. The final and perhaps most significant goal of this study is to bring relevant information and interpretations to those concerned with initiating and executing reforms in the delivery of health care services. In striving to this end, I realize that much of the following is speculative, even primitive; future scholarship undoubtedly will redefine the causes and consequences of many diseases and pathologies that I have cited in the book. New problems, priorities, and personalities will bring on the redefinition of community needs and preferences. Organizations and institutes will change. Nor are the conceptualization and analysis upon which my assessments and recommendations rest likely to escape revision. However, I believe that trades must be made between rigor and elegance on the one side, and pertinence and utility on the other, if analyses are to be produced that can escape being blown into a dusty archive by the windstream from social change. The intent of this work is to apply social science techniques and perceptions to a set of major social concerns, and I hope that it is persuasive as well as instructive.

I am indebted to many people for their advice and assistance. Dr. Peter West and Lewis Rosenbaum of the Orange County, California, Student Health Project set in play the series of events that have culminated in these pages. While I have been assisted by almost threescore former and present students, special thanks are given to Robin Morris Nicholson, Barry Johnson, James Allen Constantino, Shirley Komoto, and Susumu Yokoyama. Allyn Sinderbrand read the entire manuscript, and it is better for her intelligent and perspective suggestions. Among my colleagues, J. J. Thompson, June Cooper, and Jay Stevens have given encouragement and useful criticism. But above all, I have had the exceptional good fortune to have known and worked throughout this project with Lloyd Inui, Director of the Asian American Studies Program, California State University at Long Beach. His suggestions have deeply influenced my analysis, and his understanding of the Asian communities I have attempted to transmit through Chapters 2 and 3. Support for various stages of this work is gratefully acknowledged from the Student Health Organization, the Center for Health Manpower Education, California State University at Long Beach, and the CSULB Foundation. Finally, the interest and encouragement of Dr. Paul Torrens brought this volume into print.

Chapters 2 and 4 were adapted from Jerry L. Weaver and Lloyd T. Inui, "Information About Health Care Providers Among Urban Low-income Minorities," *Inquiry* **12** (Dec. 1975), pp. 330-343, and from Jerry L. Weaver, "Mexican American Health Care Behavior: A Critical Review of the Literature," *Social Science Quarterly* **54** (June 1973), pp. 85-102, respectively.

Jerry L. Weaver

Contents

4 Mexican American health care behavior, 55

5 Poverty and health in black and white, 71

6 Women and the health industry, 91

CHAPTER 1 **Class and community**

A cardinal feature of the period in which we live is the rapidity with which social, economic, and political institutions change. Technological innovation since World War II is partly responsible, but so is the evolution of public opinion and attitudes. For instance, contemporary society demands a much higher standard of humane treatment. Whether it is the treatment of animals or the treatment of criminals, American society refuses to accept as legitimate types of brutality and violence that 2 or 3 decades ago went unnoticed. New definitions of what is legitimate are also evident in the political arena where government regulates, subsidizes, and legislates in spheres and degrees unthought of in the first half of the twentieth century.

All of these agents of change have had a profound impact on the organization and delivery of health care. The most advanced technology of just a few years ago is suddenly obsolete; new drugs pour from the pharmaceutical houses; innovative surgical procedures appear with the regularity of new automobile models from Detroit. Solo practitioners, especially the family doctor, have very largely been displaced at the center of the personal health care industry by specialists; the physician's office has evolved into the prepaid health plan and the medical center. Government's responsibilities and role in the promotion of the nation's health grow at what seems an expotential rate, with billions of dollars being selectively directed into the health industry and politicians apparently vying with one another to introduce new health-related schemes; during the 1973-1974 Congressional season more than 75 different proposals for national health insurance were introduced. Regulatory agencies such as the Food and Drug Administration and the Federal Trade Commission advance new rules in the name of environmental, occupational, and consumer protection. Even the Supreme Court has taken a hand in the health game by redefining the private/public boundaries to move control of abortion decisions a little more firmly into the hands of the individual woman and her physician.

Thus, contemporary health policy makers must make their decisions not only in the light of complex medical technology and procedures but also in the light of competing social, economic, and political demands, needs, and priorities.

Role of social scientists

Social scientists can perform a useful task for policy makers by analyzing and interpreting social conditions and trends. This work requires that scientists not only compile basic data and impressions but blend their facts and ideas into information available to those responsible for making allocations of public resources.

To perform their role in the policy process, social scientists pull their subject out of its natural milieu, reduce it to a set of abstractions, and then attempt to demonstrate how these abstractions are related to what is going on in the real world. Every stage of this process is fraught with the possibility of error. C. Wright Mills, himself a master craftsman at the social science bench, bids social scientists to serve their calling with "the sociological imagination": the ability to avoid or reduce errors by grasping society's historical and biographical forces as well as the relations between the two within society. Social scientists then will not only escape the methodological blunders of the narrow gauge empiricist and the short-sightedness of failing to link the present subject continuously and closely to historical reality, but will come to realize that many personal problems cannot be solved merely as "troubles" but must be understood in terms of public issues—and in terms of the problems of history making.[1]

Conceptual ambiguity and conceptual clarity

The aim of this book is clarification of some issues involving the health care problems and preferences of a large part of the American society. In so doing, I hope not only to fill in some presently blank areas in the sociological map but also to generate for policy makers useful information and persuasive arguments. Concepts are the paints of the social analyst, elements he uses to create his impressions and convey his message. The selection and employment of concepts is arbitrary but subject to evaluation by two criteria. Is the usage logical? That is, within generally accepted epistemological standards, does the present combination of concepts make sense? Is the meaning readily available to those the social scientist wishes to communicate with? The second criterion for judging the use of concepts is economy. Has the social scientist been given enough to understand the user's meaning but not so much as to waste time in unproductive further ruminations? Is the effort adequate to the author's purpose? Now, some might suggest a third criterion. Is the effort elegant? Does it possess style and demonstrate an appreciation for sophisticated communication? I would argue, however, that if the first two rules are rigorously applied, then elegance of expression will come; and without logic or economy, no amount of elegance is worth the effort.

Concepts sometimes have idiosyncratic meanings. As George Orwell showed, love is hate, war is peace, and so forth. And concepts fade; that is, they become less powerful, often because their meaning is allowed to blur. These warnings are especially important because in this book I shall deal with a wide range of materials, from the social sciences and from the medical and biological sciences, drawn from a number of observers. Each has its own conceptual arrangements, so that while the reader may see a familiar term, its meaning may differ in important ways. A case in point, and a concept often encountered in this analysis, is "class."

Social class

We read that America has a "two-class medical system," or that the lower class has distinctive health problems, or that class influences how long and how well we live. What can we understand from such employments of the concept class? This, in turn, depends on what the writers mean by their use of the term. A close look reveals several substantially different meanings of class.

Class according to Marx

Although class is a central concept in Karl Marx's writings, he actually offers no coherent explication of the notion. A review of Marx's work reveals that when he uses the term, he is referring to any aggregation of persons who perform the same function in the organization of economic production. This incumbency produces profound psychological consequences that determine the beliefs and actions of the individual. Thus, economic position leads to the development of class consciousness, or the complex of attitudes, opinions, even distinctive life styles, which are the action components of social change. It is the position that the individual occupies in the social organization of production that indicates to which social class that individual belongs. Indicators of the distribution of material good and prestige symbols, such as education, income, or occupation, while they may reflect in some way the organization of production, are not identical with it. "Hence, the income or occupation of an individual is *not,* according to Marx, an indication of his class-position."[2] Two men might share the same occupation, but because one works in a small shop that he owns and the other works in a large factory for wages, they share only the occupation, not the same social class.

Modern revisionists

Marx formulated his notion of social class in order to provide a theory of history that was essentially democratic, free from dependence on great men or divine direction. In his formulation of class consciousness he found a powerful polemical device for rallying and recruiting the masses to his vision of social change. But because his writings also form one of the foundations for modern sociology, a discipline devoted to studying human beings in social groups, many sociologists and other social scientists have attempted to use social class as a tool for scholarly social analysis.

Max Weber, perhaps the single most influential twentieth century sociologist, revised the central role of social class in determining social behavior by removing economic position from the cornerstone assigned it by Marx. Weber argued that the distribution of power within a community was not, as Marx saw it, merely a question of economic position, but a consequence of one's place in three distinct orders: the economic, the social, and the political. In the first we find "classes," in the second "status groups," and in the third "parties."[3]

Weber sees class as merely one possible direction for communal action. It lacks the all-determining salience that Marx gave us. In Weber's formulation, class consciousness gives over to an impulse for economic interest, that is to say, interests involved in the existence of the "market." Interest depends on the nature of one's competitive relationship in the economy and is determined by whether one is a debtor or creditor, buyer or seller, worker or employer. There are three markets in which class interests are determined: the credit market, the commodity market, and the labor market. It follows, then, that people may find themselves involved in three markets simultaneously, or two, or one, or none as their economic situation changes; with each change in their market involvement, their class membership changes. For example, "Anyone who participates in all three markets is a member of three distinct economic classes and may participate in class conflict along three different axes."[4]

While Weber's formulation serves beautifully his original pursuit of building a general theory of social change, for the social scientist attempting to analyze the behavior or structure of a particular group of people in a reasonably specific time frame (such as a study of a local community power structure during one mayor's term in office), the possibility of fluctuating class membership inherent in Weber's formulation poses a major handicap. How is he to interpret or explain and individual's or group's motivation in terms of variegated class membership? It is little wonder, therefore, that most analysts have forsaken Marx's formulation because it is too simplistic and Weber's because its complexity pushes one into a narrow, static analysis. Instead, class now is often operationally defined in terms of income, occupation, or education; or it is avoided altogether in favor of "socioeconomic status," which is generally ascertained by ethnicity, consumption patterns, or place of residence.

It is important to note that when Marx is abandoned, the motivational components of his formulation are generally not replaced. That is, when social analysts make socioeconomic status, income, occupation, or some other structural condition their measure of position in a stratified social system, they usually have no theoretical foundation for adducing that a particular set of attitudes or values will be shared by those so characterized. Consequently, it is spurious reasoning to assume that individuals who fall into a particular stratum hold any motivational or psychological trait in common; rather, all the analyst can say is that certain individuals have the same objective characteristic. Aside from this attribution, little or nothing can be assumed about the probability of collective action.

Nor does the use of education, income, or occupation reveal the extent of biographic difference within the stratum. This lacuna imposes a heavy burden on us, because modern social research has revealed that there are substantial behavioral and attitudinal variations associated with race, age, sex, religion, geographic region, and other demographic characteristics. As we shall see, much of the important differences within our national society follows demographic cleavages. These social differences must be recognized if a clear picture of health needs is to emerge.

Social class and health

Suppose you were the Secretary of Health, Education, and Welfare and you were asked to formulate a comprehensive national policy to provide solutions for the health problems of the nation. How useful in your planning and designing of specific programs would you find materials developed by social scientists who employ the concept social class? Your assistants could produce hundreds upon hundreds of scholarly articles, monographs, and books that purport to analyze and discuss class differences, but what would you *know* about American society after reading them? Would you be in possession of solid, convincing evidence upon which to direct the expenditure of billions of tax dollars and vast amounts of other public resources?

As a cabinet-level decision maker, you would be the target of pressure from various constituencies and special interests to take action that they see as most beneficial to themselves and their clients. Labor, industrial groups, cities, ethnic groups, politicians—the list of claimants is endless. You need to be alert not only to these demands but also to unrepresented constituencies who, though weak and inarticulate, nevertheless have real needs and interests. In other words, your decision not only requires political acumen, it requires substantive information.

Multidimensional measures

Information comes in all sorts of conceptual forms and must be critically examined. Upon examination, we find that the value of some information Is suspect. A typical treatment of one segment of the population, what Rainwater[5] calls the "lower class," is based on the following definition and description:

> Our concern is with ways in which the characteristics of lower class persons influence their behavior in connection with the issues of health, illness, and the utilization of medical services. The group characterized below constitutes 25 to 30 percent of the population of the country. It includes that segment of the society usually referred to by the term "lower lower class" or "lower working class" (some 15 percent of the population) and a portion of the stable working class just superior to them in social status. A considerable body of research suggests that this group at the bottom of the social-status, occupational, income, and educational hierarchy has certain distinctive ways of looking at the world and of relating to it, as well as distinctive problems of adaptation to the world. Inevitably, these distinctive world views and modes of adaptation influence the ability of working-class people to take advantage of the standard services of the society, whether these be in the private or public sector.[*]

If we take the time to reread this description of what constitutes the lower class, we are left with little clarification of who Rainwater is writing about. The lower class constitutes the "lower lower class" and some undetermined portion of the "stable working class." (We have no clue as to the difference between a "lower" and a "stable" member of the working class except that the latter is "superior" to the former.) But in the final sentence we find another term, "working-class people," which presumably incorporates the lower lower and the aforementioned stable workers. The only indicator that the author offers for sorting individuals into their class is a composite social status, occupational, income, and educational hierarchy. These are precisely the characteristics that Marx warns us *not* to use in assigning class, and Weber has made educational attainment a dimension of social status, which he conceptualizes as theoretically equal in significance and separate from class. And if you are poorly educated but annually earn $75,000 whoring, in other

[*]Lee Rainwater, "The Lower Class: Health, Illness, and Medical Institutions," in Rainwater (editor), *Social Problems and Public Policy: Inequality and Justice* (Chicago: Aldine Publishing Co., 1974), p. 179.

words, low on two out of three criteria, are you a candidate for the lower class? A hopeless definitional muddle.

As for "distinctive world views," while we can accept that in principle individual outlooks vary (as much empirical evidence documents), there certainly is no view ubiquitous to the 25% to 30% of the population that compose the lower class. Rainwater is guilty of a slight of hand when he writes that "a considerable body of research suggests that *this group* . . . has certain distinctive ways of looking at the world. . . ." (Emphasis added.) There is no such thing; rather, there are many studies of particular populations that he aggregates into the lower class that show distinctive attitude, opinion, and behavioral profiles. They are distinctive, that is, to particular ethnic and racial groups, age cohorts, and geographic communities. The studies to which Rainwater alludes document just the opposite of his contention, and they illustrate how futile it is to generalize a "common world view" to a quarter or a third of the American population.

Income

Unlike the British, who report vital statistics by occupation and thus provide the basis for elaborate comparisons, the United States seems to shy away from classifying the population, preferring instead to use income differentials as the major unit of reporting comparative health and welfare indicators. This standard reporting technique may be in some measure responsible for the popularity of using "poverty/nonpoverty" comparisons to illustrate social problems. In any event, a sizeable number of readings exist that focus on income as their central analytical device.[6]

In 1974 the federal government set $5,000 as the poverty line for an urban family of four. Approximately 24.3 million individuals, 11.6% of the total population, were said to live in poverty. This includes 15.7% of all individuals 65 and older; 8.9% of Anglos; and 31.4% of the Black community.[7] By dividing the population along this income line, analysts are able to isolate and examine a large group of individuals whose collective health profiles reflect the multiple pathologies that Straus calls the "clustering principles."[8] James suggests that multiple health problems are the result of the "avalanche phenomenon": untended little problems multiply into complex, life-threatening or even terminal conditions before they are presented for treatment.[9]

Bauer writes that "persons with incomes of less than $5,000 have more limitation of activity, more disability, and more hospital episodes than the total population. Unfortunately they have fewer resources for obtaining medical care: fewer have hospital insurance and of course they have less cash to pay expenses on their own."[10]

Table 1-1 shows that the poor are hospitalized more frequently and for longer periods. Using different but comparable data, Lefcowitz shows that those who can least afford to lose work days do so more often than the more affluent; and since the latter are more likely to be covered by disability insurance or sick pay, the actual out-of-pocket cost to the poor is substantially greater. "Men 25-44 years old lose twice as much time from work if their income is less than $3,000 than if it is over $10,000. Among men 45-64 years old,

Table 1-1. Health characteristics of persons with family income under $5,000 compared with the total population: United States, 1968

Characteristic	Income under $5,000	Total population
	Percent	
Limitation of activity from chronic conditions	20.9	10.9
Hospital episodes	11.4	9.6
Hospital insurance	58.9	79.8
	Number per person	
Restricted-activity days	23.7	15.3
Bed-disability days	9.4	6.3
Short-stay hospital days	1.6	1.0
Short-stay hospital days per episode	13.8	10.4
Physician visits	4.5	4.2

Data from Mary Lou Bauer, "Health Characteristics of Low-Income Persons," *Vital and Health Statistics* **10** (July 1972), p. 12.

those with less than $3,000 income lose more than twice as many days as men with more than $10,000 family income. Thus, precisely among primary wage earners, the differential cost of illness is greater."[11] Aday takes the analysis of lost days significantly further by controlling for the independent effects of the unequal distribution in the income groups of age and sex. The adjusted profiles show that "families earning under $3,000 averaged 11.2 bed days per person in 1971 compared with only 5.1 for those earning $15,000 or more...."[12] The same groups reported 29.6 and 12.1 restricted-activity days per person, respectively. Aday's findings make an important contribution to our understanding of the ramifications of income, because she has adjusted for the overrepresentation of the young and the elderly in the lower income levels. Both ends of the adult age continuum have a high propensity for bedcare conditions: for many young women, maternity; for many elderly, the final stages of chronic or debilitative diseases. After removing the distortion introduced by unequal representation of age cohorts in the two income groups, we see a much clearer picture of the health factors associated with poverty.

The idea that the poor suffer substantial economic losses from illness and infirmity is only one aspect of the financial impact of health. National surveys and particular case studies have found that low income families spend a greater portion of their income for health care than higher income families spend.[13] This high level of out-of-pocket expenses may result from the higher rates of communicable diseases, chronic conditions, occupational disabilities, and infant and childhood morbidity.[14]

Given the steadily rising indices of health care costs over the past decade, the poor are also asked to shoulder a relatively larger part of the burden of inflation. As we see in Table 1-1, proportionately fewer low income families have insurance, and the idea that the poor's medical bills are covered by public or private assistance is incorrect. Out of the 48 million individuals with a family income of less than $5,000 in 1968, only 12.6%, or 6.1 million

Table 1-2. Indices of medical care prices: 1965-1973 (1967 = 100)

Year	Total medical care	Drugs and prescriptions	Physicians' fees	Obstetrical cases	T and A	Dentists' fees	Optometric exam and eye glasses	Hospital semi-private room
1965	89.5	100.2	88.3	89.0	91.0	92.2	92.8	76.6
1969	113.4	101.3	112.9	11.35	110.3	112.9	107.6	127.9
1970	120.6	103.6	121.4	121.8	117.1	119.4	113.5	143.9
1971	128.4	105.4	129.8	129.0	125.2	127.0	120.3	160.8
1972	132.5	105.6	133.8	133.8	129.9	132.3	124.9	173.9
1973	137.7	105.9	138.2	138.2	132.8	136.4	129.5	182.1
Rate of increase 1965-1973	53.8	5.6	56.5	55.1	45.9	47.9	39.5	137.7

Data from U.S. Bureau of the Census, *Statistical Abstract of the U.S., 1974* (Washington, D.C.: U.S. Government Printing Office, 1974), p. 68.

persons, received some type of aid. (Of those receiving aid, 70% reported public assistance.) "The majority of persons receiving aid were females, white, under 25 years, residents of SMSA's [Standard Metropolitan Statistical Areas], and members of families where the head of the family had less than a high school education and the family income was under $3,000. Almost half of the aid group were children under 17 years."[15] The price spirals summarized in Table 1-2 weigh especially hard on many poor and near poor because they simply do not fit into the various categorical programs that characterize our public assistance effort. The reality for these people is that they have one too few children, earn $20 a month too much, or are five years too young. So they must pay all or nearly all of their health bills.

It may be that some part of the chronic disability and illness that contribute to the disadvantageous health profiles of the poor stems from an unwillingness to take timely remedial action or from a tendency to ignore minor symptoms, to endure and finally accept pain and poor health as a normal part of their lives.[16] (There is a large body of literature that documents the variety of definition of what constitutes "good health."[17]) But what is passed off as subculture, fatalism, indifference, or laziness may be a reflection of hard reality: the simple geographic and economic unavailability of providers. Rainwater notes that "lower class people (often with a considerable amount of realism on their side) will be inclined to slight health difficulties in the interest of attending to more pressing ones, such as seeing that there is food in the house. . . ."[18] That the availability of funds has a direct bearing on service utilization has been reported by Richardson. He found that receipt of Medicare and Medicaid tends to erase the negative effects of poverty on visiting a physician following an illness episode.[19] It may be that much of what passes as indifference to pain or lack of concern about one's health may be the poor's inability to *buy* health care.

The quality and style of health care that the poor obtain may also bear on their willingness to invest their very limited resources in treatment. While the availability and utilization of providers will be explored more thoroughly in succeeding chapters, the general outline of the poor's health care providers can be sketched briefly here.

Herman argues that private practitioners are not available to the poor in adequate numbers and those who are in practice are not of generally high quality. "The greatest disadvantage of private practitioners is that the care provided may not be of high quality. A number of recent surveys have indicated that substantial proportions of general practitioners were providing inadequate care, and it may be assumed that this is even more common among overworked physicians in low-income areas."[20]

The principal providers of health care for the urban poor are the outpatient clinics and emergency rooms of community and public hospitals. In-depth studies have been conducted to determine the clientele and quality of care of these facilities. The studies reveal that the unemployed, minority, and public assistance recipients obtain fragmented, episodic treatment devoid of continuity, showing little concern for chronic but nonthreatening problems, and indicating slight consideration for the preferences and feelings of the patient and patient's family.[21] Brook and Stevenson assess the care received by a sample of patients from a Baltimore emergency room as both inefficient and inadequate.[22] Hurley's review of accounts of the treatment of the poor concludes that it is "clearly second-rate."[23]

What appears to bring forth these negative evaluations is not so much the technical skills or physical plant that the poor encounter; rather, it is the inconsiderate treatment they receive from the health providers themselves. The bureaucratic nature of clinics and emergency rooms with their insistence on forms and routine, on impersonal application of procedures, on bending the client to fit the organization, is a major source of complaints. In part this friction arises because "the lower-class person simply lacks knowledge of the rules of the game. . . . It is the lack of knowledge of the system's technicalities and backstage regions that is responsible for the lower-class person's inability to manipulate a bureaucratic system to his advantage."[24] Consequently, the experience with the institution is remembered as a bad trip.

Most patients in hospitals and clinics, however, are unfamiliar with procedures and must struggle to assert their personal preferences in the face of bureaucratic regimentation. And, as Hollingshead and Redlich have shown, hospital employees and physicians are responsive to the particularities of middle- and upper-class patients.[25] Hurley, who sees the indifference and hostility of the facility toward the poor as indicative of a strong class bias, states:

> More is involved in this situation than rigid adherence to bureaucratic standards. Ample evidence suggests that lurking behind this adherence is a strong class bias. The poor have described it best; the mother of a polio victim put it this way: "Well, they don't tell you anything hardly. They don't seem to want to. I mean you start asking questions and they say, 'Well, I only have about three minutes to talk to you.' And then the things that you ask, they don't seem to want to answer you. So I don't ask them anything anymore."[26]

Friedson,[27] Koos,[28] Strauss,[29] and others have pointed out the class bias of the professional health workers and their impatience, even contempt for the poor.

In the face of financially ruinous and ego-attacking experiences, it should not be regarded as even slightly remarkable, as Hurley puts it, that the poor frequently turn to chiropractors,[30] over-the-counter drugs, "folk medicine," or choose to ignore minor health problems. To consider such behavior as indicative of a preoccupation with their bodies or as part of a highly valued and stubbornly defended subculture[31] is to miss the central feature of the lives of the poor: they do not have much money and must survive with what is available to them. Patent medicines, chiropractors, neighbors, and pharmacists are often closer and less expensive than "scientific" providers.

Social position

Marx and Weber agree that societies confer differential status to individuals depending on their possession of what is considered meritorious. They agree that position in a status hierarchy and class membership are different phenomena. Weber offers the following distinction between class and status. "With some over-simplification, one might thus say that 'classes' are stratified according to their relations to the production and acquisition of goods; whereas, 'status groups' are stratified according to the principles of their *consumption* of goods represented by special 'styles of life.'"[32] Measures of status relate to social position, not social class. Yet this fine theoretical distinction has not stayed the interchangeable use of status for class.

Hollingshead has popularized what is now a widely accepted index of social status: the Two Factor Index of Social Position, which utilizes occupation and educational attainment of head of households.[33] Other analysts combine education and income for their measure of socioeconomic status (SES). Using such measures as these of social position, Antonovsky decides that the "inescapable conclusion is that class influences one's chance of staying alive."[34]

Lefcowitz argues that education is a causal factor in individual health status and medical care utilization, and he offers a good deal of data to sustain his claim. For example, as we see in Table 1-3, there is far greater variation within income strata from educational level to education level than between income strata of the same educational level.[35]

Other observers report similar strong associations between health characteristics and education. MacMahon, Kovar, and Feldman, using the educational levels of both parents and the family's income in the year prior to birth or infant death, say, "All three indexes showed a strong association with risk of infant death, this risk being between 50 and 200 percent higher in the lowest socioeconomic class than in the middle and upper classes."[36] They go on to conclude, "It appears, therefore, that within the lower categories of SES, family income, education of mother, and education of father have independent and approximately equal predictive values in relation to infant mortality."[37] Other health characteristics that are thought to vary with level

Table 1-3. Percent of population using selected types of medical specialists and practitioners by family income and education of head of household, July 1963–June 1964

Type of visit and income	Years of education			Percentage differences (cols. 1 and 3)
	Under 9 years	9 to 12 years	13+ years	
Pediatric				
Under $4,000	4	15	30	650
$4,000 and over	10	20	38	280
Percent difference	150%	33%	26%	
Obstetrics-gynecology				
Under $4,000	2	7	11	450
$4,000 and over	4	10	16	300
Percent difference	100%	43%	45%	
Ophthalmological				
Under $4,000	4	5	10	150
$4,000 and over	5	6	11	120
Percent difference	25%	20%	10%	
Optometric				
Under $4,000	7	7	13	85
$4,000 and over	9	10	9	0
Percent difference	28%	42%	−30%	

Adapted from Myron J. Lefcowitz, "Poverty and Health: A Re-examination," *Inquiry* **10** (March 1973), p. 5.

of education are information about health symptoms,[38] general morbidity,[39] dental practices,[40] and rate of using personal health care services.[41]

It is not surprising that health indicators vary with education; after all, with the major exception of the Black community,[42] educational attainment is tightly associated with income and place in the occupation hierarchy. Thus, what we have is a complex cluster variable in which education, occupation, and income are interrelated. This cluster of factors is not independent of other major variables: age, sex, race and ethnicity, family size, religion, place of residence (rural to central city), and other variables that social scientists have found associated with biographic and psychological particularities. This is not to argue that education may not emerge as the single most powerful predictor of health care behavior; it is simply premature to assert that such is the case before more rigorous analytical techniques are applied to well-constructed samples of the national population.

Sociocultural identity

While most discussants of class or status tend to treat their strata as undifferentiated masses, several observers have explored the sociological variations within the lower income or lower status groups. Perhaps because of the obvious fact that racial and ethnic minorities are disproportionately found among the "lower classes," such populations as the Italians, Irish, Chicanos, Puerto Ricans, Blacks, and recent urban migrants from impoverished rural regions (such as "Southern Mountain people") have drawn the attention of anthropologists and medical sociologists.[43] Almost uniformly, the health care behavior of these segments of the lower classes has been characterized as "folk medicine," "health care subculture," or "traditional beliefs." This behavior is said to reflect the values, attitudes, and traditions of sociocultural groups.

One of the leaders in this sociocultural school, Edward A. Suchman, concludes that significant differences are found among ethnic groups in response to illness and in general medical behavior. These differences, Suchman argues, stem from the power of the individual's primary group to introduce and reinforce folk ways. In general, the form of social organization is found to be more important than ethnicity or social class in relation to sociomedical behavior.[44] That is, behavior is constrained by the expectations and directives of the social groups that have significance for the individual.[45] Thus the more completely his family, clan, or communal group accounts for the individual's socialization and the less he is assimilated into the national society, the greater the likelihood that traditional health care practices (folk medicine) will prevail.[46]

When occupation is substituted for other measures of social position, it turns out that blue-collar workers in large Eastern metropolitan areas demonstrate an underutilization of "scientific" health care providers. Because many of these workers are ethnic minorities, especially of Eastern and Southern European origins, Suchman cites folk health orientation to explain their behavior.[47]

For all of the research that has been done of low income, low status ethnic minorities, there is surprisingly little solid information or even informed speculation about the *direct* impact of sociocultural status on health. One carefully thought-through and well-executed analysis of the impact of sociological and biological factors is the work with infant mortality records conducted by Helen C. Chase. In discussing the higher mortality of non-Anglo infants, she observes, "The neonatal mortality rates of white and nonwhite infants . . . may be viewed as the net result of two factors operating simultaneously: differences in weight-specific mortality rates, and differences in the proportions of infants in specified birth weight groups. When considering trends, a third element is introduced, namely, the changes in these two factors over time."[48] "There is a significant difference between the mean birth weight of groups of infants in the United States. It is not clear whether the difference is due entirely to socioeconomic or biological factors, or to a combination of the two factors. . . . In view of the complexities of other sociological and human physiological factors, it would indeed be surprising if the difference in mean birth weight between white and all other infants could be attributable *in toto* to either of these two factors."[49]

Limits of "class"

We see from a review of efforts to tie class as a single comprehensive factor to health behavior that it is too weak to stand much intellectual tugging. It is too weak because it is too loosely woven; regardless of whether the criterion is income, occupation, or education, the strata these indices mark off contain groupings of individuals far too diffuse to make interstrata comparisons meaningful.

The ambiguity that arises from stratifying the population along single variables reflects the absence in America of clearly defined social and economic divisions. Dahrendorf saw this condition and wrote that "the participants, issues, and patterns of conflict have changed, and the pleasing simplicity of Marx's view of society has become a nonsensical construction. If ever there have been two large, homogeneous, polarized, and identically situated social classes, these have certainly ceased to exist today, so that an unmodified Marxian theory is bound to fail in explaining the structure and conflicts of advanced industrial societies."[50] Conceptualizing the society in terms suggested by Weber does not generate precision either. Objective positions in the economic, social, or political hierarchies of our society seem to have little bearing on political, economic, or social behavior.

This is not to say that America is a vast, undifferentiated, mass society of isolated, alienated creatures or, alternatively, an egalitarian utopia. There are real lines of cleavage in our society, real differences in economic, social, and political orientations. For the most part, these cleavages reflect life-styles, not education; attitudes toward symbols of political authority, not partisan loyalties; and who one spends leisure time with, not how one earns a living.

Community as an analytical tool

One of the fallouts of the questioning and reappraisal of American institutions that took place during the Johnson and Nixon administrations is the growing recognition that the cement that held the political system together from the Great Depression through Vietnam has pretty well lost its adhesive strength. Litt refers to the New Deal politics of this period as "accommodation politics" whose stock-in-trade was individual benefits: contracts, jobs, in the word of Samuel Gompers, "More!"[51] This system of rewarding specific interests or individuals was based on an attitude of short-run, pragmatic compromise.[52] But it was not well suited to handling massive collective claims advanced by Blacks and other non-Anglo groups, feminists, antiwar protesters, and those whose aims were nothing less than a major exchange of individual, generally economic, allocations for collective cultural and psychological values. When millions of people began to believe the slogans of the War on Poverty, the dream of Martin Luther King, and the demands for a moral society made by the Berrigan brothers, social scientists began to see America's divisions in terms of pro- and anti-counterculture, protest, and law and order.

Closer examination uncovered persistent sociological patterns in these alignments. These patterns, instead of following income or status lines, cut across traditional lines. The earliest clearly discernible configurations to be identified were ethnic and racial minorities.

Observers such as Glazer and Moynihan,[53] Wolfinger,[54] Parenti,[55] Litt,[56] and Altshuler,[57] to mention a few examples, called to our attention that America was not one nation, indivisible, as exponents of the melting pot analogy had taught. "Though the differences among them have grown more subtle over time, the major ethnic groups in American life continue to act as magnets for their members. Most social and family life continues to take place within them. And thus they retain distinctive identities, carrying norms of child rearing, politics, religion, and so on from one generation to the next."[58] Altshuler goes on to underline the implication of ethnicity for social analysis: "The ethnic dimension—a combination of the closely linked variables of religion, national origin, and race—cuts across those of income and occupation. . . ."[59] Even within a fairly narrow occupational stratus, such as the Detroit workers Leggett studied, ethnicity is associated with major behavioral and attitudinal variations.[60]

The name that we give the phenomenon of people, clearly acculturated into the styles and customs of the larger society yet asserting an independence, an unwillingness to assimilate and lose its distinctiveness in the mass culture, is *community*. This conceptualization of community is rooted in the image developed by Rousseau and brought into social science by Durkheim, reflects Tönnies's *Gemeinschaft,* and has been defined by Horowitz as constituting (1) people who share in similar activities and in upholding similar values and virtues; (2) people who share common problems and act jointly and amiably to solve them; (3) people who individually engage in dissimilar activities, but many of these prove to be interdependent; and (4) people who share a strong psychological identification among themselves. Community, then, is a psychological phenomenon, not a geographic entity. It is formed out of shared experiences and shared preferences and values, not boundary markers and bricks and mortar.[61]

In the present endeavor we must keep in mind that community is an analytical contrivance; a contrivance to help us order a great mass of impressions, accounts, and data, a contrivance used to communicate our conclusions and recommendations. As was the case with class, the concept of community will not be verified here through empirical research. The appropriate question is: Does using it bring greater clarification of the health behavior and health care needs of a large part of the American population?

Minority communities in American society

In the following chapters, attention will be turned to the urban poor. In place of class or status criteria for delimiting the subjects, however, the population will be arranged into communities. People who are not poor will occasionally be incorporated in this arrangement; for example, the Japanese community contains a sizable number of affluent individuals. Yet social position, whether class or status determined, has less bearing on the problems facing Japanese (and certainly Blacks, perhaps Chicanos) than they have in the majority Anglo population. One of the advantages derived from using community as an organizing principle is that we see how much is distorted and overlooked when we lump members of different communities together in conventional socioeconomic categories.

Along with the Japanese, Black, Chicano, and Pilipino* communities, the

---

*"Pilipino" is used throughout the book because there is no phonetic "ph" or "f" sound indigenous to the Philippine language. The present spelling represents a recognition of the identity and history of the Pilipino people in America. See Jesse Quinsaat (editor), *Letters in Exile: An Introductory Reader on the History of Pilipinos in America* (Los Angeles: UCLA Asian American Studies Center, 1976).

particular health needs and concerns of two emerging communities—women and the elderly—will be examined. Just as the outlines of the ethnic and racial communities began to emerge 10 years ago when the smoke of the melting pot was blown away, now it may be that large numbers of women and the elderly in the United States are recognizing their interdependence, common problems, and joint destinies and are forming small but growing communities. At any rate, there are sufficiently grave health difficulties confronting women and the elderly to warrant their separate examination in a volume meant to generate increased illumination of the health problems of our society.

Taken either singly or collectively, the communities to be examined qualify for the label "minority." This designation has nothing to do with their proportion of the national population. Although several are fractional parts of the total, women are a numerical majority; and taken together, the communities make up over two thirds of the American society. Nevertheless, they rate the minority designation because, for all of their raw numbers, they lack *political* power and influence. On one side, the communities do not have political brokers such as interest groups, political parties, or major mass media to present their claims and represent their demands in the decision-making process. In turn this reflects their underendowment of money, legitimacy, prestige, information, and other resources valued by decision makers. This political poverty is both cause and consequence of the institutions, traditions, and ideologies that dominate political life in the United States.[62] In any event, it is the absence of power and influence to implement self-determination that makes Blacks, Chicanos, the elderly, Japanese, Pilipinos, and women minority communities. It is one of my central hypotheses that much of the health disadvantage suffered by these communities stems from their lack of political resources and that many problems would be quickly eradicated if they enjoyed anything near the political strength the principles of democratic politics suggest they deserve. At bottom, the collective disadvantages that will be summarized are neither "personal problems" nor "social pathologies": their causes and their solutions must be sought in the American political process.

Although the communities to be analyzed are indicative in their health problems of similar populations not reviewed (Chinese, native Americans, recent urban immigrants from rural poverty) or have little-noticed health needs that demand illumination and official recognition (cosmetic poisoning of women, hypertension of Blacks, or cancers among Japanese), the underlying purpose for comparing and contrasting minority communities is to inform the majority—and in particular makers of public policy. This stratagem of focusing light outside in order to illuminate the interior derives from my assessment of the impact on American society of the rise of ethnic studies programs and consciousness-building efforts of women, gays, and other minority groups during the late 1960s and early 1970s: Black studies, to take one example, did not teach Black students much about being black in America, but Black studies has taught Anglos a great deal about being white. To make this lesson as clear as possible, I shall offer whenever practical, vital and health data from Anglo populations, data that offer a benchmark for charting minority/majority comparisons.

Teaching Anglos about being Anglo is what studies of non-Anglos do best. The same may be said for majority/minority relations when the understanding of these statuses based on relative power discussed above is used. I shall try to advance this teaching by suggesting a rough and incomplete vision of the relationship of the one to the many captured in another medium by the Japanese writer Kobo Abé in his classic *The Woman in the Dunes:* the participation of the individual in the struggle for collective survival is what gives meaning to the individual's existence, as well as the individual's enterprise. This may well be the lesson those who control and direct American society, yet seem so often to live in but share no part of it, are being offered by minority communities.

Class is often a useful tool to categorize people and talk about some kinds of human relationships. People, however, do not live, work, and die in classes. Class conveys no dynamic interaction. Community, however, holds out the hope of relating to people and of integrating their individual psychological, social, economic, and political selves together in a collective identity. In this sense the concept allows both the analyst and the decision maker to see that individual problems, as Mills expressed it and as Abé implied, are really problems of society that can be dealt with only as public issues, and only at the level of history making.

Notes

1. C. Wright Mills, *The Sociological Imagination* (New York: Grove Press, Inc., 1959).
2. Reinhart Bendix and Seymour Martin Lipset, "Karl Marx' Theory of Social Class," in Bendix and Lipset (editors), *Class, Status and Power: A Reader in Social Stratification* (New York: The Free Press, 1953), p. 29.
3. Max Weber, "Class, Status, Party," in H. H. Gerth and C. Wright Mills (translators and editors), *From Max Weber* (New York: Oxford University Press, 1958), pp. 180-195.
4. Norbert Wiley, "America's Unique Class Politics: The Interplay of Labor, Credit, and Commodity Markets," in Hans Peter Dreitzel (editor), *Recent Sociology No. 1: On the Social Basis of Politics* (New York: Macmillan, Inc., 1969), p. 192.
5. Lee Rainwater, "The Lower Class: Health, Illness, and Medical Institutions, " in Rainwater (editor), *Social Problems and Public Policy: Inequality and Justice* (Chicago: Aldine Publishing Co., 1974), p. 179.
6. See Patricia A. Leo and George Rosen, "A Bookshelf on Poverty and Health," *American Journal of Public Health* **59** (April 1969), pp. 591-607; Anselm Strauss, "Medical Organization, Medical Care, and Lower Income Groups," *Social Science and Medicine* **3** (1969), pp. 143-177; Edward G. Stockwell, "Socioeconomic Status and Mortality in the United States," *Public Health Reports* **76** (Dec. 1961), pp. 1081-1086; John Kosa, Aaron Antonovsky, and Irving K. Zola (editors), *Poverty and Health: A Sociological Analysis* (Cambridge: Harvard University Press, 1969); Paul M. Roman and Harrison M. Trice, *Schizophrenia and the Poor* (Ithaca, N.Y.: Cornell University, School of Industrial Relations, 1967); C. H. Goodrich, M. C. Olendski, and G. G. Reader, *Welfare Medical Care* (Cambridge: Harvard University Press, 1970); Mary W. Herman, "Health Services for the Poor and Neighborhood Health Centers," *Hospital Administration* **17** (Spring 1972), pp. 50-64; Rodger L. Hurley, *Poverty and Mental Retardation: A Causal Relationship* (New York: Vintage Books, 1969).
7. *Los Angeles Times,* part I (24 July 1975), p. 24.
8. Robert Straus, "Poverty as an Obstacle to Health Programs in Our Rural Areas," *American Journal of Public Health* **55** (Nov. 1965), p. 1776.
9. George James, "Poverty as an Obstacle to Health Progress in Our Cities," *American Journal of Public Health* **55** (Nov. 1965), p. 1759.
10. Mary Lou Bauer, "Health Characteristics of Low-Income Persons," *Vital and Health Statistics* **10** (July 1972), p. 2.

11. Myron J. Lefcowitz, "Poverty and Health: A Re-examination," *Inquiry* **10** (March 1973), p. 10.
12. Lu Ann Aday, "Economic and Noneconomic Barriers to the Use of Needed Medical Services," *Medical Care* **8** (June 1975), p. 448.
13. Murray A. Tucker, "Effect of Heavy Medical Expenditures on Low Income Family," *Public Health Reports* **85** (May 1970), p. 419; Grover Wirick and Robin Barlow, "The Economic and Social Determinants of the Demand for Health Service," in *The Economics of Health and Medical Care: A Conference Volume* (Ann Arbor: University of Michigan, 1964), pp. 5-125; Charlotte Muller, "Income and the Receipt of Medical Care," *American Journal of Public Health* **55** (April 1965), pp. 510-521; Joel Alpert, John Kosa, and Robert J. Haggerty, "A Month of Illness and Health Care Among Low Income Families," *Public Health Reports* **82** (Aug. 1967), pp. 705-713; George E. Schneider and Susan Fox, "Health Care Coverage and Out-of-Pocket Expenditures of Detroit Families," *Inquiry* **10** (Dec. 1973), pp. 49-57.
14. See Monroe Lerner, "Social Differences in Physical Health," in Kosa, Antonovsky, and Zola (editors), *Poverty and Health*, pp. 69-112; Robert L. Eichhorn and Edward G. Ludwig, "Poverty and Health," in Hanna H. Meissner (editor), *Poverty in the Affluent Society* (New York: Harper & Row, Publishers, 1966), pp. 172-180; Selig Greenberg, "The Legacy of Neglect," *The Progress* **35** (Feb. 1971), pp. 21-35; Mostafa H. Nagi and Edward G. Stockwell, "Socioeconomic Differentials in Mortality by Cause of Death," *Health Service Reports* **88** (May 1973), pp. 449-455; Lois Pratt, "The Relationship of Socioeconomic Status to Health," *American Journal of Public Health* **61** (Feb, 1971), pp. 281 201.
15. Bauor, "Health Characteristics," p. 4.
16. Compare with "Low income persons tend to endure, adjust, and finally accept pain and poor health as a normal part of their lives." From Dixie L. Leyhe, Foline E. Gartside, and Donald Procter, "Medi-Cal Patient Satisfaction in Watts," *Health Services Reports* **87** (April 1972), p. 355.
17. See Benjamin D. Paul (editor), *Health, Culture and Community* (New York: Russell Sage Foundation, 1956); Vera Rublin (editor), "Culture, Society and Health," *Annals of the New York Academy of Sciences* **84** (Dec. 1960); Ozzie G. Simmons, "Social Research in Health and Medicine: A Bibliography," in Howard F. Freeman, Sol Levine, and Leo G. Reeder (editors), *Handbook of Medical Sociology* (Englewood Cliffs, N.J.: Prentice-Hall, Inc., 1963), pp. 493-581.
18. Rainwater, "Lower Class," p. 180. Also see William Ryan, *Blaming the Victim* (New York: Pantheon Books, Inc., 1971), for the argument that income, not culture, is the principal determinant of behavior.
19. William C. Richardson, "Measuring the Urban Poor's Use of Physicians' Services in Response to Illness Episodes," *Medical Care* **8** (March-April 1970), pp. 132-142; Lawrence Berger and Alonzo S. Yerby, "Low Income and Barriers to the Use of Health Services," *New England Journal of Medicine* **278** (7 March 1968), pp. 541-546.
20. Mary W. Herman, "The Poor: Their Medical Needs and the Health Services Available to Them," *The Annals* **399** (Jan. 1972), p. 209. On the technical competence and attitudes toward their patients of the health care providers the poor encounter, see James L. Walsh and Ray H. Elling, "Professionalism and the Poor—Structural Effects and Professional Behavior," *Journal of Health and Social Behavior* **9** (March 1968), pp. 16-28; Alonzo S. Yerby, "The Disadvantaged and Health Care," *American Journal of Public Health* **56** (Jan. 1966), pp. 5-9; Wendy G. Brooks, "Health Care and Poor People," in Barry A. Passett and Edgar S. Cahn (editors), *Citizen Participation: Effecting Community Change* (New York: Praeger Publishers, Inc., 1971), p. 113; Eli Ginzberg and others, *Urban Health Services: The Case of New York* (New York: Columbia University Press, 1971).
21. E. Richard Weinerman, "Yale Studies in Ambulatory Medical Care, IV: Outpatient—Clinic Services in the Teaching Hospital," *New England Journal of Medicine* **272** (6 May 1965), pp. 947-954; Joel J. Alpert and others, "Types of Families Using an Emergency Clinic," *Medical Care* **7** (Jan.-Feb. 1969), pp. 55-61; Anselm L. Strauss, "Medical Ghettos," in Strauss (editor), *Where Medicine Fails* (Chicago: Aldine Publishing Co., 1970), pp. 9-26; E. Richard Weinerman and others, "Yale Studies in Ambulatory Medical Care, V: Determinants of Use of Hospital Emergency Services," *American Journal of Public Health* **56** (July 1966), pp. 1037-1056; Julius A. Roth, "Utilization of the Hospital Emergency Department," *Journal of Health and Social Behavior* **12** (Dec. 1971), pp. 312-320.

22. Robert H. Brook and Robert L. Stevenson, Jr., "Effectiveness of Patient Care in an Emergency Room," *New England Journal of Medicine* **283** (22 Oct. 1970), pp. 904-907.

23. Rodger L. Hurley, "The Health Crisis of the Poor," in Hans Peter Dreitzel (editor), *The Social Organization of Health* (New York: Macmillan, Inc., 1971), p. 106.

24. Gideon Sjoberg, Richard A. Brymer, and Buford Harris, "Bureaucracy and the Lower Class," in Francis E. Rourke (editor), *Bureaucratic Power in National Politics,* ed. 2 (Boston: Little, Brown and Co., 1972), p. 402.

25. August B. Hollingshead and Frederick C. Redlich, *Social Class and Mental Illness* (New York: John Wiley & Sons, Inc., 1958).

26. Hurley, "Health Crisis of the Poor," p. 108.

27. Eliot Friedson, *Professional Dominance: The Social Structure of Medical Care* (Chicago: Aldine Publishing Co., 1970).

28. Earl L. Koos, *The Health of Regionville* (New York: Columbia University Press, 1954).

29. Strauss, "Medical Ghettos," *passim.*

30. Hurley, "Health Crisis of the Poor," p. 110.

31. These cultural interpretations are dealt with in Chapters 4 and 9.

32. Weber, "Class, Status, Party," p. 193.

33. See Philip M. Moody and Robert M. Gray, "Social Class, Social Integration, and the Use of Preventive Health Services," in E. Gartly Jaco (editor), *Patients, Physicians and Illness,* ed. 2 (New York: The Free Press, 1972), p. 256.

34. Aaron Antonovsky, "Social Class, Life Expectancy and Overall Mortality," *Milbank Memorial Fund Quarterly,* part I **45** (April 1967), pp. 31-73.

35. Lefcowitz, "Poverty and Health," p. 10.

36. Brian MacMahon, Mary G. Kovar, and Jacob J. Feldman, "Infant Mortality Rates: Socioeconomic Factors," *Vital and Health Statistics* **22** (March 1972), p. 1.

37. *Ibid.,* p. 4. Also see Edward G. Stockwell, "Infant Mortality and Socioeconomic Status: A Changing Relationship," *Milbank Memorial Fund Quarterly* **40** (Jan. 1962), pp. 101-111.

38. Serena E. Wade, "Trends in Public Knowledge about Health and Illness," *American Journal of Public Health* **60** (March 1970), pp. 485-491.

39. Charles Kadushin, "Social Class and the Experience of Ill Health," *Sociological Inquiry* **34** (Winter 1964), pp. 67-80; Ruth M. French, *The Dynamics of Health Care* (New York: McGraw-Hill Book Co., 1968); Irving Leveson, "The Challenge of Health Services for the Poor," *The Annals* **399** (Jan. 1972), pp. 22-29; Wayne E. Smith, "Factors Associated with Age—Specific Death Rates, California Counties, 1964," *American Journal of Public Health* **58** (Oct. 1968), pp. 1937-1949.

40. Jeannette F. Rayner, "Socioeconomic Status and Factors Influencing the Dental Health Practices of Mothers," *American Journal of Public Health* **60** (July 1970), pp. 1250-1258.

41. John A. Ross, "Social Class and Medical Care," *Journal of Health and Human Behavior* **3** (Spring 1962), pp. 35-40; Stanislav V. Kasl and Sidney Cobb, "Health Behavior, Illness Behavior and Sick Role Behavior, I: Health and Illness Behavior" **12** (Feb. 1966), pp. 246-266, and "II: Sick Role Behavior," *Archives of Environmental Health* **12** (April 1966), pp. 531-541; Richard Auster, Irving Leveson, and Deborah Saracheck, "The Production of Health: An Exploratory Study," *Journal of Human Resources* **4** (Fall 1969), pp. 411-436; M. A. Glasser, "A Study of the Public's Acceptance of the Salk Vaccine Program," *American Journal of Public Health* **48** (Feb. 1958), pp. 141-146; Leila Calhoun Deasy, "Socioeconomic Status and Participation in the Poliomyelitis Vaccine Trial," *American Sociological Review* **21** (April 1956), pp. 185-191.

42. Jerry L. Weaver, "Educational Attainment and Economic Success: Some Notes on a Ghetto Study," *Journal of Negro Education* **40** (Spring 1971), pp. 153-162; Christopher Jencks and others, *Inequality: A Reassessment of the Effect of Family and Schooling in America* (New York: Harper & Row, Publishers, 1972).

43. Irving K. Zola, "Culture and Symptoms: An Analysis of Patients Presenting Complaints," *American Sociological Review* **31** (Oct. 1966), pp. 615-630; Beatrice Berle, *Eighty Puerto Rican Families in New York: Health and Disease Studied in Context* (New York: Columbia University Press, 1958); Herbert J. Gans, *The Urban Villagers: Group and Class in the Life of Italian-Americans* (New York: The Free Press, 1962); Oscar Lewis, *La Vida: A Puerto Rican Family in the Culture of Poverty—San Juan and New York* (New York: Random House,

Inc., 1965); Ari Kiev, *Curanderismo: Mexican-American Folk Psychiatry* (New York: The Free Press, 1968); Lyle Saunders, *Cultural Differences and Medical Care: The Case of the Spanish-Speaking People of the Southwest* (New York: Russell Sage Foundation, 1954); Margaret Clark, *Health in the Mexican-American Culture* (Berkeley and Los Angeles: University of California Press, 1959); Elmer L. Stavening, Judith G. Rabkin, and Harris B. Peck, "Migration and Ethnic Membership in Relation to Social Problems," *American Behavioral Scientist* 13 (Sept.-Oct. 1969), pp. 57-87; John C. Norman (editor), *Medicine in the Ghetto* (New York: Appleton-Century-Crofts, 1969); Ellen J. Stekert, "Focus for Conflict: Southern Mountain Medical Beliefs in Detroit," in Américo Paredes and Ellen J. Stekert (editors), *The Urban Experience and Folk Tradition* (Austin: University of Texas Press, 1971), pp. 95-136; Gordon MacGregor, "Social Determinants of Health Practices," *American Journal of Public Health* 51 (Nov. 1961), pp. 1709-1714; Sheldon G. Lowry, Selz C. Mayo, and Donald G. Hay, "Factors Associated with the Acceptance of Health Care Practices Among Rural Families," *Rural Sociology* 23 (June 1958), pp. 198-202.

44. Edward A. Suchman, "Socio-Medical Variations Among Ethnic Groups," *American Journal of Sociology* 70 (Nov. 1964), pp. 319-331.

45. Edward A. Suchman, "Social Patterns of Illness and Medical Care," *Journal of Health and Human Behavior* 6 (Spring 1965), pp. 2-16.

46. Nathan Glazer, "Paradoxes of Health Care," *Public Interest* 22 (Winter 1971), pp. 62-77; Nancy Milo, "Values, Social Class and Community Health Services," *Nursing Research* 16 (Winter 1967), pp. 26-31; Jerry Solon, "Sociocultural Variations Among a Hospital's Outpatients," *American Journal of Public Health* 56 (June 1966), pp. 884-895; Mark Zborowski and E. Herzog, *Life is with the People* (New York: Columbia University Press, 1952); J. Cassel, "Social and Cultural Considerations in Health Innovation," *Annals of the New York Academy of Science* 57 (1963), pp. 739-747.

47. Daniel Rosenblatt and Edward A. Suchman, "Blue-Collar Attitudes and Information toward Health and Illness" and "The Underutilization of Medical-Care Services by Blue-Collarites," in Arthur B. Shostak and William Gomberg (editors), *Blue-Collar World: Studies of the American Worker* (Englewood Cliffs, N.J.: Prentice-Hall, Inc., 1964), pp. 324-333, 341-349.

48. Helen C. Chase, "Infant Mortality and Weight at Birth: 1960 United States Birth Cohort," *American Journal of Public Health* 59 (Sept. 1969), p. 1625.

49. Helen C. Chase, "A Study of Infant Mortality from Linked Records: Comparison of Neonatal Mortality from Two Cohort Studies, United States, January-March, 1950 and 1960," *Vital and Health Statistics* 20 (June 1972), p. 40.

50. Ralf Dahrendorf, *Class and Class Conflict in Industrial Society* (Stanford: Stanford University Press, 1959), p. 57.

51. Edgar Litt, *Beyond Pluralism: Ethnic Politics in America* (Glenview, Ill.: Scott, Foresman and Co., 1970), pp. 157-158.

52. See Theodore J. Lowi, *The End of Liberalism: Ideology, Policy, and the Crisis of Public Authority* (New York: W. W. Norton & Co., Inc., 1969); James P. Young, *The Politics of Affluence: Ideology in the United States since World War II* (San Francisco: Chandler Publishing Co., 1968).

53. Nathan Glazer and Daniel P. Moynihan, *Beyond the Melting Pot* (Cambridge: MIT Press, 1963).

54. Raymond E. Wolfinger, "The Development and Persistence of Ethnic Voting," *American Political Science Review* 59 (Dec. 1965), pp. 896-908.

55. Michael Parenti, "Ethnic Politics and the Persistence of Ethnic Identification," *American Political Science Review* 61 (Sept. 1967), pp. 717-726.

56. Litt, *Beyond Pluralism, passim.*

57. Alan A. Altshuler, *Community Control: The Black Demand for Participation in Large American Cities* (New York: Pegasus [Publishing], 1970).

58. *Ibid.,* p. 93.

59. *Ibid.,* p. 94.

60. John C. Leggett, *Class, Race, and Labor: Work-class Consciousness in Detroit* (New York: Oxford University Press, 1968).

61. Irving Louis Horowitz, *Three Worlds of Development: The Theory and Practice of Interna-*

tional Stratification, ed. 2 (New York: Oxford University Press, 1972), p. 273. On Rousseau and Durkheim, see Sheldon S. Wolin, *Politics and Vision: Continuity and Innovation in Western Political Thought* (Boston: Little, Brown and Co., 1960); Ferdinand Tönnies, *Community and Society* (Charles P. Loomis, translator and editor) (New York: Torchbooks, 1957). For an account of community in action, see William F. Whyte, *Street Corner Society* (Chicago: University of Chicago Press, 1955).

62. Richard C. Edwards, Michael Reich, and Thomas E. Weisskopf (editors), *The Capitalist System and A Radical Analysis of American Society* (Englewood Cliffs, N.J.: Prentice-Hall, Inc., 1972); Michael Parenti, *Democracy for the Few* (New York: St. Martin's Press, Inc., 1974); John Walton and Donald E. Carns (editors), *Cities in Change: Studies on the Urban Condition* (Boston: Allyn & Bacon, Inc., 1973); Warren Bloomberg, Jr., and Harry Schmandt (editors), *Power, Poverty and Urban Policy* (Beverly Hills: Sage Publications, Inc., 1968).

CHAPTER 2

Information about health care providers

The continuing discussion of the state of America's health care has concentrated mainly on structural aspects of the consumer/provider relationship. Prohibitively high costs, impersonalism, cultural and racial discrimination, physical distance and inaccessibility, long waits, and poor care are all traits allegedly common to medical center, clinics, prepaid medical plans, solo and group practices, and other health care providers.[1] However, concentrating on these structural lacunae and shortcomings tends to hide another fundamental aspect of health care utilization: the consumer's awareness of available services and how to gain access to them. This information is a prerequisite for obtaining services and ranks with structural reforms in strategic importance.

Where do low income urban dwellers get their information about health service providers? What are the preferences for care among available sources of treatment? Our concern here is with people about whom the United States government recently wrote:

> On nearly every index that we have, the poor and the racial minorities fare worse than their opposites. Their lives are shorter; they have more chronic and debilitating illnesses; their infant and maternal death rates are higher; their protection, through immunization, against infectious diseases is far lower. They also have far less access to health services— and this is particularly true of poor and non-white children, millions of whom receive little or no dental or pediatric care.[2]

Our aim is to ascertain what minority communities know about available health care providers.[3] One might seek this knowledge by asking direct questions such as: "Is there a place where one's child can receive a preschool smallpox immunization?" or "Is there a place where one can go to get a bad cut tended?" This type of interrogation usually obtains the desired results since most people, in the quiet of their living rooms, can remember having seen or heard about such a facility. The question is whether these responses would give a clue as to where the person would actually go for help. That is, the armchair respondent still may not recall the provider if confronted with a health-related problem. Answers to direct questions of this type may provide only abstract information: names and places that would not be considered in an actual decision-making situation.

Seeking the information people actually bring to problem-solving situations leads to another approach. Respondents can be placed in a hypothetical decision-making situation by asking where they would recommend a friend or family member to go for treatment in each of five fairly common situations. The reasoning is that responses to these problems reveal preferences that, in turn, reflect the knowledge of what is actually available to the person as sources of care. After the responses of those interviewed are aggregated, a profile emerges of the group's awareness of alternative health care providers. With the group's information profiles, we can proceed to determine the sources or origins of information by inquiring how the respondent learned about the provider recommended as a source of treatment.

This two-stage approach to health care information reveals distinctly different communication patterns within the communities under examination and suggests that alternative methods of disseminating information about health care services are called for in order to reach the diverse components of the American society.

Class, ethnicity, and health

Previous studies of the sources and content of information about health care have argued that social class is related to variations in level, accuracy, and origins. For example, Feldman reports that the ability to identify the symptoms of cancer, polio, and diabetes increases with increase in educational attainment, socioeconomic status, and income.[4] Since education may very well be a prerequisite to obtaining managerial, technological, and professional employment, it is not surprising that education seems a controlling variable. Rosenblatt and Suchman tie education to class and class to differential information in a study that reports a generally lower level of information about scientific medicine among blue-collar respondents.[5]

Class apparently correlates not only with different levels of accuracy but also with distinct sources of health-related information. Koos suggests that the residents of "Regionville" gain their information about providers and symptoms from face-to-face contacts with physicians, friends, and family members.[6] Ianni reports that in the lowest social stratum, printed matter is the most frequently cited source of health care information; television as a source declines steadily and significantly as class declines; and physicians are sources of information for those of higher status.[7] Feldman challenges this finding and argues that printed and broadcast media are principal sources for the more highly educated while the less educated rely on personal contacts. Disputing Koos and Ianni, Feldman concludes that "there are a number of other surveys which duplicate our findings that professional sources of health information rank well below the mass media and conversations with friends."[8]

Class is not the only axis that divides the overall population, however. Sinehart reveals that ethnicity is related to differential sources of information: non-Anglos and less well educated Anglos gain information from the broadcast media; middle-class Anglos and "well-educated" non-Anglos from newspapers, periodicals, and other printed matter.[9]

Even given the fact that "well educated," "middle class" and "less well educated" are hardly powerful delimiters or useful tools for analytical discourse, Sinehart's emphasis on ethnicity as an independent variable is well taken. Some of the literature will be reviewed that points to the conclusion that even when class is equalized, ethnicity is still related to variations in health care behavior and conditions. Here the crux of our concern is the interrelationship of ethnicity and class.

In the following study of the preferences for health care and the sources of information about providers in minority communities, three conditions guide the enterprise. First, the work has to produce information that would be useful to individuals and groups attempting to improve the organization and delivery of personal health care services. Second, the work should be innovative: that is, rather than repeating research already done, something new should be tackled. And third, the work should yield theoretically interesting results.

These three conditions were met through a research design that incorporates five different samples from an urban population: Anglos who are under 65 years of age, Anglos who are over 65 years of age, Blacks, Pilipinos, and Japanese. The latter two groups have largely been overlooked by students of health care behavior. Indeed, Pilipinos (like other fragmentary Asian and Latin American communities in the United States) have been ignored by scholars, politicians, and community service organizations, in part because many have been subsumed under the Spanish-surname census category. As the following brief summaries reveal, each of the groups has acute health care needs and problems, some of which could be remedied by more adequate dissemination of information about providers and services throughout the group.

Low income Anglos

When we read that poverty Blacks have a postneonatal mortality of 15.6 per 1,000 live births compared with 7.6 for nonpoverty Blacks, the comparison of poverty area Anglos (7.8) and nonpoverty Anglos (4.9) seems much less striking.[10] But when we look only at poverty/nonpoverty Anglo comparison, we readily see that the poor Anglo's baby has a 60% higher chance of dying. If it lives, the under-$5,000 income Anglo's child will average 3.3 physician visits per year; the over-$5,000 income bracket Anglo's child will average 4.2.[11] Moreover, low income Anglos, like other medically disadvantaged groups, are assigned to hospital wards, treated as teaching material, and are "subject, at every stage and every way, to inferior medical care and human indignity." If they turn up at an outpatient clinic or emergency room, along with their non-Anglo peers, they will be greeted with "indignity, abuse, and disregard."[12]

The elderly

The elderly share with the ethnic minorities distinctive health care needs. For example, in 1971 the per capita health care expenditures for persons 65 and older was $861; for those under 65 it was $250.[13] Perhaps these disparate outlays reflect the fact that persons over 65 are twice as likely as those under 65 to have one or more chronic conditions, that the elderly average seven visits to a physician each year compared with five for younger persons, that the elderly are more frequently admitted to hospitals, and that their average length of stay is about twice as long as that for younger persons.[14] When expenditure figures are combined with the social and economic discrimination and prejudice leveled against them, the roughly 10% of the national population who are 65 and over may be said to resemble a minority group.[15] In the following analysis 65-and-older Anglos are treated as a distinct community, and their preferences and information profiles are compared with those of other minorities.

Blacks

Blacks, living in either poverty or nonpoverty, are repeatedly reported to have higher levels of many illnesses and a lower rate of physician and hospital utilization than Anglos.[16] In a Chicago study, poverty Black infant mortality was almost double that of the poverty Anglo: 45.5 and 22.2 per 1,000 live births, respectively. Postneonatal mortality of the same groups was 15.6 and 4.9 per 1,000 survivors to 28 days—a threefold increase among the poverty Blacks.[17] Several studies suggest that after the variables for class, income, and age are controlled, Blacks have important disadvantages in several health care areas.[18]

Pilipinos

With the repeal in 1965 of the national origin's quota system for immigration, the Pilipino population in the United States began to climb rapidly. In 1960 the Census Bureau reported 176,310 Pilipinos living in the United States; a decade later the Census Bureau found 343,060—a 100% increase. Moreover, the pace of immigration has picked up over the last few years: 6,093 in 1966, 10,865 in 1967, 16,731 in 1968, 20,744 in 1969, 31,203 in 1970, 28,471 in 1971, 29,376 in 1972, and 30,799 in 1973.[19] Many of the recent immigrants are relatives of earlier immigrants who join the latter in the agricultural areas of central California; others are associated with the U.S. Navy and settle in San Diego, Oakland, San Pedro, Seattle, and other coastal cities. A small percent are partners in international marriages, often with Anglo or Black members of the military. A larger fraction is Pilipino technicians and professionals—several thousand are nurses and physicians—who come to the United States to begin careers.[20] From the 1970 census it appears that a large number of Pilipinos (recent and long-term residents) are lower income, working class.[21] Besides sharing the disabilities of the overall low income population, some Pilipinos are only partially acculturated and many elderly have acute difficulties in obtaining health care.[22] Moreover, the Pilipino community does not seem to provide comprehensive internal support and services to its members; apparently the community is highly fragmented along class and place-of-origin as well as other axes.[23] This fragmentation compounds the problems of the aged and medically needy by compromising efforts at communitywide research, planning, and development of delivery systems.

Japanese

There are approximately 600,000 American citizens or resident aliens of Japanese extraction living in the United States. While the Japanese are largely concentrated in Hawaii and California, there are sizeable populations in other states. Many Japanese share with Chinese, Thais, Koreans, and other Asians cultural particularities and limitations in English fluency that aggravate other problems of gaining health care.[24] But in some ways the Japanese are distinctive among Asian Americans. For instance, unlike the urban Chinese who are largely ghettoized in "Chinatowns" within major cities,[25] the Japanese—thanks in part to their internment in concentration camps during World War II—are much more dispersed in suburbs and working class neighborhoods. The Japanese community has emerged out of the camps to win an important measure of economic success; in 1970 its median family income was $12,515 compared with $10,610 for the Chinese, $9,318 for the Pilipino, and $9,590 for the total U.S. population.[26] But even with this relative affluence, health problems of many elderly Japanese are complicated by poverty, loneliness, boredom, and other aspects of isolation.[27]

Relation of ethnicity to health care information

Our aim here is to explore the impact of ethnicity on provider preference and source of information about health care services. In order to test this hypothesis, we must control for the effects of other variables such as income, local availability of providers, and information in the mass media. In part, this control was achieved by selecting people to be studied from the same environment.

With the use of 1970 census data, clusters of low income members of each target population were located within the southern California region. In principle, every respondent had access to the same English-language mass media, the same local transportation system (or nonsystem), and the same types of providers (such as county hospitals, public health clinics, general proprietary hospitals). With the exception of the Pilipino sample who lived 25 miles away, all respondents were drawn from contiguous neighborhoods. Thus situational and ecological factors were equalized.

As Table 2-1 reveals, the five samples contain basically the same distribution of major socioeconomic and demographic characteristics. Using the conventional indicators of social class (education, occupation, income), we see that the samples contain about equal proportions of poverty, working, and small-business individuals. Overall, with minor and insignificant exceptions, the samples parallel each other in class composition. With class, demographic, and situational factors roughly controlled through the sampling procedure, we can examine the weight of ethnicity on information patterns.

When neighborhoods of prospective respondents were located, teams of trained college students of the same ethnicity were dispatched. Approximately half of the Japanese and Pilipinos who consented to be interviewed conducted the session in Japanese and Tagalog, respectively. Bilingual interviewers coded these questionnaires in English. The refusal-to-be-interviewed rate among Anglos, Pilipinos, and Japanese was about 10%. Among the Blacks called upon, the refusal rate was nearly 50%—on some blocks as high as eight out of ten. Many of the Blacks' homes were located in a high crime, extreme poverty area, and their occupants may have been reluctant to open their doors and reveal their possessions and themselves to unfamiliar callers. Although there is no way to demonstrate that the Blacks who refused to be interviewed are essentially the same as those who cooperated, the refusal rate probably introduced little or no meaningful bias. Block-based quota sampling was

Table 2-1. Selected socioeconomic characteristics

	Anglo 64 and younger	Anglo 65 and older	Black	Japanese	Pilipino
Female respondents	72.2%	67.2%	70.4%	66.7%	42.9%
Mean family size of sample	2.9	1.4	4.2	3.6	3.6
Educational attainment°					
Less than sixth grade	2.1%	4.8%	7.6%	2.2%	12.2%
Sixth to eighth grade	7.6	33.3	8.6	11.8	13.8
Ninth to twelfth grade	18.8	9.5	21.4	18.4	9.0
High school diploma	36.8	22.2	23.9	30.9	14.8
Some college	27.1	23.8	29.9	27.2	18.5
College degree(s)	7.6	6.4	8.6	9.5	31.7
Occupational status†					
Executive and proprietors of large concerns and major professionals	4.2%	6.3%	.8%	3.5%	3.2%
Managers and proprietors of medium-sized businesses and lesser professionals	11.8	9.4	10.2	5.7	6.3
Administrative personnel of large concerns, owners of small businesses and semiprofessionals	4.9	6.3	6.1	6.7	10.1
Owners of small businesses, clerical and sales, technicians	25.3	15.6	25.4	42.9	22.2
Skilled workers, foremen	11.8	17.2	9.3	7.8	7.9
Semiskilled workers	25.3	18.8	22.0	18.6	18.0
Unskilled workers	16.7	26.4	27.2	15.8	32.3
Income‡					
Less than $2,000	10.1%	16.4%	14.1%	8.6%	9.5%
$2,000 to $3,999	23.2	50.8	13.3	8.6	12.1
$4,000 to $5,999	18.9	13.1	17.8	10.9	15.9
$6,000 to $7,999	13.0	11.5	15.9	14.1	11.5
$8,000 to $9,999	10.9	4.9	16.8	10.9	10.9
$10,000 to $11,999	6.5	—	9.7	17.2	13.7
$12,000 to $14,000	5.1	—	5.3	16.4	8.8
More than $14,000	12.3	3.3	7.1	13.3	17.6
Total number of cases	144	64	125	141	189

°Includes non-American equivalents.
†Based on principal occupation of head of household prior to retirement.
‡Combined income from all sources and members of household during 12 months preceding interview.

employed, and the interviewers remained on a block until filling their quota, usually 10 interviews. Moreover, other research has found that among poverty Blacks, there are no significant differences among refusals and those interviewed.[28] It is my judgment that the present Black sample provides a valid sample of the parent community.

Recommendations for treatment

As noted previously, each respondent was presented five hypothetical situations and asked: "Where would you suggest a friend or member of your family go in each of the following situations: has a badly cut leg, needs a typhoid shot or smallpox inoculation, has been nervous or emotionally upset, wants advice about a pregnancy problem, and wants information about venereal disease?"

The responses should be read as expressions of preferences made in the context of sociological and economic as well as medical considerations. However, they can also be interpreted as indications of information in utilizable form; these are the places people think about and are willing to suggest as solutions to problems. Overall, the responses are illustrative of the problem-solving information in the community.

Table 2-2 reveals a fairly clear-cut divergence between reliance on private practitioners and public providers. The under-65 Anglo, Black, and Pilipino samples more often recommend public health clinics and emergency rooms for treatment of each of the five needs than do the Japanese and elderly Anglo samples. The Japanese and elderly Anglos consistently prefer the family physician or general practitioner for treatment in each case except that of treating a badly cut leg. Even in this case the Japanese and elderly Anglo samples are much less willing to recommend an emergency room, falling behind the other groups by 25% to 30%.

These profiles are divergent for a number of reasons. Some of the variation in private/public selection reflects the relatively greater mobility of the Black, young Anglo, and Pilipino samples. The three groups that most often mention clinics or emergency rooms show the highest percent of respondents having lived in their present residence 1 year or less. Conversely, the elderly Anglo and Japanese groups far surpass the others in reports of 10 years' or longer continuous residency. When the relationship between length of residence and recommendation was examined, it was found that the likelihood of mentioning a public provider or emergency room decreased with increased longevity. It would be expected that newcomers to a city or those who have moved into a new neighborhood would take some time in locating a physician and establishing a family doctor bond. Newcomers would, however, be able to recommend clinics and emergency rooms since they are "always around."

Moreover, numerous studies have shown that the propensity to obtain treatment from clinics and emergency rooms varies inversely with income[29]; since relatively more Blacks and younger Anglos fall into the lowest income strata, this disproportion may account for some of the variation.

While nearly two thirds of the elderly Anglo sample reports earning less than $4,000, however, it has a much higher rate of *not* selecting clinics and

Table 2-2. Would recommend a friend or family go for treatment of cited problem (by ethnicity)

	Anglo 64 and younger	Anglo 65 and older	Black	Japanese	Pilipino
Badly cut leg					
Family doctor; general practitioner	13.6%	26.6%	13.3%	40.3%	27.0%
Emergency room of a hospital	78.5	57.8	80.0	51.5	57.7
Outpatient clinic	4.2	6.3	0	2.8	3.2
Other; no response	3.7	9.3	6.7	5.4	12.1
Needs shots					
Family doctor; general practitioner	47.9	51.6	37.5	66.0	33.3
Emergency room of a hospital	3.5	4.7	1.7	4.3	6.9
Outpatient clinic	6.3	7.8	5.0	4.3	9.5
Public health office or clinic	36.1	25.0	45.0	22.0	42.3
Free clinic	4.9	1.6	10.0	1.4	6.9
Other; no response	6.2	9.3	0.8	2.0	1.1
Nervous, emotionally upset					
Family doctor; general practitioner	34.0	50.0	34.2	43.3	31.2
Specialist depending on the problem	35.4	15.6	33.3	31.2	28.0
Emergency room of a hospital	4.2	6.3	5.8	7.8	13.2
Outpatient clinic	4.2	3.1	1.7	2.8	4.8
Public health office or clinic	3.5	4.7	7.5	4.3	9.0
Minister or priest	9.7	12.5	14.2	2.8	9.5
Other; no response	9.0	7.8	3.3	7.8	4.3
Pregnancy problem					
Family doctor; general practitioner	52.1	60.9	50.8	50.4	42.9
Specialist depending on the problem	10.4	4.7	5.8	17.7	12.2
Emergency room of a hospital	1.4	1.6	3.3	2.1	8.5
Outpatient clinic	2.8	4.7	5.8	2.1	9.0
Public health office or clinic	15.3	7.8	15.0	7.1	15.9
Free clinic	13.9	9.4	14.2	10.6	9.5
Other; no response	4.1	19.1	5.1	10.0	2.0
Venereal disease					
Family doctor; general practitioner	35.4	43.8	28.3	43.3	29.1
Specialist depending on the problem	2.1	3.1	5.0	0.7	12.7
Emergency room of a hospital	2.1	4.7	2.5	3.5	5.3
Public health office or clinic	35.4	26.6	38.3	27.0	32.3
Free clinic	21.5	9.4	23.3	13.5	10.1
Other; no response	3.5	12.4	2.6	12.0	10.5
Total number of cases	144	64	125	141	189

emergency rooms for treatment. Factors other than economic seem germane here.

In part, the elderly Anglo sample's preference for a family physician may reflect traditional American folklore. Historically the solo practitioner has been the predominant provider to the working and middle classes—indeed, in most of the United States, has been the only source of care. And medical care, like driving a new car, is a privilege one must (and should) pay for. Also, the traditional belief that welfare and charity recipients are slackers and failures probably works to preclude consideration of public providers. Although this particular variation of Social Darwinism is weakening, it was still virulent during the pre–World War II era among the middle masses of the Midwest, the origins of many of the present elderly Anglo sample. This prestige and ego-protecting bias is probably reinforced by the identification of public providers with non-Anglo minorities: Blacks, or Chicanos in California and the Southwest. Thus, the elderly Anglos (and others as well) may seek to avoid what is seen as lower class, socially disreputable facilities that, because they serve inferior people, *must* dispense inferior care.[30]

Younger Anglos, perhaps, are less victimized by their parents' and grandparents' biases against public providers. Selection of free clinics, for example, was almost exclusively made (in all four samples) by the 25-and-younger respondents. The younger Anglos have matured in a society that has proliferated the public sources of health care. Public assistance is now commonly given. Nearly one third of the younger Anglo sample receive Medicaid or some other form of public assistance; thus they are far more familiar with public social services than are the older generations and probably stigmatize it much less.

For many low income people, public clinics and emergency rooms offer internists, pediatricians, and other specialists who are not available privately.[31] Haynes and McGarvey write, "Of the 19 physicians reported to be in the immediate area of John Hopkins University (a Baltimore Black ghetto) in 1968, 13 were general practitioners, 5 were internists, and 1 was a pediatrician. Of the 106 practitioners in the Watts area of Los Angeles, only 17 were specialists. . . . In a poor section of Washington, D.C., there are 40 physicians but only 1 is a pediatrician." They conclude, "In general, the percentage of specialists in the poverty areas is lower than that in the nonpoverty areas and even this figure is inflated because the percentage of board-certificated specialists is even lower."[32]

Pilipinos share with Blacks a higher rate of recommending public providers. While the ramifications of poverty and the unavailability of private providers contribute to the Pilipinos' profile, two other factors have special salience for their preferences. The first is the relatively large number of the sample that is elderly, retired agricultural laborers. These men spent 30 or 40 years moving from place to place, thus having little time to establish a relationship with a family physician. What care they received, and their medical histories reveal it to be minimal, often came at a public health clinic or in an emergency room after an accident or prolonged secondary infection. (As we shall see in a moment, "personal experience" is the source of much of the Pilipinos' information about providers.)

The second condition is the absence of Pilipino physicians and other providers *in private practice.* Private practice is the key because the Pilipino community, along with the Black, counts in its midst a number of health care providers. Indeed, the Republic of the Philippines is a large exporter of health professionals to the United States—4,752 physicians reported between 1968 and 1974.[33] But few Pilipino physicians, just as few Black physicians and dentists, tend to be found in private ghetto practice. Both are more often encountered as residents or interns at teaching hospitals or urban medical centers, that is, in emergency rooms and outpatient clinics. For Pilipinos and Blacks, the likelihood of encountering a "brother" or "sister" is greater at the public facility.

Unlike the Pilipinos, the Japanese opt for the family physician. This may appear contradictory to those who see certain similarities in the two groups. Both are cultural as well as ethnic minorities. Many members speak little or no English; those who are marginally assimilated often have distinctive diets; both communities have been victimized by discrimination, prejudice, and violence; and many Japanese and Pilipinos live in semighettos or reside in clusters in urban centers.[34]

But these similarities must not obscure several profound differences. Almost all Pilipino physicians are immigrants from the Islands; they tend to locate outside the local community, and their patients generally are non-Pilipino. The Japanese community contains locally produced providers: there are numerous *Nisei* (the first U.S.-born generation, the sons of the *Issei* pioneers) and *Sansei* (the second generation U.S.-born, sons of the Nisei) physicians, dentists, pharmacists and nurses, and various specialists. And the Japanese patronize these community members; trips of 20, 30, even 50 miles to visit a Japanese dentist or physician are commonplace.

Why do the Japanese prefer private providers? Many respondents said that their customary physician, dentist, and pharmacist[35] are Japanese, so that when they indicated a preference for a private practitioner, in effect the Japanese respondent was saying that he or she would recommend a Japanese physician to a friend or family member.

The recommendation of Japanese physicians to friends or family (that is, very likely to another Japanese) reflects a broader sociopsychological pattern. The Japanese who are either little acculturated or barely assimilated into the dominant society have a range of support open to them that the much more fragmented Pilipino community denies its members. As Kitano expresses it, "Many Japanese still need the ethnic structure and the justification for the cradle-to-grave services (e.g., a Japanese doctor will be on hand at delivery; a Japanese priest will perform over the burial; and in between, one lives a life of friends, dating and marriage primarily with other Japanese) provided by the ethnic community. . . ."[36] Kitano points out that this dependence on the ethnic community for physical and psychological support varies with generation and class; the older and lower classes of the present sample rank very high in relative dependence.[37]

But lest we think of the present Japanese sample as wholly or even largely unacculturated or unassimilated, it must be pointed out that many fully acculturated middle-aged and college-educated middle-class individuals are incorporated within. These segments are comparatively free from many of the financial and psychological conditions that restrain their more traditional kinsmen. Yet it was found that the preference pattern of the Japanese sample was largely undisturbed by variations in socioeconomic characteristics. Why, then, the continuing preference across the community for Japanese providers?

The acculturated and assimilated Japanese may be drawn to the community provider, not because they need him, as their parents or grandparents may, but because they prefer to receive treatment from a fellow Japanese. In some cases this preference is based on pride: "He's as good a doctor as any Anglo; I'll patronize him because I feel pride in *our* accomplishment." Others see the Japanese provider as less risky: "Since he largely depends on the community for his livelihood," the Japanese patient speculates, "he is less likely to exploit me, to overcharge or mistreat me, because if I complain, the community will quickly know about my dissatisfaction." Others, perhaps somewhat less cynically, see the politeness, patience, and gentleness of the (stereotype) Japanese as a promise of more humane treatment. Finally, there are the Japanese who have been seared directly or vicariously by the internment or other acts of discrimination and who simply do not trust non-Japanese in any relationship, let alone one as intimate as health care.[38]

Sources of information

Table 2-3 suggests another dimension to the preference for Japanese physicians by Japanese patients: the presence in the community of an active referral network. After each respondent was asked for a recommendation of a provider for the previously mentioned health problems, each was asked; "Where did you learn about this provider?" Sixty percent of the Japanese indicated a friend or member of the family (Table 2-3). No other group

Table 2-3. Sources of information about health care providers

Source	Anglo 64 and younger	Anglo 65 and older	Black	Japanese	Pilipino
Television or radio	8.5%	6.1%	6.8%	5.9%	4.9%
Newspapers	6.0	5.8	6.2	5.2	4.4
Friends of members of the family	29.1	19.6	23.8	58.4	28.8
Personal experience (such as previous visit)	42.8	48.3	55.3	17.4	48.9
Recommended by a physician	7.4	10.5	5.5	4.8	5.5
School	4.4	6.1	2.4	4.8	3.1
Booklets, pamphlet, or other literature	0.9	1.8	—	0.7	3.1
Telephone book	0.9	1.8	—	2.8	1.3
Total number of cases*	705	275	587	680	891

*Combined frequencies; no responses, don't knows, and "others" eliminated.

mentioned half as often this source of information about providers. This overwhelming reliance on family and friends underscores the ethnocommunal structure Kitano and others have pointed to among the U.S. Japanese population.

The source-of-information data also highlight a basic difference between the Japanese and Pilipino communities: while the former relies on family and friends, the latter reports "personal experience" as the source of information (three times more often than among the Japanese). This may reflect the isolation of many elderly Pilipino males and the absence of nuclear families. The men who migrated as agricultural laborers, cannery workers, and the like in the 1920s and 1930s were not permitted to marry mainland women because of miscegenation laws; at the same time, Pilipino women were excluded after 1934 by the Tydings-McDuffie Law, otherwise known as the Philippine Independence Act. Only after World War II did many Pilipinos find it somewhat less difficult to form families.

However, even when the presence of many elderly single males in the Pilipino population is taken into account, the fact remains that nearly half of the present sample is female and that many of these have resided in their present dwelling for a decade or more. Unless we are willing to overlook that obvious residential isolation, cultural particularities, language problems, and other distinguishing traits of the Pilipino population and consider them "Anglicized" because their reliance on personal experience is equivalent to that of the Anglo and Black samples, it seems reasonable to ascribe the difference between the information networks of the Japanese and Pilipino groups to the absence in the latter community of an integrative and interactive ethnic structure.

Looking at the lack of difference in sources of information between the Anglo and Black samples, we find that citing the mass media does *not* increase among the latter; nor does mentioning media increase with higher educational attainment in any sample. The similarities in the profiles of the Anglos and Blacks indicate that both gain their information in the same manner: from their experiences. Yet the Black sample more frequently selects public providers. Unless we are willing to believe that Blacks simply are unaware of private providers and, therefore, have experienced only public ones, the argument that Blacks are unable to cope with bureaucratic, technological medicine is clearly inapplicable; the public providers that Blacks have experienced and *continue to recommend* are the most highly bureaucratized of the preferred alternatives. The Black sample may not enjoy or even prefer these providers, but they do appear sufficiently confident with them to suggest them as sources of care for friends or family. We shall pursue the reasons for Black selection of public providers in Chapter 5.

Using the community for health education

Looking to see what people know about sources of treatment reveals a pervasive pattern of ignorance and misinformation. The recommendation of emergency room care for emotional problems, venereal disease, pregnancy problems, inoculations, and other nonemergency elective procedures is a clear misapplication of that provider.[39] Of a more serious nature is the absence of information about free clinics, the immunization and inoculation programs of the local public health department, local venereal disease clinics, and crisis intervention programs. Because these specialized programs are designed to remove nonemergency cases from the overcrowded emergency rooms and to serve critical needs of the poor and medically indigent, their relative anonymity is doubly unfortunate.[40] Since these programs rely for outreach on media exposure, their invisibility may be attributed to the failure of the media to inform effectively tens of millions of people.

After the significance of ethnicity on information and preference patterns is observed, the temptation is great to claim that ethnic differences are a controlling factor in developing problem-solving information and that would-be reformers and others interested in placing clients by way of providers should address each ethnic community differently. The survey results clearly illustrate the importance of ethnicity: Anglo, Black, Japanese, and Pilipino samples do differ in their provider recommendations and sources of information. But exclusive emphasis on ethnic differences is an oversimplification. In utilization and informational profiles the Black and younger Anglo samples are quite similar. Both groups can be educated about alternative sources of care at emergency rooms and public clinics because this is where they have their personal experiences. Asians, on the other hand, and other marginally assimilated groups such as Latin Americans, Anglo rural migrants,[41] native Americans, and Puerto Ricans must be educated in the context of their communities. This implies finding and then utilizing the linkages between dominant and communal societies, linkages such as vernacular community newspapers, service and social groups that may have counterpart organizations, public assistance caseworkers, and students from conventional, adult, and special education programs. If these linkages are exercised, information can be introduced into the predominant person-to-person disseminating network of the community.[42]

Even if health care information is disseminated with an eye to the way it will optimally educate and inform the various segments of the minority communities, however, no basic reform in utilization and no elementary correction in mortality and morbidity rates will be realized unless structural reforms are simultaneously made. Knowledge about providers who remain racist, inhumane, discriminatory, inaccessible, and prohibitively expensive will do little to change prevailing utilization patterns or improve health and well being. Structural reform *and* community education are prerequisites to improvement.

Notes

1. For an example of a structural critique, see Barbara and John Ehrenreich, *The American Health Empire* (New York: Vintage Books, 1971).
2. U.S. Department of Health, Education, and Welfare, *Towards a Comprehensive Health Policy for the 1970's. A White Paper* (Washington, D.C.: U.S. Government Printing Office, 1971), p. 2.
3. On low income and health care behavior, see John Kosa, Aaron Antonovsky, and Irving K. Zola (editors), *Poverty and Health* (Cambridge: Harvard University Press, 1969); Rodger

Hurley, *Poverty and Mental Retardation* (New York: Vintage Press, 1969); Philip M. Moody and Robert M. Gray, "Social Class, Social Integration, and the Use of Preventive Health Services," in E. Gartly Jaco (editor), *Patients, Physicians, and Illness,* ed. 2 (New York: The Free Press, 1972), pp. 250-261; Myron J. Lefcowitz, "Poverty and Health: A Re-examination," *Inquiry* **10** (March 1973), pp. 3-13; Irving Leveson, "The Challenge of Health Services for the Poor," *The Annals* **399** (Jan. 1972), pp. 22-29; Wayne E. Smith, "Some Factors Associated with Age-Specific Death Rates, California Counties, 1964," *American Journal of Public Health* **58** (Oct. 1968), pp. 1937-1949; Lois Pratt, "The Relationship of Socioeconomic Status to Health," *American Journal of Public Health* **61** (Feb. 1971), pp. 281-291.

4. Jacob J. Feldman, *The Dissemination of Health Information* (Chicago: Aldine Publishing Co., 1966).

5. Daniel Rosenblatt and Edward A. Suchman, "Blue-Collar Attitudes and Information Toward Health and Illness," in Arthur B. Shostak and William Gomberg (editors), *Blue-Collar World: Studies of the American Worker* (Englewood Cliffs, N.J.: Prentice-Hall, Inc., 1964), pp. 324-333; Otto Reid, Patricia Arnaudo, and Aurilla White, "The American Health-Care System and the Poor: A Social Organization Point of View," *Welfare in Review* **6** (Nov.-Dec. 1968), pp. 1-12.

6. Earl L. Koos, *The Health of Regionville* (New York: Columbia University Press, 1954), p. 117.

7. Francis A. Ianni, Robert M. Albrecht, and Adele K. Polan, "Group Attitudes and Information Sources in a Polio Vaccine Program," *Public Health Reports* **75** (July 1960), pp. 665-671. Compare with William Griffiths and Andie L. Knutson, "The Role of Mass Media in Public Health," *American Journal of Public Health* **50** (April 1960), pp. 515-523.

8. Feldman, *Dissemination,* p. 137.

9. James W. Sinehart, "Voluntary Exposure to Health Communication," *American Journal of Public Health* **58** (July 1968), pp. 1265-1275.

10. Monroe Lerner, "Social Differences in Physical Health," in Kosa, Antonovsky, and Zola (editors), *Poverty and Health,* p. 96.

11. William C. Richardson, "Poverty, Illness and the Use of Health Services in the United States," *Hospitals* **43** (July 1969), pp. 34-40.

12. Julius A. Roth, "The Treatment of the Sick," in Kosa, Antonovsky, and Zola (editors), *Poverty and Health,* p. 242.

13. U.S. Senate, *Developments in Aging: 1971 and January-March 1972. A Report of the Special Committee on Aging, #92-784* (Washington, D.C.: U.S. Government Printing Office, 1972), pp. 23-24; U.S. Senate, *Barriers to Health Care for Older Americans* (Washington, D.C.: U.S. Government Printing Office, 1973).

14. U.S. Senate, *Developments,* p. 23.

15. Thomas W. Elwood states, "The aged resemble minority groups when measured by socio-economic criteria." From "Old Age and the Quality of Life," *Health Services Reports* **87** (Dec. 1972), p. 920.

16. Richardson, "Poverty," pp. 34-40; Lerner, "Social Differences," pp. 69-112; Eleanor Hunt and Earl E. Huyck, "Mortality of White and Non-White Infants in Major U.S. Cities," *Health, Education and Welfare Indicators* (Jan. 1966), pp. 1-19; Ann H. Pettigrew, "Negro American Health," in Thomas Pettigrew (editor), *Profiles of the American Negro* (New York: D. Van Nostrand Co., 1965), pp. 72-79, 202-235; W. M. Young, Jr., *Poor Health in the Richest Nation* (New York: McGraw-Hill Book Co., 1964), pp. 182-211; Leslie A. Falk, "The Negro American's Health and the Medical Committee for Human Rights," *Medical Care* **4** (July-Sept. 1966), pp. 171-177.

17. Pierre De Vise and others, *Slum Medicine: Chicago's Apartheid Health System* (Chicago: University of Chicago, Community and Family Study Center, 1969), p. 3; Ralph H. Hines, "The Health Status of Black Americans," in Jaco (editor), *Patients, Physicians, and Illness,* p. 44.

18. In a study of Blacks and Anglos in Oakland, California it was found that "Blacks had a higher average diastolic and systolic blood pressures and a higher prevalence of hypertension than whites for both males and females and for all age groups. When these distributions were examined by social class, blacks in the lowest social classes had the highest blood pressures." From S. Leonard Syme and others, "Social Class and Racial Differences in Blood

Pressure," *American Journal of Public Health* **64** (June 1974), pp. 619-622. Similar results are reported by Thomas Oakes and others, "Social Factors in Newly Discovered Elevated Blood Pressure," *Journal of Health and Social Behavior* **14** (Sept. 1973), pp. 198-204; F. Gilbert McMahan, Philip A. Cole, and Jerome R. Ryan, "A Study of Hypertension in the Inner City. A Student Hypertension Survey," *American Heart Journal* **85** (Jan. 1973), pp. 65-71; Ernest Harbur and others, "Socioecological Stressor Areas and Black-White Blood Pressure: Detroit," *Journal of Chronic Diseases* **26** (Sept. 1973), pp. 595-611. For other studies that suggest an independent ethnic factor when socioeconomic class is controlled, see Paul B. Cornely and S. K. Bigman, "Cultural Considerations in Changing Health Attitudes," *Medical Annals of the District of Columbia* **30** (April 1961), pp. 191-199; Wylda Cowles and Steven Polgar, "Health and Communication in a Negro Census Tract," *Social Problems* **10** (Winter 1963), pp. 228-236; Joseph R. Hochstim, D. A. Athanasopoulos, and John H. Larkins, "Poverty Area under the Microscope," *American Journal of Public Health* **58** (Oct. 1968), pp. 1815-1827; Lawrence Podell, *Studies in the Use of Health Services by Families on Welfare: Utilization of Preventive Health Services* (Springfield, Va.: National Technical Information Service, 1970, PB 190391); Jerry L. Weaver, "Health Care Costs as a Political Issue: Comparative Responses of Chicanos and Anglos," *Social Science Quarterly* **53** (March 1973), pp. 846-854.

19. U.S. Immigration and Naturalization Service, *Annual Report for Fiscal 1973* (Washington, D.C.: U.S. Government Printing Office, 1974), p. 56. Emmigration controls, imposed in 1971 by the Marcos dictatorship, recently have been eased—prsentaging another increase in Pilipino arrivals in the United States.

20. See Royal F. Morales, *Makibaka: The Pilipino American Struggle* (Los Angeles: Mountainview Publishers, 1974), pp. 69-89.

21. In the 1970 national census, 33.7% of the enumerated Pilipinos were laborers, farm workers, or service employees. Almost one fifth of all Pilipino families are 24% or more *below* the federal poverty level. From U.S. Bureau of the Census, *Census of Population. Subject Reports Final Report PC (2)-16. Japanese, Chinese, and Filipinos in the United States* (Washington, D.C.: U.S. Government Printing Office, 1973), pp. 158-160.

22. A study of elderly Pilipinos in Seattle found three principal barriers to health care services: (1) the unavailability of Pilipino physicians, (2) unavailability of Pilipino nurses and receptionists, and (3) lack of financial help. The first two points relate to communication barriers created by English-only personnel and the lessening of psychological stress that comes from being treated by one's own kind. From *Health Assessment of Elderly Pilipinos in International District, Seattle, Washington* (Seattle: Demonstration Project for Asian Americans, 1973).

23. "Filipinos coming from the same town or locality banded together and contributed to the central fund that would by utilized for hospital expenses and funerals. In 1970 there are at least 13 such organizations in Stockton, California, each looking out for the welfare of its members. Altogether there are more than 47 Filipino groups." From Lillian Galego, Laurena Cabanero, and Brian Tom, *Roadblocks to Community Building: A Case of the Filipino Community Center Project. Working Paper #4* (Davis: University of California, Asian American Research Project, 1970), pp. 12-13. In January 1974 there were reportedly 1872 clubs, councils, associations, and organizations in the United States; 102 in Los Angeles County alone. From Alex A. Esclamade, publisher of the *Philippine News*, personal communication.

24. For a comprehensive and current review of the various Pacific and Asian communities, see Lloyd Inui and Franklin Odo, *Asian American Experience* (Long Beach: California State University, Asian American Studies Program, 1974).

25. For studies of the health problems of Chinatown Chinese, see Frederick P. Li and others, "Health Care for the Chinese Community in Boston," *American Journal of Public Health* **62** (April 1972), pp. 536-539; L. P. Lee, A. Lim, and H. K. Wong, *San Francisco Chinese Community Citizen's Survey and Fact Finding Committee Report,* abridged edition (San Francisco: H. G. Garle, 1969), pp. 91-122; Timothy R. Brown and others, *Mental Illness and the Role of Mental Health Facilities in Chinatown* (Los Angeles: Resthaven Community Mental Health Center, Report #6, 1972); Stuart H. Cattell, *Health, Welfare and Social Organization in Chinatown, New York City* (New York: Community Service Society of New York City, 1962); Gil Lum, *A Draft of the Proposed Comprehensive Health Program for the Chinatown–North Beach Target Area* (San Francisco: North East Medical Services, Inc.,

1969); Glen Chinn and Linda Newcomb, *On the Feasibility of Training Asians to Work with Elderly Asians: A Preliminary Assessment of Needs and Resources Available to Asian Elderly in Seattle, Washington* (Seattle: Training Project for the Asian Elderly, 1973).

26. U.S. Department of Health, Education, and Welfare, *A Study of Selected Socio-Economic Characteristics of Ethnic Minorities Based on the 1970 Census. Vol. II: Asian Americans* (Washington, D.C.: U.S. Government Printing Office, 1974), p. 105.

27. Richard A. Kalish and Sam Yuen, "Americans of East Asian Ancestry: Aging and the Aged," *Gerontologist* 11 (Spring 1971), pp. 36-47; Trent Bassent, "An Aging Issei Anticipates Rejection," in Georgene Seward (editor), *Clinical Studies in Cultural Conflict* (New York: The Ronald Press Co., 1958), *passim;* Thomas Maretzki and Linda D. Nelson, "Psychopathology among Hawaii's Japanese: A Comparative Study," in William Caudill and Ysung-Yi Lin (editors), *Mental Health Research in Asia and the Pacific* (Honolulu: East-West Center Books, 1969), *passim.*

28. See Jacob Benus, "The Problem of Non-Response in Sample Surveys," in John B. Lansing and others, *Working Papers on Survey Research in Poverty Areas* (Ann Arbor: University of Michigan, Institute for Social Research, 1971), pp. 20-59.

29. Richardson, "Poverty," pp. 220-226; Joel J. Alpert and others, "Types of Families Using an Emergency Clinic," *Medical Care* 7 (Jan.-Feb. 1969), pp. 57-58; E. Richard Weinerman and others, "Yale Studies in Ambulatory Medical Care: Determinants of Use of Hospital Emergency Services," *American Journal of Public Health* 56 (July 1966), pp. 1037-1056.

30. John M. Goering and Rodney M. Coe, "Cultural Versus Situational Explanations of the Medical Behavior of the Poor," *Social Science Quarterly* 51 (Sept. 1970), pp. 309-319; Ozzie G. Simmons, *Social Status and Public Health* (New York: Social Science Research Council, 1958), p. 8.

31. "The 3,000 bed County Hospital, locally known as the 'Big House,' was found to be eight miles distant and one hour of public transporation away from Watts residents. *Yet it was in effect the only hospital available to most of these low income people.*" From David B. Starkweather and Arnold I. Kisch, "The Life Cycle Dynamic of Health Service Organizations," in Mary F. Arnold, L. Vaughn Blankenship, and John M. Hess (editors), *Administering Health Systems: Issues and Perspectives* (Chicago: Aldine Publishing Co., 1971), p. 320. Also see Anselm L. Strauss (editor), *Where Medicine Fails* (Chicago: Aldine Publishing Co., 1970); Eli Ginsberg and others, *Urban Health Services: The Case of New York* (New York: Columbia University Press, 1971).

32. M. Alfred Haynes and Michael R. McGarvey, "Physicians, Hospitals, and Patients in the Inner City," in John C. Norman (editor), *Medicine in the Ghetto* (New York: Appleton-Century-Crofts, 1969), p. 120.

33. Compiled from annual fiscal year reports of immigrants admitted by country or region of last permanent residence, U.S. Immigration and Naturalization Service.

34. George Farmer, *Education: The Dilemma of the Oriental-American* (Los Angeles: University of Southern California, School of Education, 1969); Ford H. Kuramoto, *Aging Among the Japanese Americans* (Los Angeles: University of Southern California, Gerontology Center, 1971); White House Conference on Aging, *Special Concerns Session Report on the Asian American Elderly* (Washington, D.C.: U.S. Government Printing Office, 1971).

35. Nisei pharmacists may also play an important curative role, especially offering aid for psychosomatic complaints. See Stanford M. Lyman, "Generation and Character: The Case of the Japanese American," in Hilary Conroy and T. Scott Miyakawa (editors), *East Across the Pacific: Historical and Sociological Studies of Japanese Immigration and Assimilation* (Santa Barbara: Clio Press, 1972), pp. 301-302.

36. Harry H. L. Kitano, *Japanese Americans: The Evolution of a Subculture* (Englewood Cliffs, N.J.: Prentice-Hall, Inc., 1969), p. 145.

37. *Ibid., passim;* Stanford M. Lyman, "Japanese-American Generation Gap," *Society* 10 (Jan.-Feb. 1973), pp. 55-63.

38. Kitano's observation about why so few Japanese receive public assistance cogently summarizes the factors related to recommending private (Japanese) practitioners: "It is difficult to pinpoint why the Japanese have seldom been on 'relief.' It may have stemmed in part from 'shame,' in part through ignorance of such programs, and in part from alternatives available within the ethnic community." From Kitano, *Japanese Americans,* p. 76.

39. Half or more of the emergency room visits analyzed were for nonurgent problems. From Alpert and others, "Types of Families using an Emergency Clinic," p. 56.

40. Jerome L. Schwartz, "First National Survey of Free Medical Clinics, 1967-1969," *HSMHA Health Reports* **86** (Sept. 1971), pp. 775-787. Anglo patients are predominant in street and sponsored centers, whereas neighborhood clinics serve mainly the minority patient.

41. Ellen J. Stekert, "Focus for Conflict: Southern Mountain Medical Beliefs in Detroit," in Américo Paredes and Ellen J. Stekert (editors), *The Urban Experience and Folk Tradition* (Austin: University of Texas Press, 1971), pp. 95-136.

42. Since these and other linkages between the dominant and minority communities and within the minority communities would reach different cohort, occupational, residential, and kinship groups, this recommendation does not reinforce the "fallacy of the single pyramid," which assumes (incorrectly) that information and motivation can trickle down to the public at large if the agency worker is successful in getting a few "key" leaders to endorse his or her program. Rather than relying on a few notables, the linkage approach places its emphasis on individuals and organizations that have contacts across the spacial as well as socioeconomic and demographic dimensions of the community, and especially on individuals *within* the low income and disadvantaged segments. Thus, the linkage approach assumes a major commitment to self-help, self-determination. For a discussion of the single pyramid fallacy, see Cowles and Polgar, "Health and Communication," pp. 235-236.

CHAPTER 3 Social patterns and health care problems of Asian Americans

No group in the American population is treated with a greater lack of understanding or is victimized by more stereotypes than the various peoples who are lumped under the label "Asian Americans." For census and record-keeping purposes, the government confers the "other" designation on many of them. The mass media portrays Asians as clean, neat, frugal people who smile, giggle and say "ah so!" or as maniacs who smash boards and people with their hands and feet. At other times, Asian Americans are labeled the "model minority" and the "quiet Americans" and are thought to be free from individual or collective disadvantages and unfulfilled aspirations because they rarely demonstrate disapproval or dissatisfaction.[1]

The very term Asian American, originally used in lieu of "Oriental," becomes a dysfunctional stereotype when it is used, because it conceals the heterogenity of the groups so labeled. In fact, the immigrants from the Asian/Pacific basin are as diverse and unique as the peoples who have immigrated from Europe. The Chinese, Japanese, Korean, Indonesian, Guamanian, Samoan, Pilipino, Vietnamese, Thai, and their neighbors each have an ancient heritage, culture, and history of their own. Yet until recently these groups were treated as comprising a monolithic entity, and only now are the distinctive characteristics of the separate Asian communities gaining recognition.

Among the developments that have made the Asian peoples more visible is the dramatic increase in the size of several communities. As Table 3-1 reveals, this growth is a consequence of the elimination in 1965 of immigration restrictions on Asians. Some new immigrants experience short-term disruption and adjustment difficulties that bring them to the attention of social workers, educators, domestic relations courts, health workers, and other officials. But most new arrivals quickly enter the labor force. Many open businesses (such as food markets and restaurants) that form the nucleus for transforming their neighborhoods into ethnic enclaves. For example, this is precisely the history of the Korean community's emergence in the Olympic-Western area of Los Angeles.

Another aspect of the new visibility is a growing group consciousness, an awareness of being Asian, of being distinctive. This awareness is coupled with a pride in oneself and one's community, and a determination to live in dignity. With awareness often comes a desire to recognize community problems and to take corrective action. In many cases concern leads to study projects that investigate and document housing, health, and employment deficiencies, and cultural exploitations.

Table 3-1. Immigration and population increase of Asian Americans

| Group | Immigrants (1965-1973)° | | Asian American population | | |
	Number	Percent increase	1960 (number)	1970 (number)	Percent increase (1960-1970)
Chinese	128,858	326.2	236,084	435,062	84.2
Japanese	37,250	71.7	473,170	591,290	24.9
Koreans	83,886	959.1	—	126,000†	80.0
					(1970-1974)
Pilipinos	177,912	883.9	181,614	343,060	88.8

°U.S. Immigration and Naturalization Service Reports for Fiscal Year 1973 (Washington, D.C., 1974).

†*A Study of Selected Socio-Economic Characteristics of Ethnic Minorities Based on the 1970 Census.* Vol. 2: Asian Americans (Arlington, Va.: Urban Associates, Inc., n.d. [1974]), p. xviii.

Although this consciousness and articulation have led to many positive results, there remains the necessity to identify the origins of many problems and to develop appropriate responses. I shall illustrate this thesis by an examination of the health care problems of two major Asian populations: the Japanese and the Pilipino.

The point of this comparison is twofold. First, focusing on the Japanese and Pilipino communities reveals the differences between the social conditions of long-established, fairly stable populations and those experiencing tremendous recent growth. Second, the comparison illustrates the distinctive social and physical pathologies within the different Asian American populations. The analysis suggests that fundamentally dissimilar social organization is an important yet little recognized variable in determining the nature of health (and other social) problems as well as the efficacy of remedial approaches.

Japanese community

There are approximately 600,000 American citizens or resident aliens of Japanese extraction living in the United States. While 70% are concentrated in Hawaii and California, there are sizeable communities in other states.[2] Unlike the largely urban Chinese population that is ghettoized in "Chinatowns" in major cities of both coasts, the Japanese are much more dispersed in the suburbs. However, significant numbers of Japanese are found in the inner cities of Seattle, Los Angeles, and the San Francisco Bay Area. These "Little Tokyos" contain many elderly Japanese as well as concentrations of ethnic restaurants and markets, Japanese language schools, theaters featuring Japanese films, and other cultural institutions.

The growing spatial separation of the Japanese has diminished the wide range of economic, social, and cultural networks that combined families, generations, classes, and neighborhoods both vertically and horizontally prior to World War II. Nevertheless, many Japanese presently living in outlying districts continue to maintain their ties with their kin, Japanese businesses and cultural institutions, and community service and social organizations.

Although there are Japanese who break out, a large majority (probably not less than two thirds of the population) remain closely tied to the community. This self-selected communalism is reinforced by a feeling of mistrust toward the dominant society and its institutions—a mistrust rooted in 7 decades of discrimination capped by the 1942 relocation of the mainland Japanese by the federal government.[3]

Pilipino community

One of the fastest growing populations in the United States, the Pilipino community is swelling with new immigrants. From 1965 when the national origins quota was amended and the Philippines reported only 2,489 emigrants to the United States to 1973's figure of 30,799, the size of the resident population has doubled. At current rates of growth, Pilipinos will outnumber both the Japanese and Chinese by 1980.

Some recent arrivals are relatives of earlier immigrants and have joined them in the agricultural areas of central California; others have gone to the middle west or eastern states. But most Pilipino immigrants have settled in the Pacific West, especially San Diego, Oakland, San Pedro, Los Angeles, and Seattle. Here the unskilled, dependents, and the elderly often move in with earlier arrivals. "Little Manilas" have appeared in several cities. Many contemporary sojourners are highly educated professionals who rapidly merge into suburbia. But it appears that a large number of immigrants (at least 40% of all males 16 years old and over) are lower income, working class.[4]

Table 3-2 demonstrates important differences between the Japanese and Pilipino communities. Although several hundred Pilipinos came to the United States in the 1910s and 1920s to pursue advanced education, a large number soon joined their countrymen who had been recruited as agricultural laborers in the fields and canneries of the West Coast. The post–1965 immigrants are predominantly university educated, but many are denied access to their former professions (the case with many health care professionals) because their limited English fluency brings failure at licensing board exams (Table 3-3).[5] This creates an anomalous and emotionally trying situation: although the mean educational attainment of the Pilipino population (12.3 years) compares favorably with that of the Japanese (12.6 years), the former are often kept from the positions and income for which they feel their education apparently prepared them. According to the 1970 census, Pilipinos are more often encountered in laboring and semiskilled occupations than the white-collar middle-class jobs into which the Japanese have moved.[6]

This summary of the main sociological characteristics of the Japanese and Pilipino communities suggests a pervasive pattern of cultural particularities and limited integration into the dominant society. Much of this communalism results from the social, economic, and cultural preferences of Japanese and Pilipinos. This is certainly a proper choice to be made by members of a free society; but in exercising the option, Japanese and Pilipinos (and other minorities as well) apparently face certain health care problems. As the following review illustrates, some of the most dangerous afflictions seem to be associated with their communal subcultures; others may stem from the

Table 3-2. Selected characteristics of Japanese and Pilipino populations in the U.S.

Characteristic	Japanese	Pilipino
Occupational status of head of household		
I Professionals, technicians	21.9%	21.8%
II Managers, administrators	13.6	3.6
III Sales, clerical, craftspersons	35.4	26.7
IV Operatives	8.9	14.2
V Laborers, services, private household workers	14.9	26.6
VI Farmers, farm managers, farm workers	5.3	8.1
Mean family income	$13,511	$6,322
Educational attainment of head of household		
Eighth grade or less	16.4%	30.2%
Ninth to eleventh grade	11.8	14.0
High school diploma	36.9	22.4
College (including degrees)	34.9	33.4

Data from U.S. Bureau of the Census, *Census of Population: 1970. Subject Reports. Final Report PC(2)-16. Japanese, Chinese, and Filipinos in the United States* (Washington, D.C.: U.S. Government Printing Office, 1973).

Table 3-3. Immigration of Pilipino health care professionals, 1968-1973

Occupation	1968	1969	1970	1971	1972	1973	Pilipinos as a percentage of immigrants from all countries, 1968-1973
Professional and student nurses	891	796	954	1,564	1,589	1,281	19.2
Optometrists	24	29	55	38	28	46	67.2
Pharmacists	151	294	262	269	244	283	43.9
Physicians and surgeons	706	785	770	980	782	729	16.3
Dentists	140	198	198	179	159	158	43.7

Data from U.S. Department of Justice, Immigration and Naturalization Service, *1973 Annual Report.* Many migrants are attracted by the advertisement in Philippine newspapers and professional periodicals of relatively well-paying positions. Unfortunately, stiff licensing examinations prove an insurmountable obstacle. See California Advisory Committee to the U.S. Commission on Civil Rights, *A Dream Unfulfilled: Korean and Pilipino Health Professionals in California* (Los Angeles, May 1975).

inability of the national health system to recognize and deal with the needs of Japanese and Pilipinos.

Morbidity and mortality among Japanese Americans

Several students of Japanese American health conditions have reported persistent mortality differentials between Japanese and Anglos. Gordon, for instance, claims that the overall mortality is and has been more favorable for Japanese.[7] Kitano alleges that in California the Japanese child at birth can expect to live about 6 to 7 years longer than the Anglo and 10 to 11 years longer than the Black. As a group, the Japanese are thought to have the lowest infant mortality as well as the lowest mortality throughout their life span.[8] But a careful review of available published sources reveals that the claim of greater longevity for Japanese in the United States rests on data that may be drastically distorted because of omissions and classifying errors.

California's vital statistics, which are the basis for most longevity and mortality projections, are based on cross-sectional analysis of birth and death reported for particular populations. That is, the total of all reported Japanese births is divided into the number of infant deaths occurring 0 to 28 days and 29 days to 12 months after birth to determine neonatal and infant mortality, respectively. A similar computation of *reported* births and deaths is used to fix life expectancy. This procedure *assumes* that the Japanese reported dying also had their births credited to the Japanese community and that all births and deaths are recorded. Yet members of the community repeatedly claim that both births and deaths, especially neonatal deaths, are not reported. During the 1920s and 1930s Japanese living in rural regions lost many babies whose deaths, like their births, were unattended by physicians. These events might be reported to the nearest Japanese Consulate so that the records of the family back in Japan could be kept accurate, but many Japanese saw no reason to report the events to the local authorities.

Accurate vital statistics also suffer from confusion on the part of registrars about the proper category for offspring of mixed marriages; is the child of a Japanese woman and an Anglo man listed by the mother's or father's ethnic group? Perhaps even less care and concern can be expected if the decision is being made about death certification.

Classification errors and unreported births or deaths that confound the cross-sectional technique remain a continuing problem. This is seen when data that employ the traditional methodology are compared with those from a method that effectively avoids classifying and reporting errors. Breslow and Klein, using data generated by traditional methods, offer a set of infant death rates that report the alleged Japanese advantage.[9] But Norris and Shipley,[10] using data from a carefully delimited population born in 1965 and followed through 1967, reveal that when matched cohorts of Japanese and Anglos are compared, the advantageous rate of the Japanese evaporates:

Death rate per 1,000 live births, 0 to 11 months

	Breslow and Klein	*Norris and Shipley*
Anglo	18.8	19.3
Black	30.1	32.3
Japanese	13.2	22.0

Both analyses are based on California experience for the 1965-1967 period. Since the "official" infant mortality is demonstratively unreliable, we may reasonably question the accuracy of other comparative longevity figures.

With this caveat about the reliability of statistics in mind, let us review the morbidity profile of the Japanese population. Although much of the research reported in medical journals deals with Hawaiian Japanese, the findings (within the limits noted) at the very least are suggestive of trends in the mainland population.

Cancer

The unusual rates of specific site cancers among Japanese have attracted a score or more of discussants. Haenszel and Kurihara state that if the U.S. Anglo population is taken as descriptive of the national norm, the Japanese have definitely higher rates of esophagus, stomach, liver, and biliary passage cancers.[11] Among Hawaiians, 1947-1954 records report the following comparative site frequencies per 100,000 populations[12]:

	Large intestine	Stomach	Prostate	Uterine, cervical
Anglo	18.6	18.7	25.4	19.6
Japanese	10.0	48.6	2.8	19.4
Pilipino	4.0	4.5	2.7	16.3

The incidences of stomach cancer are linked, albeit as yet inconclusively, to the presence of talc-treated rice in the traditional diet. In the United States the rice preferred by the Japanese is given, for cosmetic and preservation reasons, a treatment of powdered talc—a substance that contains asbestos. The association of asbestos (a known irritant) and cancer has given rise to a good deal of speculation, including "the hypothesis that the carcinogenic agent causing the high incidence of Japanese stomach cancer in asbestos-containing talc on rice appears . . . to satisfy the charcteristics of the known epidemiology of that form of cancer. . . ."[13]

Perhaps an escape from worrying about cancer is offered by changing the diet. But no, the evidence is to the contrary.

Cancers of the colon, rectum, and large bowel, once rarely reported for Japanese, are increasingly being found among Japanese Americans; indeed, the rate approximates that of the Anglo population.[14] Haenszel and associates report that the frequencies of bowel cancer among Hawaiian Japanese of both the first (Issei) and second, that is, first Hawaii-born generation (Nisei), "who at the time of the interview had discontinued the daily practice of taking one or more Japanese-style meals, were roughly double those for individuals persisting in this practice. . . ."[15] After a careful analysis of diet patterns, it was found that increased consumption of dairy products, certain vegetables, and particularly the eating of beef is closely associated with increased probability of large bowel cancer. Wynder and associates report very similar associations between the consumption of fats and fresh fruit and higher incidents of cancer of the colon.[16]

Apparently, some of the cancer mortality and morbidity are related to environmental factors (such as new diet) because several site rates are changing. Quisenberry and associates report that among Hawaiian Japanese women the rate of breast cancer doubled between 1947-1954 and 1960-1962.[17] And while breast cancer has been thought a rare malignancy among Japanese women in California, a recent analysis of the tumor registry for the San Francisco Bay Area reveals a strong upward shift in breast cancer incidents for Japanese women. Buell says that "because the result was foreshadowed in the incidence data for Japanese women in Hawaii in 1960-1964, the shift must be generally true for Japanese-American women." He goes on to conclude that the trend supports those who conclude that the great difference in breast cancer rates between Western and Asian populations is environmentally rather than genetically determined.[18] If this hypothesis is accepted, it has profound implications for the hundreds of thousands of Asian women who emigrated from areas where breast cancer is of little concern because of its infrequency—and for health professionals whose responsibility it is to educate the public about newly emerging risks.

Cardiovascular-renal disease

The changing rates found for cancers are also encountered with heart disease and associated problems. Research reporting data from Hawaii for the late 1950s reveals a lower-than-Anglo rate for cardiovascular-renal disease among Japanese but higher rates of hypertension and cerebrovascular accidents.[19] In the 1960s, however, Wenkam and Wolff found an increasing rate of heart disease, and they associate the increase with the change to high-protein, high-fat diets.[20] Labarthe, Kim, and Ehrlich offer 1964 Hawaiian data that reveal a mean cholesterol level significantly elevated among 171 Japanese plantation workers. This research tends to support the speculation of an upward trend of heart disease associated with changing food consumption patterns.[21] Larsen and Bortz indicate that serum cholesterol values of younger Japanese in Hawaii resemble those of Anglos; the conclusion reached is that saturated fats should be reduced.[22] Keys points to the association between acculturation (as represented by nontraditional food habits) and heart disease when he writes that for every heart attack in Japan, there are four in Hawaii and ten in the U.S. mainland among Japanese.[23] Gordon reports similar findings for Japanese men in Japan, Hawaii, and the mainland.[24]

Lactose

Dairy products apparently are associated with a range of health concerns aside from heart disease. Nandi and Parham conclude that Asians should avoid milk drinking because they are more intolerant than other racial groups to lactose. Asians seem to lack enzymes to break down successfully the molecular structure of milk.[25]

Hodgkin's disease

This malady rarely has been reported among Asians, perhaps because of poor diagnosis or indifferent reporting. However, Mason and Fraumeni suggest that the shifts in mortality among U.S. Japanese toward the rates prevailing in the Anglo populations are noted at all ages. They subscribe the increase to environmental influence.[26]

Psychopathologies

Stanford Lyman, a close observer of the Japanese community, attributes a wide range of health problems to psychosomatic diseases—ulcers, colitis, psoriasis, and falling hair—which occur with unusual frequency among Nisei.[27] Quisenberry and associates report the incidence of benign ulcers in Hawaiian Japanese men to be 1 1/2 times greater than in Anglo males, a condition they attribute to psychosomatic problems occurring more frequently among Japanese.[28] Lyman claims that "many of my Nisei friends have informed me that they silently suffer abdominal pains. Others are startled and ashamed of seemingly incurable mottled fingernails and falling hair."[29] These observations are supported by clincial research that reveals that Japanese have the highest rates of depression among ethnic groups studied.[30]

Impressionistic accounts from social workers and those involved with the struggle against drug abuse and suicide suggest a dangerously widespread syndrome of alienation, depression, and self-destructive tendencies among Japanese teenagers. Iga points to stresses arising inside the family.[31] Meredith argues that failure to meet Anglo physical standards results in pathologies: "Third generation Japanese Americans demonstrate a profile of introversion linked with heightened anxiety levels, and manifest greater deference and submissiveness with a tendency . . . to express greater body dissatisfaction than their Caucasian counterparts."[32] Young Japanese women apparently are especially troubled. Reports from the Los Angeles County Coroner's office reveal that in the earlier 1970s the majority of Japanese youths dying from drug overdoses were women. Although not out of proportion, the incidents of drug use, delinquency, and suicide/overdose deaths as well as psychological and emotional problems frighten many Japanese parents and are a real source of concern to the community.[33]

Health problems of the elderly

Most of the Issei who left Japan sought their fortunes in the fields of California and plantations of Hawaii, but they intended to return to Japan. When it became apparent that they would not immediately return, many wrote home and requested that their parents arrange a suitable marriage; some immigrants received pictures of their unknown brides so that they could identify them when the women disembarked in San Francisco, Los Angeles, or Seattle. Consequently, unlike the Pilipino, the Japanese pioneer generation contains a large number of elderly females.

Even with families and a well-integrated ethnic community, thousands of elderly Japanese men and women live alone and lack money for transportation, recreation, food, personal health care, and other health-related goods and services. Moreover, this financial barrier is reinforced by cultural traits—particularly the inability to speak English and a deeply held preference for Japanese food—so that many elderly Japanese are prevented from obtaining care in nursing homes, acute care facilities, and other health care institutions.[34]

Other barriers to institutional care include the ineligibility for public assistance by lack of citizenship, lack of information, and confusion attendant on contacts with bureaucratic agencies. Underutilization of existing services was revealed in a 1968 survey of 131 Issei living in Los Angeles's Little Tokyo. Of 78% and 31% who reported enrollment in Medicare and Medicaid, respectively, only 30% and 23% indicated that they used the benefits available to them.[35] Given the general disabilities that afflict the elderly plus the added burden on the Issei of the higher frequencies of particular diseases (such as certain site cancers), good health cannot be a persuasive explanation for this underutilization.

Morbidity and mortality among Pilipino Americans

If being from the Philippine Islands is only an historical event and has no inherent biological or epidemiological significance, then the Pilipinos need not be considered subject to special health care needs; they can continue to be treated (or ignored) as they have been traditionally. But there seems to be mounting evidence that being Pilipino makes one subject to special diseases, illnesses, and health care needs. Let me briefly summarize some of the studies that suggest that there is an ethnic health condition.

Hyperuricemia

Hyperuricemia (or gouty arthritis) apparently afflicts the adult male Pilipino far more often than others. For example, Decker and Lane report that the incidence of gouty arthritis among adult males admitted to a large Hawaiian hospital between 1954-1959 was 2.5% among Pilipinos but only 0.13% among all other patients.[36] Healey and associates, after an exhaustive review of available data from the United States, Hawaii, and the Philippine Islands, conclude, "Thus it is clear that Pilipinos who were born in the Philippine Islands and have immigrated to the United States show a high frequency of hyperuricemia and of gouty arthritis . . . One hypothesis is that many Pilipinos have, as a racially determined characteristic, an inability to handle the higher purine loads imposed by the diet taken in the United States."[37] That living in the United States imposes a special risk on Pilipinos is suggested further by the finding that adult males in the Islands, unlike their Pilipino American counterparts, do not show an elevated mean level of serum uric acid, the agent of hyperuricemia and gouty arthritis.[38]

Cardiovascular-renal disease

While gouty arthritis has been reported largely in males, Pilipinas are said to have a much higher rate of cardiovascular-renal disease. Bennett, Tokuyama, and McBride found that coronary disease is less prominent among Pilipinos than among other Hawaiians; however, hypertension and cerebrovascular accidents are more in evidence among Pilipino than Japanese males. But Pilipino women show the highest rate of cardiovascular-renal disease of any group studied.[39]

Research reported by Adamson suggests that the amount of serum cholesterol, a substance thought to be associated with heart disease whose level in the blood is associated with eating beef, eggs, milk products, and other foods (as well as other factors), varies with place of residence: rural Pilipinos in Hawaii have a much lower level, while their urban cousins report a level equal to that of urban Anglos.[40]

Screening for heart disease and associated pathologies, usually thought to be health problems of upper middle-class Anglo businessmen, is now being taken very seriously by those concerned with the health of the low income Black population: the Black's rates of heart disease and high blood pressure equal and exceed those of the Anglo.[41] A similar concern about heart disease is warranted for urban Pilipinos.

Amyotrophic lateral sclerosis

Matsumoto and associates report that both the incidence and mortality rates from motor neuron disease among Pilipinos are excessive compared with those for Anglos and Japanese in Hawaii.[42]

Cancer

Most cross-ethnic comparisons of the incidence and types of cancers report a low, more favorable rate for Pilipinos. However, Quisenberry has found that Pilipinos in Hawaii demonstrate primary cancer of the liver much more often than any other ethnic group and more than twice as often as males of all races.[43]

Thyrotoxic periodic paralysis

Bernard, Larzon, and Norris argue that there is cause to suspect that thyrotoxic periodic paralysis, a form of paralysis that may go unreported because of the temporary nature of the condition, may be found among Pilipinos because their ethnic background predisposes them to it.[44]

Diabetes mellitus

In a study of 38,103 residents of Oahu, Hawaii, conducted in 1958-1959, Sloan found that the age-adjusted diabetes prevalence rate for Pilipinos was three times greater than that of the Japanese and slightly higher than that of the Anglo.[45]

Venereal disease

Although no precise data exist, several conditions are indicated that are associated with high rates of VD. Some of these are: the presence of thousands of single men, who were living in labor camps or low income inner city hotels, who had been prevented for years by law and prevailing opinion from marrying non-Pilipinas and by immigration laws from bringing brides from the Islands, and who were encouraged by bosses to use prostitutes.

Industrial diseases and incapacities

Most of the Pilipino pioneers settled in coastal cities and followed careers in shipyards, canneries, and related maritime occupations, or worked as migratory farm workers or in packing and processing plants. For many of the former, long years on and around the sea have led to arthritis, pulmonary disabilities, or chronic bronchial conditions. Agriworkers suffer from the cumulative effects of pesticide poisoning or from the hours spent wielding a short-handled hoe—a favorite instrument of the growers that forces its users to remain bent over nearly parallel to the earth as they weed and cultivate.

Since most of the pioneers were very poorly paid, the rigors of great physical labor have been compounded by inadquate diet, poor housing and little or no treatment of accidents or illnesses.[46]

Psychopathologies

From the handful of reports available that describe the living conditions of the elderly Pilipino, a picture emerges of isolation, poverty, deprivation, and heroic struggle to maintain human dignity in the face of pressures and obstacles of crushing weight. But because these people prefer not to deal with social service bureaucrats, or because caseworkers, admission officers, and other welfare professionals either ignore or cannot locate them, there is no comprehensive description of the nature and extent of mental and emotional problems among the elderly Pilipino. However, when we combine what we have read with what we have seen and suspect, the plight of many thousands in Seattle, San Francisco, Stockton, Delano, San Pedro, and San Diego may be tragic.[47]

When the problems of the elderly, the adjustment difficulties, identity crises, drug and drinking problems of recent migrants, plus the psychological and emotional stress and terror suffered by many Pilipina partners in international marriages are considered, research into the mental health needs of the Pilipino community is a regrettably too long ignored priority.[48]

Utilization of health care providers

The preceding summary of the mortality and morbidity patterns of Japanese and Pilipinos suggests that members of the two communities face distinctive personal health care problems. Perhaps the outstanding examples of this ethnic particularity are the frequency of cancer of the stomach among Japanese and the presence of hyperuricemia among Pilipinos. In addition, both communities share psychopathologies that have as one origin the exploitation and racism visited on them by the dominant society. And because many of the older generation were prevented by low wages from accumulating personal savings for a comfortable retirement, their health care bills are especially onerous.

Availability and quality of health care services have a bearing on the mortality and morbidity that we have seen, since many conditions could be contained or cured if they were diagnosed and treated early. Thus, concern for the health care needs of Asian Americans takes us to the question of health services utilization patterns of the communities. In the following section, we shall examine the utilization of providers by two samples of the Japanese and Pilipino communities.

In order to have an independent benchmark for assessing the utilization patterns of low income urban Asian Americans, I shall include the profile of a comparable Anglo sample interviewed during May 1973. The three samples contain basically identical distributions of the major demographic variables (females, educational attainment, age, occupation), except that the Japanese sample's income profile is slightly shifted toward the higher range.

Table 3-4 shows that of the three groups, the Japanese report the highest

Table 3-4. Percent of samples reporting contact between family and major health care providers during preceding 6 months

	Anglo	Japanese	Pilipino
Visited a dentist	45.2%	68.1%	52.4%
Visited a physician	85.6	73.0	72.5
Had been a patient in a hospital	26.9	12.1	20.1
Total number of cases	208	141	189

Table 3-5. Percent of samples characterizing selected health care costs as "too high"

	Anglo	Japanese	Pilipino
Hospital costs	89.4%	83.6%	81.2%
Dentist bills	64.9	65.0	71.0
Physician fees	68.7	60.0	71.5
Cost of medicine	73.1	65.7	62.9
Total number of cases	208	141	189

rate of contacts with dentists. Since studies in Hawaii reveal that Japanese have more dental caries than other groups,[49] need plus higher incomes plus the presence of several nearby Japanese dentists may account for this higher utilization. The lowest level of hospitalization has also been found among the Japanese in Hawaii. The explanation commonly offered is that traditional Japanese (that is, most Issei and many Nisei) strive to avoid showing "weakness" or incapacity by being abed. As we shall see in a moment, other interpretations featuring limited income, fear of hostile bureaucrats, and language barriers may be contributing factors in low hospitalization rates. Such factors may also contribute to the lower than Anglo utilization rates among Pilipinos.

Costs as a barrier to utilization

The Asian samples are as willing as the Anglo to characterize costs of personal health services as "too high." Since this attitude is consonant with the Asian's low utilization rates, Table 3-5 tends to support the notion that perceived high costs are a barrier to seeking health care.

Although the attitudes and opinions of the respondents cannot be interpreted as meaning that they do not seek health service because they feel themselves unable to pay for it, it does seem a fair inference that many individuals forego regular checkups and elective procedures, perhaps even terminate medication or extended therapy, because of pressure on their budgets.

Institutional barriers

All low income people are constrained in obtaining health care by the physical availability of providers. More and more health providers, especially solo practitioners and specialists, are leaving the inner city or the rural regions in favor of the comforts and rewards of suburban locations. Hospitals, clinics, and private offices are often several hours away by bus or not accessible at all to those without private automobiles, and lack of transportation often means nonutilization. For example, a study of the health care behavior of elderly Pilipinos in Seattle found that those with cars obtained care more regularly; those who had to rely on public transportation reported fewer contacts as the distance to the provider increased.[50]

For many Japanese and Pilipinos, however, the physical location of a provider may be less significant in utilization decisions than *who* is offering the treatment. Our research shows that Japanese, regardless of age or degree of acculturation, tend to seek out Japanese physicians, dentists, and other health care providers.

Whether it is because of language problems, fear of racist discrimination, or rough treatment from Anglos, a preference for one's own kind, or the belief that a member of the community will be more humane, less expensive, and more polite, Asian Americans express a preference for treatment by their ethnic brothers and sisters. But what about the Japanese and Pilipinos who cannot locate a physician? And what happens to the other Pacific and Asian (or Mideastern, Latin American, or other) peoples who have no representative among the local health care providers? Naturally, they obtain services; yet it would be an interesting and useful project to see if the *frequency of utilization* increases when an ethnic provider or bilingual, bicultural facility becomes an available alternative.

Culture and communalism

The preceding analysis suggests that degree of assimilation and acculturation are related to distinct health care needs. For example, the traditional Japanese diet increases the likelihood of several health problems. Preference for ethnic peers and social and cultural institutions may drastically reduce the types and numbers of health care providers from whom the individual is able to obtain services: many elderly Japanese and Pilipinos who otherwise might be candidates for admission to board-and-care homes or convalescent hospitals continue to live alone because they are unable to locate an acceptable institution.

Assimilation and acculturation are linked to what E. H. Erikson characterizes as the "crisis of identity": sharing cultural and cognitive traits with two or more societies but not being fully at ease or accepted in any.[51] This gives rise to elevated stress and may be related to the increasing incidents of hypertension, suicide, and emotional difficulties of individuals among the second and third U.S.-dwelling Japanese and Pilipino generations. Perhaps identity problems are related to the high frequency of psychosomatic complaints.

The cultural traits of the Japanese and Pilipinos are conveyed and reinforced by their communities. While most individuals are capable of successful interaction with the Anglo society, many prefer to remain inside the community networks as much as possible. This preference is reflected in the selection of health care professionals. But insofar as there are limited community providers, many Japanese and Pilipinos avoid visits to specialists and delay contacts with providers until compelled to seek assistance. Given the frequency of cancer, heart disease, and other potentially explosive maladies, delayed treatment and ignored minor symptoms may lead to unnecessary suffering or death.

Communalism also affects the flow of information about personal health matters. In the preceding chapter we saw that information about health care providers is gained from friends and family members much more often by Japanese and Pilipinos than is the case in the Black or Anglo communities. Since elderly Japanese and Pilipinos report that more of their contacts are among their generational cohorts rather than with younger members of the community or individuals of other groups, it is probable that information about new health-related programs or providers rarely reaches the elderly, both because of their physical isolation and their language barrier.

If the communalism of many Japanese and Pilipinos opens them to certain health hazards and reduces the range of available providers, their ethnostructure also provides a great deal of indisputable worth. The multiplicity of social contacts plus their continuity and strength nurture a deep-seated feeling of in-group solidarity: individuals can relax, express themselves, and communicate with sympathetic, empathetic peers. They can take comfort from the knowledge that emotional and physical dependencies will be accepted and reciprocated. Perhaps this was best summed up by a member of a Pilipino community organization when she said that her association had recently paid the funeral expenses of six or seven elderly Pilipinos who had no family in the United States—had paid the expenses while the oldtimers were still alive so that "they can rest easy during their last months on earth."

The Japanese and Pilipinos (and other Asians as well) would have acute health care difficulties even if they were fully assimilated into the Anglo society; we have seen that increased frequencies of cancers and heart disease are associated with Anglicized diet. What we see now is the need to recognize the specific health care consequences of cultural differences and communalism and take action to deal with them. Moreover, just as many of the pathologies suffered by the Japanese and the Pilipino are distinct, so are the organizational patterns and cultural traits that form the context in which remedial action must take place. These distinctive social patterns are obstacles only to efforts that attempt to deal with Asian groups as a monolithic entity. When this distinctiveness is recognized and community structures understood, social patterns become avenues to educating and mobilizing the different populations for better health care.

Notes

1. Harry L. Kitano and Stanley Sue (editors), "Asian American: A Success Story?" *Journal of Social Issues* 29 (1973), topical issue; Bill Hosokawa, *Nisei: The Quiet Americans* (New

York: William Morrow & Co., Inc., 1969); Harry L. Kitano, "Passive Discrimination: The Normal Person," *Journal of Social Psychology* **70** (Oct. 1966), pp. 23-31; Ronald O. Haak, "Co-opting the Oppressors: The Case of the Japanese-Americans," *Transaction* **7** (Oct. 1970), pp. 23-31; Bok-lim C. Kim, "Asian-Americans: No Model Minority," *Social Work* **18** (May 1973), pp. 44-53.

2. U.S. Bureau of the Census, *Japanese, Chinese, and Filipinos in the United States* (Washington, D.C.: U.S. Government Printing Office, 1973).

3. Harry L. Kitano, *Japanese Americans: The Evolution of a Subculture* (Englewood Cliffs, N.J.: Prentice-Hall, Inc., 1969); William Petersen, *Japanese Americans: Oppression and Success* (New York: Random House, Inc., 1971).

4. Royal F. Morales, *Makibaka: The Pilipino American Struggle* (Los Angeles: Mountainview Publishers, 1974); *A Study of Selected Socio-economic Characteristics of Ethnic Minorities Based on the 1970 Census,* Vol. 2: *Asian Americans* (Arlington, Va.: Urban Affairs, Inc., 1974); Sonia Wa-Lovits, "Filipinos in California" (unpublished M.A. thesis, University of Southern California, 1966); Sr. Marie Bergamini, "An Assessment of International Nursing Students in the United States: A Case Study of Philippine Experience" (unpublished Ph.D. dissertation, University of California, Berkeley, 1964).

5. U.S. Department of Justice, Immigration and Naturalization Service, *1973 Annual Report* (Washington, D.C., 1974).

6. For a useful guide to literature on the Pilipino community, see Philip B. Whitney, "Filipinos in the United States," *Bulletin of Bibliography* **29** (July-Sept. 1972), pp. 73-83.

7. Tavia Gordon, "Mortality Experience Among the Japanese in the United States, Hawaii, and Japan," *Public Health Reports* **72** (June 1957), pp. 543-553; Gordon, "Further Mortality Experience Among Japanese Americans," *Public Health Reports* **82** (Nov. 1967), pp. 973-984.

8. Kitano, *Japanese Americans,* p. 130.

9. Lester Breslow and Bonnie Klein, "Health and Race in California," *American Journal of Public Health* **61** (April 1971), pp. 763-775.

10. Frank Norris and Paul W. Shipley, "A Closer Look at Race Differentials in California's Infant Mortality, 1965-67," *HSMHA Health Reports* **86** (Sept. 1971), pp. 810-814.

11. William Haenszel and Minoru Kurihara, "Studies of Japanese Immigrants. I. Mortality from Cancer and Other Diseases Among Japanese in the United States," *National Cancer Institute Journal* **40** (Jan. 1968), pp. 43-68.

12. Walter B. Quisenberry, "Sociocultural Factors in Cancer in Hawaii," *Annals of the New York Academy of Sciences* **84** (8 Dec. 1960), pp. 795-806.

13. R. R. Merliss, "Talc-treated Rice and Japanese Stomach Cancer," *Science* **173** (17 Sept. 1971), pp. 1141-1142; Merliss, "Talc and Asbestos Contaminant of Rice," *Journal of the American Medical Association* **216** (28 June 1971), p. 2144; H. Bohlig, P. Dalquen, and E. Hain, "Epidemiology of Asbestos-Induced Diseases," *Internist* (Berlin) **13** (Aug. 1972), pp. 318-325; "Mainly Good News About Asbestos," *Food and Cosmetic Toxicology* **10** (Aug. 1972), pp. 574-578; Hitoshi Matsudo, Norman M. Hodgkin, and Akira Tanaka, "Japanese Gastric Cancer: Potentially Carcinogenic Silicates (Talc) from Rice," *Archives of Pathology* **97** (June 1974), pp. 366-368; William E. Smith, "Asbestos, Talc and Nitrates in Relation to Gastric Cancer," *American Industrial Hygiene Association Journal* **34** (May 1973), pp. 227-228.

14. Nung Won Choi, "Ethnic Distribution of Cancer of the Gastrointestinal Tract in Manitobe," *American Journal of Public Health* **58** (Nov. 1968), pp. 2067-2081; William Haenszel and Emily A. Dawson, "A Note on Mortality From Cancer of the Colon and Rectum in the United States," *Cancer* **18** (March 1965), pp. 265-272; Grant N. Stemmermann, "Cancer of the Colon and Rectum Discovered at Autopsy in Hawaiian Japanese," *Cancer* **19** (Nov. 1966), pp. 1567-1572; E. L. Wynder and others, "Environmental Factors of Cancer of the Colon and Rectum. 2. Japanese Epidemiological Data," *Cancer* **23** (May 1969), pp. 1210-1220.

15. William Haenszel and others, "Stomach Cancer Among Japanese in Hawaii," *National Cancer Institute Journal* **51** (Dec. 1973), pp. 1765-1779.

16. Wynder and others, "Environmental Factors of Cancer of the Colon and Rectum," pp. 1210-1220.

17. William B. Quisenberry and others, "Ethnic Differences in Cancer in Hawaii," *Progress in Clinical Cancer* **4** (1970), pp. 48-61.

18. Philip Buell, "Changing Incidence of Breast Cancer in Japanese-American Women," *National*

Cancer Institute Journal **51** (Nov. 1973), pp. 1479-1483; Richard Doll, Calum Muir, and John Watherhouse (editors), *Cancer Incidence in Five Continents,* Vol. 2 (Geneva: UICC, 1970); Brian MacMahon, Philip Cole, and James Brown, "Etiology of Human Breast Cancer: A Review," *National Cancer Institute Journal* **50** (Jan. 1973), pp. 21-42.

19. Charles Bennett, G. H. Tokuyama, and T. C. McBride, "Cardiovascular Renal Mortality in Hawaii," *American Journal of Public Health* **52** (Sept. 1962), pp. 1418-1431; Tavia Gordon, "Further Mortality Experience," pp. 973-984; Nils P. Larsen and Walter M. Bortz, "Arteriosclerosis: A Comparative Study of Caucasian and Japanese Citizens in the Hawaiian Islands, 1959," *Journal of the American Geriatrics Society* **8** (Nov. 1960), pp. 867-872; Joseph Stokes and others, "Coronary Disease and Hypertension in Hawaii: Racial Distribution in 1,167 Men," *Hawaii Medical Journal* **25** (Jan.-Feb. 1966), pp. 235-240.

20. Nao S. Wenkam and Robert J. Wolff, "A Half Century of Changing Food Habits Among Japanese in Hawaii," *American Dietetics Association Journal* **57** (July 1970), pp. 29-32; Robert Moellering and David R. Bassett, "Myocardial Infarction in Hawaiian and Japanese Males on Oahu—a Review of 505 Cases Occurring Between 1955 and 1964," *Journal of Chronic Diseases* **20** (Feb. 1967), pp. 89-101.

21. Darwin R. Labarthe, Peter M. Kim, and S. Paul Ehrlich, Jr., "Coronary Risk Factors of Male Workers on a Kauai, Hawaii Plantation: Comparison of Data for Japanese and Filipinos," *Public Health Reports* **85** (Nov. 1970), pp. 975-980.

22. Larsen and Bortz, "Arteriosclerosis," pp. 867-872; Ancel Keys and others, "Lessons from Serum Cholesterol Studies in Japan, Hawaii, and Los Angeles," *Annals of Internal Medicine* **48** (Jan. 1958), pp. 83-94.

23. Ancel Keys, "10 Heart Attacks in the United States for 1 in Japan," *American Heart* **16** (Spring 1966), p. 6.

24. Gordon, "Mortality Experience Among the Japanese in the United States," pp. 543-553; David R. Bassett and others, "Coronary Heart Disease in Hawaii: Dietary Intake, Depot Fat, 'Stress,' Smoking, and Energy Balance in Hawaiian and Japanese Men," *American Journal of Clinical Nutrition* **22** (Nov. 1969), pp. 1483-1520; Hiroo Kato and others, "Epidemiologic Studies of Coronary Heart Disease and Stroke in Japanese Men Living in Japan, Hawaii, and California: Serum Lipids and Diets," *American Journal of Epidemiology* **97** (June 1973), pp. 372-385; Jeanne L. Tillotson and others, "Epidemiology of Coronary Heart Disease and Stroke in Japanese Men Living in Japan, Hawaii, and California: Methodology for Comparison of Diet," *American Journal of Clinical Nutrition* **26** (Feb. 1973), pp. 177-184.

25. Myung H. Chung and Douglas B. McGill, "Lactase Deficiency in Orientals," *Gastroenterology* **54** (Feb. 1968), pp. 225-231; Minal A. Nandi and Ellen S. Parham, "Milk Drinking by the Lactose Intolerant," *American Dietetic Association Journal* **61** (Sept. 1972), pp. 258-261.

26. Thomas J. Mason and Joseph F. Fraumeni, Jr., "Letter: Hodgkin's Disease Among Japanese Americans," *Lancet* **1** (9 Feb. 1974), p. 215.

27. Stanford M. Lyman, "Generation and Character: The Case of the Japanese-American," in H. Conroy and T. Scott Miyakawa (editors), *East Across the Pacific: Historical and Sociological Studies of Japanese Immigration and Assimilation* (Santa Barbara: Clio Press, 1972), pp. 279-314.

28. Quisenberry and others, "Ethnic Differences in Cancer in Hawaii," pp. 48-61.

29. Lyman, "Generation and Character," pp. 279-314.

30. John Lamont and Carol Tyler, "Racial Differences in Rate of Depression," *Journal of Clinical Psychology* **29** (Oct. 1973), pp. 428-432.

31. Mamoru Iga, "The Japanese Social Structure and the Source of Mental Stress of Japanese Immigrants in the United States," *Social Forces* **35** (March 1957), pp. 271-278.

32. Gerald M. Meredith, "Sex Temperament Among Japanese American College Students in Hawaii," *Journal of Social Psychology* **77** (April 1969), pp. 149-156.

33. Kim, "Asian-Americans," pp. 44-53; Yukio Okano and Bernard Spika, "Ethnic Identity, Alienation, and Achievement in Japanese-American Families," *Journal of Cross-cultural Psychology* **2** (Sept. 1971), pp. 273-282; Proceedings of the First National Conference on Asian American Mental Health, April 27-29, 1972, San Francisco, Calif.

34. Richard A. Kalish and Sharon Moriwaki, "The World of the Elderly Asian American," *Journal of Social Issues* **29** (1973), pp. 187-193; Arthur K. Ito, "Institutionalization—Ethnic Elders Need More Than Medical Care" (paper presented to the Institute on Minority Aging, California

State University, San Diego, June, 1974); Richard A. Kalish and Sam Yuen, "Americans of East Asian Ancestry: Aging and the Aged," *Gerontologist* **2** (Spring 1971), pp. 36-47; Sheridan Tatsuno, "The Political and Economic Effects of Urban Renewal on Ethnic Communities: A Case Study of San Francisco's Japan Town," *American Journal* **1** (March 1971), pp. 33-51.

35. Issei Survey, *Los Angeles' "Little Tokyo"* (Summer 1968), available from the Japanese American Studies Center, UCLA.

36. John L. Decker, James J. Lane, and William E. Reynolds, "Hyperuricemia in a Male Filipino Population," *Arthritis and Rheumatism* **5** (April 1962), pp. 144-155.

37. Louis A. Healey, Jr., and others, "Hyperuricemia in Filipinos: Interaction of Heredity and Environment," *American Journal of Human Genetics* **19** (March 1967), pp. 81-85.

38. Louis A. Healey, Jr., "Ethnic Variations in Serum Uric Acid. I. Filipino Hyperuricemia in a Controlled Environment," *Arthritis and Rheumatism* **9** (April 1966), pp. 288-294.

39. Bennett, Tokuyama, and McBride, "Cardiovascular Renal Mortality in Hawaii," pp. 1418-1431.

40. Lucile F. Adamson, "Serum Cholesterol Concentrations of Various Ethnic Groups in Hawaii," *Journal of Nutrition* **71** (May-Aug. 1960), pp. 27-36.

41. See Chapter 5.

42. Nobutero Matsumoto and others, "Epidemiologic Study of Amystrophic Lateral Sclerosis in Hawaii: Identification of High Incidence Among Filipino Men," *Neurology* **22** (Sept. 1972), pp. 934-940.

43. Quisenberry, "Sociocultural Factors in Cancer in Hawaii," pp. 795-806.

44. J. C. Bernard, M. A. Larson, and F. H. Morris, Jr., "Thyrotoxic Periodic Paralysis in Californians of Mexican and Filipino Ancestry," *California Medicine* **116** (Feb. 1972), pp. 70-74.

45. Norman R. Sloan, "Ethnic Distribution of Diabetes Mellitus in Hawaii," *Journal of the American Medical Association* **183** (Feb. 1963), pp. 419-424.

46. Morales, *Makibaka;* Carey McWilliams, *Brothers Under the Skin* (Boston: Little, Brown and Co,. 1943).

47. Glenn Chinn and Linda Newcomb, "On the Feasibility of Training Asians to Work With Asian Elderly" (Seattle: Training Project for the Asian Elderly, March 1973); "Health Assessment of Elderly Filipinos in International District" (Demonstration Project for Asian Americans, Seattle, 1972); Lillian Galedo, Laurena Cabanero, and Brian Tom, "Roadblocks to Community Building: A Case Study of the Filipino Community Center Project. Working Paper #4" (Asian American Research Project, University of California, Davis, Nov. 1970); "Letters Home" (Filipino American Studies Center, Asian American Studies Program, UCLA, 1976).

48. Fred Cordova, "The Filipino-American: There's Always an Identity Crisis," in Stanley Sue and Nathaniel W. Wagner (editors), *Asian-American Psychological Perspectives* (Palo Alto: Science and Behavior Books, 1973), pp. 136-139; Donald F. Duff and Ransom J. Arthur, "Between Two Worlds: Filipinos in the U.S. Navy," *American Journal of Psychiatry* **123** (Jan. 1967), pp. 836-843; H. Elton Hooper, "A Filipino in California Copes with Anxiety," in Georgene H. Seward (editor), *Clinical Studies in Cultural Conflict* (New York: The Ronald Press Co., 1958) pp. 265-290.

49. Wenkam and Wolff, "A Half Century of Changing Food Habits Among Japanese in Hawaii," pp. 29-32.

50. Demonstration Project, "Health Assessment of Elderly Filipinos in International District."

51. See Erik H. Erikson, *Childhood and Society* (New York: W. W. Norton & Co., Inc., 1950); Erikson, *Young Man Luther: A Study in Psychoanalysis and History* (New York: W. W. Norton & Co., Inc., 1958); compare with Lucian W. Pye, *Politics, Personality, and Nation Building: Burma's Search for Identity* (New Haven: Yale University Press, 1962).

CHAPTER 4

Mexican American health care behavior

Along with the alarm and rhetoric about the state of America's health there has emerged a less dramatic but perhaps ultimately more profound awareness that solutions to health care problems require the consideration and integration of vastly complex interdisciplinary sources of knowledge and theory: engineering, social sciences, laboratory sciences, philosophy, and ethics must be combined with traditional health care curricula and considerations. One consequence of this increasing interdisciplinary concern is the growing role of anthropological and sociological research and theory in the training of providers of health care and the design and staffing of facilities.

In this chapter we shall review one segment of social science literature that is increasingly coming to the attention of health care professionals: reports and analyses of health care behavior of Mexican Americans. This review is intended to provide more than a useful primary bibliography; my aim is to raise questions about the scope, methodology, content, and reliability of this literature—to analyze its utility for the work of scholars, policy makers, and practitioners who are concerned with providing health care services to America's second largest minority community.

Health care as subculture

Scholarship is a cumulative endeavor; we build on the work of our predecessors, supposedly eliminating their errors, ideally making some small contribution to knowledge by consecutive review and refinement. But inherent in the follow-on style of work is a basic caution, perhaps best captured by the lawyer's phrase *stare decisus* (let precedent rule), which seems to discourage original or innovative interpretations, especially when an established explanation exists. In the literature on the Mexican American population, evidence of this approach to scholarship can be seen: the repetition from one work to another of a central theme that the health care behavior of Mexican Americans is a consequence of (as well as a reinforcement for) a community-wide subculture.[1]

Saunders: pater familias

To call Saunders the *pater familias* of the Mexican American health care studies is both to recognize his influence on subsequent analyses and to understate his impact, since Saunders's research and hypotheses are cited throughout the subsequent literature.[2]

Saunders paints with broad strokes; he attempts to place health care in the total context of Mexican American life. To do so he marshals accounts from anthropological studies, which he supplements with work by ethnographers of Central and South American communities.[3] Onto this canvas he sketches the biographies of six New Mexican families: "fifteen adults, twenty-three children, two dogs, three cats, a few rats, mice enough to keep two of the cats sleek and contented, and an assortment of lice, bedbugs, fleas, roaches, spiders, flies, and other pests."[4]

The significance of Saunders's late-1940s work derives largely from his attempt to place health care behavior in a cultural perspective, thus establishing the basis for theories and models of behavior that become operational once the cultural conditions are observed. Saunders's theory is that there are four basic sources of health care knowledge and treatment: (1) folk medical lore of medieval Spain as refined in Mexico, (2) one or more native American tribes, (3) Anglo folk medicine, and (4) scientific medicine. While recognizing the central role of the Mexican American's particular health care culture, Saunders notes that behavior is influenced by other factors. Age and degree of participation in Anglo culture are important variables associated with different beliefs, knowledge, and practices with respect to illness and disease. But in his discussion of health behavior and attitudes, Saunders concentrates on the differences, not *within* the overall Mexican American population but *between* it and the Anglo model, especially as revealed in what he sees as the core of Mexican American health culture—folk medicine.

This folk medicine culture reflects the following attitudes and behavior: health is looked upon as a matter of chance, and it is felt that there is very little that a person can do to keep it; many diseases are caused by magic and bewitchment; mild disorders are treated by the afflicted or by another member of the family. In more serious cases, and if the disease is thought to be "natural" (in other words, not caused by magic or bewitchment), a physician may be consulted. If the complaint is thought to be other than natural, a folk healer *(curandero)* or witch *(bruja)* is seen. Since Mexican Americans are family-centered people, and since illness and treatment are very much a social event in their traditional culture, Mexican Americans will attempt to avoid hospitalization. Finally, because Spanish-speaking patients have little or no conceptualization of time, they do not adhere to time schedules or remember to return for appointments if the interval is more than a week.[5] No distinction is made among Spanish-speaking farm laborers, new migrants above the Rio Grande, Mexican American residents in Chicago, and middle-class urban dwellers in east Los Angeles.

Second generation: loyal sons and daughters

The second generation of health behavior studies rests on research conducted during the middle and late 1950s. Three of the principal contributors offer detailed ethnographies of working class rural and village populations. In their concentration on folk medicine and their cultural interpretation of behavior, the second generation closely follows Saunders's pioneering effort.[6]

Clark's monograph is a study of a Spanish-speaking enclave called *Sal si Puedes* (literally, escape if you can) on the eastern edge of San Jose,

California.[7] Health care information was obtained from 14 families of this *barrio* (neighborhood). Clark recognizes that her population is atypical in many respects of the overall Mexican American population, but she argues that it is nevertheless generalizable because such barrios produce outmigrants who must deal with the Anglo community.

Saunders's model of culturally determined health care practices provides Clark's frame of reference, and her findings largely confirm the subculture thesis: patients treat themselves, are treated by family or friends, or visit curanderos. *Mal de ojo* (the evil eye) and *brujería* (witchcraft) are responsible for many illnesses. Physicians are consulted but curanderos are also, often simultaneously. Barrio residents have definite ideas about how a medical practitioner should behave; these expectations are based largely on the traditional practices of folk healers. Barrio people are not in a great hurry about something as sobering as illness; efficiency is not considered a particularly admirable trait.

Rubel[8] and Madsen[9] present separate but largely complementary data and analyses drawn from their 1957–1961 work in Hidalgo County, Texas. Both utilize the ethnographic methods of participant observations, detailed biographies of selected informants, and familiarization with all aspects of the community. Rubel's research is intensive (he spent 2 years living and working with sixteen key informants from seven impoverished families); Madsen, while also relying on biographic accounts, attempts a more general picture of Mexican American culture in the lower Rio Grande River Valley.

Rubel's account of health care behavior deals with the now familiar concepts of natural and magical diseases, witchcraft, the use of herbs, reliance on family and curanderos, and the fatalistic attitude toward illness.[10] An issue on which Rubel develops a new perspective is health care cost and its relationship to willingness of rural Mexican Americans to visit physicians. Saunders and Clark mention the costliness of scientific health care treatment (and contrast these fees with the much lower expenditures for folk remedies) as a contributory factor in the use of curanderos; Rubel, however, argues that it is not the *amount* of the physician's fee but the fee system itself that is the principal irritation: "An important feature which contrasts lay healers with physicians is that the former are traditionally recompensed for their services in the form of gratuities, while the latter exact fees. To an important extent this distinction contributes to the widely held supposition that physicians . . . practice medicine to enrich themselves at the expense of their patients, whereas on the contrary, lay healers practice 'to help the people.' "[11]

Madsen seems to depart from the tradition of considering folk medicine and ethnicity as coterminous. He claims that acceptance of magic, witchcraft, and curanderos varies inversely with social class: the lower class sees the natural and the supernatural blended into one functional totality. Therefore, the members of this class rely heavily on supernatural techniques in dealing with illness and other problems. Conservative members of the middle class have a more secular orientation but still perceive a supernatural power pervading the universe. The conservative elite preserves a religious philosophy but scorns the superstitions of the lower class. The Anglicized upper class tends to adopt popular scientific concepts of natural order and causation. But then Madsen attenuates this class-based variability hypothesis. He asserts that many Mexican Americans are caught in the conflict between the scientific basis of modern medicine and the supernatural theories of folk medicine. This extends to the sophisticated individuals who sometimes rely on folk medicine although they may be ashamed to admit it to the outside world; even members of the community's socioeconomic elite firmly believe in punitive disease. Belief in witchcraft remains strong among the adult members of the lower classes and the lower-middle class. While skepticism is widespread in the upper-middle class, witchcraft beliefs are occasionally encountered there. Although Madsen suggests some difference in behavior related to education, occupation, and Anglicization, his discussion suggests the prevalence of folk medicine behavior throughout the Mexican American community and that the vast majority of the community (since the Anglicized upper class and elite contain only a tiny fraction of the overall population) adhere to the tenets of folk medicine.[12]

In an era of ethnologies reporting tiny samples of rural working-class or peasant Mexican Americans, Jaco's pioneering study of the incidence of mental disease among Mexican Americans is based on psychiatric treatment records from all mental institutions in the state of Texas. He examines 11,298 records of psychotic patients admitted for the first time during 1951-1952.[13]

From these data Jaco creates a comparative profile of the incidence of mental illness. The rate of first-time admissions per 100,000 population is 80 for the Anglo population, 55 for the "nonwhite" population, and 42 for the Mexican American population. The proportion of the latter committed to public institutions is about three times greater than its private treatment rate.

Although he cites Saunders to the effect that Spanish-speaking peoples of the Southwest have a different attitude toward "Anglo medicine," Jaco concludes that the low incidence rate of severe mental aberrations *cannot* be attributed to avoidance of Anglo mental facilities. When every possible source of qualified psychiatric diagnosis and treatment is encompassed, as Jaco assumes he has done, the likelihood of differences in attitudes between groups toward mental illness and their effect on incidence rates for these groups is minimized. Jaco's conclusion is that Mexican Americans simply have a significantly lower frequency of psychotic disturbances, that they are less afflicted than the Anglo.

Jaco's widely reported findings are partially supported by two later studies of admission rates to mental institutions. A review of 1960-1961 admissions to Colorado public institutions reveals that for all classes of illness (not just psychotic illness as in the Texas study) Mexican Americans have a slightly *higher* rate per 100,000 population.[14] Purely psychiatric admissions are somewhat lower, but the rate of admission for alcoholism is higher than that of the Anglo population. Data from New Mexico covering new admissions for all causes seem to confirm Jaco's hypothesis: the reported rate of Mexican American admissions is 41.8 per 100,000 population compared with 53.6 for Anglos.[15]

One issue on which all mental illness studies for this period agree is that admission is likely to vary inversely with age: the younger age groups report the highest rate. Explanations offered suggest that the younger Mexican Americans are especially susceptible to cross-cultural pressures and find themselves not comfortable in or accepted by either the traditional Mexican American or Anglo societies, a situation leading younger members of the community to develop deep psychological problems much more readily than their senior kinsmen who are settled into the traditional society. A different interpretation of the inverse relationship is that older family members are more sheltered, even hidden away, when they manifest symptoms that in the Anglo community are associated with institutionalization: it is not that fewer elderly Mexican Americans are mentally ill but that they are held within the family and tolerated to an extent not permitted in the Anglo family.

The major findings of the second generation of scholarship can be summarized as including: the Mexican American population is an undifferentiated, homogeneous mass who distrusts scientific medicine, seeks treatment from folk healers, views illness fatalistically, sees many illnesses as resulting from and only curable by magic and witchcraft; illness is a social or collective as opposed to an individual event; the Mexican American community holds a culture, one aspect of which is recognizable by a complex system of health-related traits, which forms a barrier to effective utilization of scientific health care. Rubel writes that one of the major tasks of Valley physicians is to change the Mexican American's culture. He notes that the physicians are puzzled, even dismayed, because many Mexican Americans have not completely abandoned traditional remedies for the modern preventive and curative care of the physician. The resistance to Anglicization is seen by Rubel and his contemporaries as a major obstacle to improved health.

Third generation: emergence of the Chicano

If the second generation is characterized by its uniformity in methodology, assumptions about the ubiquity of a health-care subculture and sweeping generalizations, the studies produced during the 1960s reveal almost the opposite thrust: recent efforts utilize large and small survey research as well as ethnographic data. They tend to concentrate on narrow segments of the Mexican American population, both geographically and socioeconomically. It bears noting that much of current scholarship has been inspired by and forms an integral part of *chicanismo*—the drive for power, dignity, and recognition that surfaced in the barrios, fields, and classrooms of the Southwest during the 1960s.[16] Seeing earlier studies as essentially contributing to the malaise that they are fighting, Chicano activists hoping to destroy the conventional wisdom are found alongside academics intent on testing established hypotheses, the two creating a diverse and contradictory new literature.

The single most important scholarly treatment of the nation's second largest minority, the Grebler, Moore, and Guzman volume, largely ignores health behavior.[17] However, the project out of which this volume emerges released a report that presents selected data on utilization of health delivery facilities, morbidity, and mortality.[18]

Aside from the figures concerning mental illness already mentioned, Moustafa and Weiss report from a 1960-1961 Colorado study that infant mortality is three times as great a cause of death in the Mexican American (13.6%) as in the Anglo (4.3%) populations; that Colorado Mexican Americans die younger than their Anglo counterparts, 56.7 years as compared with 67.5 years; that in San Antonio, Texas (1963) Mexican Americans have a higher rate of death at each age level except the over-75 years than Anglos, while the former's infant mortality exceeds the latter's by 28.2 per 100,000 births to 21.3; and that in California (1955) Mexican Americans report a lower physician-visitation rate per person per year (2.3) than Blacks (3.7) or Anglos (5.6) as well as the lowest frequency of hospital admission per 1,000 persons (76 compared with 82 for Blacks and 95 for Anglos). A similar lowest rate of utilization is reported for Mexican American enrollment in health insurance plans. These utilization data are attributed to (1) beliefs about illness, its causation, prevention, and treatment; (2) negative attitudes toward Anglo-oriented services, physicians, hospitals, and such programs as health insurance; and (3) Mexican American folk medicine. But the writers warn us to be skeptical of the survey data because the Mexican American's lower rate may also reflect (1) limitations on the survey instruments and interviewing procedures, especially since the majority of the Mexican American respondents are lower socioeconomic class, a stratum often found to give unreliable information; (2) problems of communication associated with language barriers; and (3) unwillingness on the part of Mexican Americans to admit illness for fear that reporting an illness might lead to an investigation by authorities.

This final point, that some Mexican Americans fear health workers or investigators, is also raised by Clark. She notes that the public health worker is a government employee and as such is related to other government workers —law enforcement officers, tax assessors, immigration authorities, truant officers, building inspectors, FBI agents, and public prosecutors—all of whom are viewed as potential threats to the security of barrio people. We shall see that there is probable cause for alarm and apprehension about the consequences of dealing with representatives of public institutions.

One of the most controversial aspects of health care behavior is the alleged negative impact of the Mexican American family. Nall and Speilberg argue that the degree of the patient's integration into the Mexican American culture, especially his presence as a member of a-functioning family unit, inhibits his acceptance of scientific treatment and thereby his speed of recovery. The authors stipulate that a "milieu effect," the product of a complex network of factors associated with the family rather than specific behavior or attitudes, acts to curtail the effectiveness of treatment.[19]

Nall and Speilberg's allegation follows the line of analysis offered by Heller: "The kind of socialization that Mexican American children generally receive at home is not conducive to the development of the capacities needed for advancement in a dynamic industrialized society. This type of upbringing creates stumbling blocks to future advancement by stressing values that hinder mobility—family ties, honor, masculinity, and living in the present—and by neglecting the values that are conducive to it—achievement, independence, and deferred gratification."[20] Similar discussions of the family's pathological environment have given rise to what one observer labeled "The Social Science Myth of the Mexican-American Family."[21]

The most elaborate development of the myth is found in Kiev's study of Mexican American folk psychiatry.[22] On the basis of 2 years' residence in San Antonio, Texas, and what he cites as contacts with four curanderos, numerous patients and informants, Kiev argues the following causes and symptoms of psychological conflicts: Oedipal patterns that appear in such traits as recklessness, resoluteness, and self-assurance and derive from machismo; and a strong masochistic tendency among women. Because the Mexican American mother continues to nurse well past infancy, Mexican American children are forever expecting to have their dependency needs gratified by the environment. Kiev concludes that the major values and traits of Mexican American culture are dysfunctional to individual well-being. He mentions sense of fatalism, adherence to traditional ways, acceptance of a mystical nonrational view of the world, emphasis on form and *dignidad,* and reluctance to accept personal responsibility as central values and assumptions of Mexican American culture that are contrary to those emphasized by psychotherapy. Implicitly, Kiev tells us that if it were not for the curandero's ability to work within the Mexican American's frame of reference, aggressive and psychotic behavior would be vastly more widespread in the barrio, much to its own and the Anglo's discomfort.[23]

Kiev's work suggests that a large number of Mexican Americans seek help from curanderos for relief of folk-defined illnesses that consist largely or wholly of psychopathological symptomatology.[24] Thus, along with the hypothesis that Mexican American families shelter mentally ill individuals, or the contrary argument of Jaco that the community has less mental illness, the reliance-on-curanderos thesis reinforces the prevailing culture-based interpretation of mental illness treatment. This line of analysis suggests several propositions, among which are: Mexican Americans perceive and define psychiatric disorder differently than Anglos; Mexican Americans are too proud and too sensitive to expose such personal problems as mental illnesses to public view; Mexican Americans avoid Anglo-oriented institutions, preferring to forego treatment, return to Mexico, or turn to the family or traditional folk healers because of their fear of contact with authorities or because they can communicate effectively only in Spanish.

Since the validity of any or all of these culture-based interpretations is of great significance to the development of mental health programs, Karno and Edgerton attempt to test these propositions with data from a randomly selected sample of 444 Mexican Americans from east Los Angeles. Using a set of vignettes to measure respondents' ability to recognize mental illness and generate solutions for handling the situation they see, Karno and Edgerton obtained the following results: Mexican Americans are more likely than Anglos to recommend that the persons described see a physician; when asked "As far as you know does a psychiatrist really help the people who go to him?" Mexican Americans somewhat more often than Anglos replied affirmatively; Mexican Americans are somewhat more optimistic about the curability of mental illness; a similar percent of both groups expresses the belief that a psychiatric clinic could help a person with a psychiatric disorder; about three out of four Mexican Americans compared with two out of three Anglos report having regular family physicians.

Looking at the treatment rate of psychiatric patients in California public institutions, Karno and Edgerton find Chicanos strikingly underrepresented. In 1966 Chicanos comprised only 3.3% of the resident population; the expected figure, given the Chicano's proportion of the state's population, would be between 9% and 10%.

Drawing together the utilization rates with their attitudinal data, the authors make these observations:

> The underutilization of psychiatric facilities by Mexican Americans (at least those who reside in east Los Angeles) is not to be accounted for by the fact that they share a cultural tradition which causes them to perceive and define mental illness in significantly different ways than do Anglos . . . We believe that the underrepresentation of Mexican Americans . . . is to be accounted for by a complex of social and cultural factors. These factors have very different weightings in their relative influence. Some of the heavily weighted factors include: a formidable language barrier; the significant mental health role of the very active family physician; the self-esteem reducing nature of agency-client contacts experienced by Mexican Americans; and the marked lack of mental health facilities in the Mexican American community itself. Of moderate weighting are such considerations as: the open border across which return significant numbers of Mexican Americans . . . Of relatively lesser weighting are such matters as folk medicine, folk psychotherapy, and "Mexican Culture" in general.[25]

The trend toward tighter sampling procedures and greater concern for such major demographic variables as class, education, age, family size, and place of residence is seen in other recent works. Sheldon reports on a 1961-1962 study of 89 Mexican American men in the Los Angeles area (greatly anglicized, to be sure: "Our modal man is called Carlos, although he may prefer to be called Charles or even Charley or Chuck by his close friends.") whom he considers to be representative of emerging middle-class Mexican Americans in the metropolis.[26] "Carlos' health is good, as is that of his family. He goes to a private doctor for medical care. Occasionally he uses public health clinics for shots or pregnancy advice for his wife. He is satisfied with the medical treatment he received from either place. He learned of the clinic that he uses through neighbors, relatives, or advice from other public agencies—not from the mass media. He carries health insurance through his office." (With an income of $12,500, Carlos's family represents about 7% of the Mexican Americans of the Southwest and enjoys an income four times greater than the 1960 average family.)

A basic tenet of the cultural interpretation of health behavior is that Mexican Americans are unwilling to be hospitalized. Madsen states that except in a crisis, hospitalization is always avoided. To be separated from the family and isolated in an Anglo world is almost intolerable. Similar views are expressed by Saunders and Clark. But in a study of Mexican Americans and Anglos, McLemore concludes that ethnicity as such has little to do with attitudes toward hospitalization.[27] He finds that educational attainment is the main independent variable: Mexican Americans and Anglos of similar educational level show greater agreement than is found within the Mexican American group.

In an analysis of results from a 1969 survey of randomly selected urban Orange County, California families, I found that Mexican Americans and Anglos express approximately the same level of preference for receiving health care from private physicians or hospitals; when the sources of actual treatment were examined, however, the survey revealed that a nearly four times greater proportion of Mexican Americans receives treatment from the area's principal public health facility.[28] I concluded that the higher rate of public provider utilization is related to previous negative experiences at the hands of Anglo medical personnel; that the presence of Spanish-speaking medical and para-medical personnel eases client-provider relations; and that low income Anglos who might be directed to the public facility by welfare workers, family, or friends in order to receive less expensive treatment avoid the facility because it is seen by them as a "Mexican" hospital.[29]

Asked if all children 17 years and younger as well as their parents receive a regular medical checkup (as opposed to remedial visits), 57% of the Orange County Mexican American and 58% of the Anglo respondents replied affirmatively; for regular dental checkups the rates are 54% and 56%, respectively. These similar rates are especially interesting since the Mexican American sample contains twice as many families reporting a total income of $6,000 or less and averaging 2.4 children compared with 1.4 for the Anglo group. But the Mexican American group's lower per capita income does not reduce health care: the likelihood of all members of the family having regular dental checkups actually *increases* with increased family size (gamma = .216) whereas the rate of checkups does not vary with Anglo family size. Similarly, increased family size is positively correlated with increased likelihood of regular medical checks in the Mexican American sample, although the correlation is weaker (gamma = .166); among the Anglo sample the likelihood of medical checkups *decreases* with increased family size.[30]

In my study I found that both groups, regardless of income, education, or family size, hold approximately as often the costliness of selected items of the health care budget to be "too high." However, there is substantial variation between the level of support that the two groups give proposals to reduce health care costs. What is significant in the response patterns is that the greater acceptance of each proposal by the Mexican American sample remains constant even when education, income, and family size are controlled. In this group of urban, middle-class Mexican Americans, ethnicity is independently related to behavioral and attitudinal variations.[31]

It is difficult to draw too heavily from the studies of the third generation. Methodological and conceptual limits are present in the mental illness surveys. And several of the other studies rest on small samples of Mexican Americans: McLemore's study contains 28 charity-ward respondents, mine 75. But clearly there are grounds to conclude that sweeping generalizations about Mexican American health behavior and attitudes are suspect. However restricted their samples, the third generation studies offer reason to believe that the often claimed significance of traditional folk health culture is overdrawn, especially with educated, urban working, and middle-class populations.

Evidence for this is offered by several recent studies that emphasize noncultural factors as major determinants of Mexican American health behavior. Karno and Edgerton mention that existing patterns of behavior are controlled by the absence of health care facilities—one cannot use Anglo services if they are not available. A related issue is the absence of Mexican Americans from the staffs of existing medical facilities. In a study of hospital occupational stratification in four cities containing large Mexican American populations, D'Antonio and Samora found that they are vastly underrepresented in the high status occupations (physicians, administrators and policy makers, nurses) while equally overrepresented in the lowest status occupations (maid, porter, unskilled labor).[32] Although Madsen challenges the notion that Mexican American physicians treat their kinsmen more respectfully and considerately than Anglo physicians,[33] Saunders, Clark, and Rubel stress the practicality of having Spanish-speaking physicians and nurses to instruct non-English–speaking patients and families. Currently the hiring of Spanish-speaking medical personnel is a major goal of Chicanos who see the employment of bilingual medical personnel as part of broader issues of social and economic emancipation toward which the community is driving.[34]

It is certainly arguable that both the lack of health care facilities and the absence of bilingual staff and administrative personnel are evidence of the overall unresponsiveness of the Anglo power structure to the needs of the barrio. Grebler and his associates describe the situation of the Mexican Americans in San Antonio, the site of several health-behavior studies: "Before World War II its politicians did not define Mexican Americans as an actual or even a potential political clientele. Investigations of the U.S. Public Health Service in 1935, for example, revealed that San Antonio's health services were largely inadequate and were operated entirely as a source of political patronage." San Antonio reports a higher rate of deaths among Mexican Americans at each age level compared with the Anglo population as well as 33% higher infant mortality. (One of Grebler's associates, Joan Moore, reports that former Texas governor John Connally assured the research team that Mexican Americans were happy Texans and had few problems of consequence not well on the way to solution.[35])

Clark calls attention to the Mexican Americans' habit of associating health workers with "authorities" and their resultant reluctance to contact them. This reluctance seems difficult to understand (after all, physicians, nurses, and public health workers are looking after our well-being) outside the context of the Mexican-Americans' relationships with other authorities who look after their well-being. During the 1930s welfare departments in Los Angeles, Detroit, St. Paul, and presumably elsewhere sought to reduce their unemployment and relief costs by "repatriating Mexicans," that is, deporting to Mexico anyone alleged to be a Mexican national who could not prove otherwise to the satisfaction of the "authorities."[36] In the 1950s a federal effort to apprehend illegal Mexican entrants, Operation Wetback, was conducted throughout the Southwest. Immigration officers, empowered to seize individuals for deportation unless the individual could prove he was not an illegal entrant, conducted sweeps throughout barrios, often at night or before dawn. Suspicious persons (that is, anyone who looked Mexican) were ordered to show proof of U.S. citizenship. Because of its large scale and allegations of rough treatment, Operation Wetback became one of the most traumatic recent experiences of the Mexican Americans in their contacts with government authority. No Mexican American community in the Southwest remained untouched. One final example of how the Anglo's attitude toward an organization of the dominant society may differ from the Mexican American's is that "everyone" knows that the U.S. Forest Service, symbolized by Smokey the Bear and portrayed heroically on the popular Lassie television series, are "good guys" protecting our national forests and the trees, birds, and animals that inhabit them. New Mexican Chicanos, however, see the forest ranger in a drab olive uniform as an American occupational trooper guarding the spoils of the Mexican American War. Resentment against the Forest Service and its personnel reached a peak when it was learned that forest personnel were used to guide police and U.S. National Guard patrols searching for Chicano activists involved in the short-lived "Tijerina Rebellion" in Tierra Amarilla, New Mexico.[37]

I will not attempt to review the literature dealing with the nature of the relationships between Mexican Americans and the educational and law enforcement institutions; rather, I think that the essence of the situation may be sensed in the following excerpts. The National Education Association:

> In some schools the speaking of Spanish is forbidden both in the classrooms and on the playground, except, of course, in classes where Spanish is taught. Not infrequently students have been punished for lapsing into Spanish. This has even extended to corporal punishment . . . The obvious theory is that a child will learn English if he is required to speak English and nothing but English, at least during those hours of the day when he is in school.[38]

William H. Parker, former Chief of the Los Angeles Police Department:

> The Latin population that came in here in great strength were here before us, and presented a great problem because I worked over on the East Side when men had to go in pairs—but that has evolved into assimilation—and it's because of some of these people being not too far removed from the wild tribes of the district of the inner mountains of Mexico. I don't think you can throw the genes out of the question when you discuss behavior patterns of people.[39]

Research aims for a new generation

We have seen that most studies of Mexican American health behavior are based on isolated villages, agricultural labor, and subsistence farming communities, or poverty-stricken urban barrios. Available studies of middle-class urban populations place great emphasis on the retention and distinctiveness of folk culture. After all, these traits make the samples "Mexican American." There are no systematic wide-ranging studies of health behavior; there is some evidence that the generalizations about the ubiquity of folk medicine are overdrawn, but neither position is able to produce much current data. Yet there are census data that tell us something about the validity of projecting from rural or agricultural populations.

The 1970 census reveals that 57% of the reported Mexican American community is U.S. born of U.S.-born parents. The community, contrary to popular notions, is more highly concentrated in cities than is the overall American population: nearly half live in central areas of large cities, 32% in suburbs, and only 15% in rural areas. Clearly, the community is neither "Mexican" nor "peasant." It is, however, young and fertile—33% of Mexican American families compared with only 17% in the total population contain four or more children. And the community holds a disproportionately large number of low income families: 25% report a total income of less than $4,000; the average Mexican American family income in 1969 was $6,962, whereas the national average was $9,590.[40] But these figures should not hide the great regional, economic, and social variations within the community, a point well illustrated by Peñalosa.[41]

The available data do not permit an unequivocal answer to the central questions before us: Is there a Mexican American health care subculture? Are the health care traits cited by Saunders, Clark, Rubel, Madsen, and others found throughout the population that traces its origins to Mexico or the pre–United States era of the Southwest? Are the health attitudes and behavior reported in rural New Mexico and south Texas culturally determined, or are they the result of isolation from scientific medicine compounded by insult and disrespect at the hands of Anglo providers? Do similar health care patterns exist but go unreported in the lower–middle class barrios of Los Angeles, Chicago, and Denver? Is there a distinctive life-style that pervades commercial, educational, social, and health behavior?

Answering these questions is of high priority because such research will provide vital information to people charged with developing, organizing, and administering health care delivery systems. Moreover, the answers to these questions will go a long way to demythify the Mexican American—a condition of slight moment to the Chicano but of potentially great consequence for Anglo-Chicano relations.

The preceding review suggests three basic issues that should be addressed by new research (such as through studies of hospital utlization, dental care, visitations to public versus private providers—the entire range of the sociology of medicine).

Health care subculture

Do individuals of Mexican heritage hold similar attitudes about illness and manifest similar preventive and curative traits regardless of age, socioeconomic status, or place of residence in the United States? In addressing this issue, the scholar must be imaginative in the use of controls: while there are numerous studies of rural and lower-class southwestern and western Mexican Americans, no research has been conducted that incorporates a cross-sectional sample of the population or encompasses Mexican Americans living in Ohio, Illinois, or Michigan. Yet studies cited above suggest that attitudes and behavior of various sectors of the community are not consonant with the "health-care-as-subculture" notion Appropriate controls would permit us to go a long way in clarifying the validity of this hypothesis.

Utilization of providers

Is utilization of public and private providers a function of cost, location, or information; or is symptomatology, socioeconomic status, or age the principal determinant(s)? We have seen claims that Mexican Americans avoid Anglo medicine, preferring to rely on curanderos, family, or friends. Other research suggests that the fee system, availability and ease of access, or the patient's education and acculturation are the controlling factors. The argument is advanced that Anglicization is a prerequisite for successful integration into the delivery system. Projects designed to this end are in operation (such as remedial education under the rubric of "aid to the culturally disadvantaged"); yet there is little clear evidence that greater utilization and better health care are outcomes of these efforts.

Community participation

Is the presence of Spanish-speaking providers and staff associated with increased utilization and higher repeat visitation rates? Does community participation in the planning, administering, and evaluating of health services affect visitation patterns? There is evidence that Spanish-speaking physicians and paramedical personnel are perhaps more abrasive to Mexican Americans than are non-Spanish speakers, but contrary findings exist that point to greater efficiency and effectiveness of programs that employ bilingual personnel. Since both private and public providers of health care are, in theory at least, client-centered systems designed to provide services to individuals in distress, it seems self-evident that their success may be judged in terms of the facility with which clients (that is, patients) gain assistance. Thus the issue of Spanish-speaking personnel dealing with Spanish-speaking clients seems of primary significance. Similarly, the inclusion of community representatives of health-planning commissions as required by the Comprehensive Health Planning Act raises the question of the effect of health services and utilization of community involvement. Indeed, the broader issue of who and what are represented through such schemes deserves the highest research priority.

These three issues certainly do not exhaust the range of questions raised or implied in the literature surveyed, but they do offer foci around which socially useful and theoretically interesting work may be done. The methodological shortcomings and conceptual inadequacies of much of the research reviewed may be avoided if the scholar combines concern, sensitivity, and technical rigor. The rapid urbanization of the Mexican American population, the growing numbers of Mexican American physicians, dentists, nurses, and other professionals and semiprofessionals, and the emergence of Chicanos and chicanismo are recent phenomena that demand these efforts. Such work will serve the interests of both the social sciences and the barrio.

Notes

1. A useful bibliography of Mexican American studies is found in Inter-Agency Committee on Mexican-American Affairs, *A Guide to Materials Relating to Persons of Mexican Heritage in the United States* (Washington, D.C.: U.S. Government Printing Office, 1969). For a guide to bibliographic sources, see Joseph A. Clark y Morena, "Bibliography of Bibliographies Relating to Mexican American Studies," *El Grito* 3 (Summer 1970), pp. 25-31.

2. Lyle Saunders's principal works include *Cultural Differences and Medical Care: The Case of the Spanish-speaking People of the Southwest* (New York: Russell Sage Foundation, 1954); Lyle Saunders and G. Hewes, "Folk Medicine and Medical Practices," *Journal of Medical Education* **28** (Sept. 1953), pp. 43-46; Lyle Saunders and Julian Samora, "A Medical Care Program for a Colorado County," in Benjamin D. Paul (editor), *Health, Culture and Community: Case Studies of Public Reaction to Health Programs* (New York: Russell Sage Foundation, 1956), pp. 377-400; Lyle Saunders, "Healing Ways in the Spanish Southwest," in E. Gartly Jaco (editor), *Patients, Physicians and Illness* (New York: The Free Press, 1958), pp. 567-569; Julian Samora, Lyle Saunders, and Richard F. Larson, "Knowledge About Specific Diseases in Four Selected Samples," *Journal of Health and Human Behavior* **3** (Fall 1962), pp. 176-185; Robert C. Hanson and Lyle Saunders, *Nurse-Patient Communication: A Manual for Public Health Nurses in Northern New Mexico* (Santa Fe: New Mexico State Department of Public Health, 1964).

3. Saunders uses the following sources: William M. Hudson (editor), *The Healer of Los Olmos and Other Mexican Lore* (Dallas: Southern Methodist University Press, 1951); Sr. Mary Lucia van der Eerden, *Maternity Care in a Spanish-American Community of New Mexico* (Washington, D.C.: The Catholic University of American Press, 1948); Howard E. Thomas and Florence Taylor, *Migrant Farm Labor in Colorado: A Study of Migratory Families* (New York: National Child Labor Committee, 1951); Florence Kluckhohn, "Los Atarqueños: A Study of Patterns and Configurations in a New Mexico Village" (Ph.D. dissertation, Radcliffe College, Cambridge, Mass., 1941); Ozzie G. Simmons, "Anglo-Americans and Mexican-Americans in South Texas: A Study in Dominant-Subordinate Group Relations" (Ph.D. dissertation, Harvard University, Cambridge, Mass., 1952).

4. Saunders, *Cultural Differences and Medical Care,* p. 12.

5. Compare with George I. Sanchez, *Forgotten People: A Study of New Mexicans* (Albuquerque: University of New Mexico Press, 1940); Ruth D. Tuck, *Not With the Fist: Mexican-Americans in a Southwest City* (New York: Harcourt Brace Jovanovich, Inc., 1946); Munro S. Edmonson, *Los Manitos: A Study of Institutional Values* (New Orleans: Middle American Research Institute, Tulane University, 1957); Florence R. Kluckhohn, "The Spanish-American of Atrisco," in Florence R. Kluckhohn and Fred L. Strodtbeck, *Variations in Value Orientations* (Evanston: Row, Peterson, 1961), pp. 175-257.

6. Besides the monographs discussed, see Sam Schulman, "Rural Health Ways in New Mexico," in Vera Rubin (editor), "Culture, Society and Health," *Annals of the New York Academy of Sciences* **84** (Dec. 1960), pp. 950-959; Julian Samora, "Conceptions of Health and Disease Among Spanish Americans," *American Catholic Sociological Review* **22** (Winter 1961), pp. 314-323; Sam Schulman and Anne M. Smith, "The Concept of 'Health' Among Spanish-speaking Villagers of New Mexico and Colorado," *Journal of Health and Human Behavior* **4** (Winter 1963), pp. 226-234.

7. Margaret Clark, *Health in the Mexican-American Culture* (Berkeley and Los Angeles: University of California Press, 1959).

8. Arthur J. Rubel, *Across the Tracks: Mexican-Americans in a Texas City* (Austin: University of Texas Press, 1966).

9. William Madsen, *Mexican-Americans of South Texas* (New York: Holt, Rinehart and Winston, Inc., 1964).

10. See Arthur J. Rubel, "Concepts of Disease in Mexican-American Culture," *American Anthropologist* **62** (Oct. 1960), pp. 795-814.

11. Rubel, *Across the Tracks,* p. 194; compare with Madsen, *Mexican-Americans of South Texas,* pp. 89-90.

12. The sensitivity to nudity and matters concerning reproduction may in part account for the low rate of prenatal care among Mexican Americans. See S. J. Reeder and L. G. Reeder, "Some Correlates of Prenatal Care Among Low Income Wed and Unwed Women," *American Journal of Obstetrics and Gynecology* **90** (Dec. 1964), pp. 1304-1314.

13. See E. Gartly Jaco, "Mental Health of the Spanish-American in Texas," in Marvin K. Opler, (editor), *Culture and Mental Health* (New York: Macmillan, Inc., 1959), pp. 467-488; E. Gartly Jaco, *The Social Epidemiology of Mental Disorder: A Psychiatric Survey of Texas* (New York: Russell Sage Foundation, 1960).

14. Colorado Commission on Spanish Surnamed Citizens, *The Status of Spanish Surnamed Citizens in Colorado: Report to the Colorado General Assembly* (Jan. 1967).
15. Cited in A. Taher Moustafa and Gertrud Weiss, *Health Status and Practices of Mexican Americans. Mexican-American Study Project, Advance Report 11* (Los Angeles: Graduate School of Business Administration, University of California, Los Angeles, 1968).
16. Chicanismo is the label given the eclectic ideology of political activism and cultural pride advanced by Chicano activists. Chicanismo focuses on the Mexican American's life experiences in the United States and attempts to reconstruct a new image for them. See Joan W. Moore with Alfredo Cuellar, *Mexican Americans* (Englewood Cliffs, N.J.: Prentice-Hall, Inc., 1970), pp. 143-156; reviews of *La Raza, Aztlán, El Grito,* and other activist-oriented publications, and John Womack, Jr., "Who Are the Chicanos?" *The New York Review of Books* 19 (31 Aug. 1972), pp. 12-18.
17. Leo Grebler, Joan W. Moore, and Ralph C. Guzman, *The Mexican-American People: The Nation's Second Largest Minority* (New York: The Free Press, 1970). The book has been variously praised or ignored by Chicano and Anglo scholars. For a representative cross section, see "The Mexican-American People: A Review Symposium," *Social Science Quarterly* 52 (June 1971), pp. 8-38. The comments by Rodolfo Alvarez, "The Unique Psycho-Historical Experience of the Mexican-American People," pp. 15-29, are especially germane to the present analysis.
18. Cited in Moustafa and Weiss, *Health Status and Practices of Mexican Americans.*
19. Frank C. Nall and Joseph Speilberg, "Social and Cultural Factors in the Responses of Mexican-Americans to Medical Treatment," *Journal of Health and Human Behavior* 8 (Dec. 1967), pp. 299-308.
20. Celia S. Heller, *Mexican American Youth: Forgotten Youth at the Crossroads* (New York: Random House, Inc., 1966), p. 35.
21. Miguel Montiel, "The Social Science Myth of the Mexican-American Family," *El Grito* 3 (Summer 1970), pp. 56-63.
22. Ari Kiev, *Curanderismo: Mexican American Folk Psychiatry* (New York: The Free Press, 1968).
23. *The Los Angeles Times,* 19 April 1971, carried a feature story, "Curandero: Evil Spirits and Mental Health," recounting a program initiated in a state mental hospital in which curandero is used in an effort to bring Chicano patients to a stage of self-confidence and motivation at which "modern" practitioners may take over. The Chicano social workers who brought the curandero to the hospital claimed 80% success level for the program. The *Times* writer noted, "The Administration of the hospital . . . has not been enthusiastic about the program. It has steadfastly maintained that it is not economically possible to have a special program for every cultural group [p. 30]."
24. On the curandero, see Octavio Ignacio Romano, "Charismatic Medicine: Folk Healing and Folk Sainthood," *American Anthropologist* 67 (Oct. 1963), pp. 1151-1171.
25. Marvin Karno and Robert B. Edgerton, "Perception of Mental Illness in a Mexican-American Community," *Archives of General Psychiatry* 20 (Feb. 1969), pp. 233-238.
26. Paul M. Sheldon, "Community Participation and the Emerging Middle Class," in Julian Samora (editor), *La Raza: Forgotten Americans* (Notre Dame: University of Notre Dame Press, 1966), pp. 125-157.
27. S. Dale McLemore, "Ethnic Attitudes Toward Hospitalization: An Illustrative Comparison of Anglos and Mexican Americans," *(Southwestern) Social Science Quarterly* 43 (March 1963), pp. 341-346.
28. Jerry L. Weaver, *Health Care Service Use in Orange County California: A Socioeconomic Analysis* (Long Beach: Center for Political Research, California State University, Long Beach, 1969).
29. Compare with John M. Goering and Rodney M. Coe, "Cultural versus Situational Explanations of the Medical Behavior of the Poor," *Social Science Quarterly* 51 (Sept. 1970), pp. 309-319; Ozzie G. Simmons, *Social Status and Public Health* (New York: Social Science Research Council, 1958), p. 8.
30. Jerry L. Weaver, "Health Care Costs as a Political Issue: Comparative Responses of Chicanos and Anglos," *Social Science Quarterly* 53 (March 1973), pp. 846-854. An unexpectedly high

rate of health service use by minorities is cited in other research. Low income Blacks in Washington, D.C. are reported to have a higher rate of medical checkups than Anglos of similar SES. See Paul B. Cornely and S. K. Bigman, "Cultural Considerations in Changing Health Attitudes," *Medical Annals of the District of Columbia* 30 (April 1961), pp. 191-199. Compare with Wylda Cowles and Steven Polgar, "Health and Communication in a Negro Census Tract," *Social Problems* 10 (Winter 1963), pp. 228-236.

31. Similar conclusions are drawn by Edward A. Suchman, "Socio-Medical Variations Among Ethnic Groups," *American Journal of Sociology* 70 (Nov. 1964), pp. 319-331. Also see Paul, *Health, Culture and Community;* Beatrice B. Berle, *Eighty Puerto Rican Families in New York City: Health and Disease Studied in Context* (New York: Columbia University Press, 1958); Sydney H. Croog, "Ethnic Origins, Educational Level, and Responses to a Health Questionnaire," *Human Organization* 20 (Summer 1961), pp. 65-69; Steve Polgar, "Health and Human Behavior: Areas of Interest Common to the Social and Medical Science," *Current Anthropology* 3 (April 1962), pp. 159-205. For a useful bibliography dealing with the sociology of health, see Ozzie G. Simmons, "Social Research in Health and Medicine: A Bibliography," in Howard F. Freeman, Sol Levine, and Leo G. Reeder (editors), *Handbook of Medical Sociology* (Englewood Cliffs, N.J.: Prentice-Hall, Inc., 1963), pp. 493-581.

32. William V. D'Antonio and Julian Samora, "Occupational Stratifications in Four Southwestern Communities: A Study of Ethnic Differential Employment in Hospitals," *Social Forces* 41 (Oct. 1962), pp. 18-24.

33. "Too often . . . Latin doctors are *iglesados* who look back on their own folk origins with contempt that is reflected in their relations with patients who cling to folk beliefs. These doctors are often more intolerant of unscientific thinking than Anglo doctors. The anglicized Latin doctor feels the patient's hostility and commonly answers with satire. This response increases the communication barrier between patient and physician and heightens Latin resentment against hostile and dominant Anglo society," from Madsen, *Mexican-Americans of South Texas,* p. 95.

34. See East Los Angeles Health Task Force, *East Los Angeles Health: A Community Report from a Project and Conference on Health Problems and Priorities in East Los Angeles,* 1970.

35. Joan W. Moore, "Political and Ethical Problems in a Large-Scale Study of a Minority Population," in Gideon Sjoberg (editor), *Ethnics, Politics, and Social Research* (Cambridge: Schenkman Publishing Co., Inc., 1967), p. 229.

36. On Los Angeles, see Carey McWilliams, "Getting Rid of the Mexicans," *American Mercury* 28 (March 1933), pp. 322-324; on Detroit, see Norman D. Humphrey, "Mexican Repatriation for Michigan—Public Assistance in Historical Perspective," *Social Science Review* 15 (Sept. 1941), pp. 505ff; on St. Paul, see Norman S. Goldner, "The Mexican in the Northern Urban Area: A Comparison of Two Generations" (M.A. thesis, University of Minnesota, Minneapolis, 1959). Cited by Grebler, Moore, and Guzman, *The Mexican-American People,* pp. 524-525.

37. Grebler, Moore, and Guzman, *The Mexican-American People,* p. 528.

38. *The Invisible Minority,* a report of the NEA-Tucson Survey on the Teaching of Spanish to the Spanish Speaking (Washington, D.C.: National Education Association, 1966). Quoted from John H. Burma, *Mexican-Americans in the United States: A Reader* (Cambridge: Schenkman Publishing Co., Inc., 1970), p. 110.

39. *Hearings before the United States Commission on Civil Rights,* San Francisco, 27 Jan. 1960. Quoted from Grebler, Moore, and Guzman, *The Mexican-American People,* p. 530.

40. U.S. Department of Health, Education, and Welfare, *A Study of Selected Socio-economic Characteristics of Ethnic Minorities Based on the 1970 Census.* Vol. I: *Americans of Spanish Origin* (Washington, D.C.: U.S. Government Printing Office, July 1974).

41. Fernando Peñalosa, "The Changing Mexican-American in Southern California," *Sociology and Social Research* 51 (July 1967), pp. 405-406.

CHAPTER 5 Poverty and health in black and white

Although it is true that the poor and the lower classes suffer disproportionately high rates of illness, disease, and disability, and that the Black population is disproportionately overrepresented among the disadvantaged, it seems certain that just being Black opens one to additional health problems. A. S. Yerby, former Health Commissioner for New York City, summarizes his experience with the Blacks' plight and the effects of race on health: "Clearly, in terms of health, there is a special disadvantage in being a Negro in the United States which transcends being poor."[1] Ryan writes that "disabilities are far more prevalent among Negroes than among Whites."[2] He attributes this to racial discrimination and its corollary, personal stress.

While there is a body of research that summarizes the health problems and needs of Blacks and offers limited Black/Anglo comparisons,[3] most of these accounts are either impressionistic, methodologically suspect, or limited to a particular disease or pathology (such as hypertension or infant mortality). For example, discussions of Black/Anglo health differences often compare aggregate samples that are not controlled for variations in age, class, or educational differences—all factors known to be associated with distinctive health profiles. Nor does simply controlling for a single demographic variable allow the significance of race to be isolated. The technique of matching low income Black and Anglo samples may produce seriously misleading findings, since the elderly are disproportionately represented among the low income Anglo strata. Thus, age may be affecting what are alleged to be racial differences. Looking at a single problem, such as sickle-cell anemia or hypertension, while revealing a very real and grave situation for the Black community, tends to distract attention from the total health situation and may lead to fragmented, often highly emotional reactions that claim resources that might be invested more profitably in attacking the broad social or economic conditions such as unemployment, discrimination, dependency, and exploitation that spawn and sustain multiple pathologies.

In other words, a realistic appraisal of the overall health situation of the Black community must treat the whole person in the context of that person's environment. At the same time, it must attempt to disentangle class and race so that the relationship between socioeconomic forces and personal attributes can be seen. Such an effort is not merely an intellectual exercise; it has genuine implications for policy makers. For instance, *if* lack of money to spend on health services is the principle reason that physicians avoid poor Black communities, then programs designed to increase the real spending power of poor people ought to be incentive enough to bring providers into the ghettos and other poor, presently underdoctored, areas. Conversely, *if* the predominately white health care establishment is populated by individuals who simply (or, rather, for a complex of reasons) do not want to associate with lower-class Blacks, even if they have money to spend, then financial incentives will have little or no effect on the availability of dentists, physical therapists, convalescent hospitals, physicians, and the like.

In this chapter I shall review the extant materials with an eye for studies that present comparable samples of Black and Anglo populations. An additional target is material that offers insights into the nature of the health problems that might be attacked through governmental action. An example of the former is found among studies of hypertension; of the latter, the analysis of the impact of diet and nutrition on infant mortality. From the collage of Black health needs, implications for national health policy will be drawn.

Ghetto health problems

That living in densely populated communities of run-down dwellings, pinched by freeways, industrial zones, or decaying commercial centers, is dangerous to one's health is a self-evident proposition.[4] Lead in the air, lead in paint, and lead in pistol barrels is only one of the hazardous "common elements" of ghetto life. Infectious diseases compound environmental threats. For example, although tuberculosis has all but vanished from the lists of American health problems, it remains conspicuously present in ghettos. Birch and Gussow report that in the mid 1960s the rate of newly detected cases of tuberculosis was 20 per 100,000 residences in the predominately white, middle-class Flushing area of New York City; in Central Harlem, only a few miles away, the rate was 226 per 100,000. In Watts, the TB rate is four times that of the rest of Los Angeles County. Similarly, ghettos contain disproportionately high rates of diphtheria, brucellosis, polio, typhoid, hepatitis, mumps, measles, and rheumatic fever.[5]

If these infectious diseases were not enough to contend with, dramatically increasing rates of cancer are being reported among Blacks. The Third National Cancer Survey of the National Cancer Institute found the incidence of cancer to be 397.2 per 100,000 for Black males, 342.6 for Anglo males, 256.8 for Black females, and 270.3 for Anglo females.[6] It may be that the alleged soaring rate for Blacks is a phenomenon of better record keeping rather than a recent explosion of cancer; alternatively, however, the dramatic increase may reflect the impact of environmental pollution and of food preservatives, colorings, and processing on the increasingly urbanized Black population.

Hypertension, cardiovascular diseases, stroke, and related pathologies of the circulatory system are reported throughout the Black population whether urban or rural. Indeed, the first indications of the magnitude of Black health problems were seen in studies published during the 1940s and early 1950s comparing rural southern Blacks and Anglos.[7] Recent research focused on the extent and severity of hypertension and related disorders among urban dwellers. As early as 1966 it was reported that "in any age group the likelihood of heart disease with hypertension is greater for Negroes than for white persons."[8] Among young Black adults seen in Harlem, 30% to 35% were affected by hypertension.[9] A study of 11,309 residents of New Orleans showed that Black males exceeded Anglo males in the prevalence of hypertension in every age cohort except the 30- to 39-year-old. Among the females, however, Blacks exceeded the Anglos' rate in every age category. Fully 71% of Black women over 50 years of age were found to be hypertensive.[10] A similar pattern was revealed in a survey conducted in Oakland: "Blacks had higher average diastolic and systolic blood pressures and a higher prevalence of hypertension than whites for both males and females and for all age groups. When these distributions were examined by social class, blacks in the lowest social classes had the highest blood pressures."[11]

Perhaps the most revealing research has been reported by Harburg and his associates.[12] Here the relationship between health and environment is starkly illustrated: Male Blacks living in areas of Detroit that were characterized by low socioeconomic status, high crime rates, high population density, high residential mobility, and high rates of marital breakup ("high stress areas") reported higher rates of blood pressure than Blacks living outside the high stress areas. This study also found that *color* was related to blood pressure. The highest aggregate blood pressure rates were reported for the sample of darkest-skinned males living in high stress areas. The significance of skin pigmentation in the etiology of hypertension has also been reported by Boyle, who saw age-adjusted increases in blood pressure associated with increased pigmentation: a significantly greater prevalence of hypertension was found in the darker compared with the lighter half of the Black study group.[13]

The origins of hypertension have been traced back to slavery, segregation, continuing discrimination, diet, and biological conditions. Whatever the origin, high blood pressure is but one of the manifestations of personal stress.[14] Kramer points to both the psychological and physiological ramifications of being Black in America when she links color and social acceptance:

> The psychological concomitant to racial visibility is personal invisibility. When a categorical status (being a "Negro") is internalized without another set of cultural values even to cause conflict, there are no social alternatives available to serve as a source of identity. . . . there is no positive response from within that can offer any psychological resolution. The resulting tension is all but intolerable. . . .[15]

It is the dilemma of being so obviously invisible that gives the writings of Ralph Ellison, Richard Wright, James Baldwin, Claude Brown and other Black artists such disarming poignancy and devastating truth.

The struggle to survive the tensions and stresses of American society is successfully waged every day by millions of Blacks; a few, however, fall victim to stroke, high blood pressure, and to suicide, drug abuse, alcoholism, and the rage that drives a Black to challenge police to use their weapons "in self-defense."[16] Other Blacks are found to have become mentally ill and are institutionalized for psychiatric care.

On the basis of their review of clinic data, Ann and Thomas Pettigrew conclude "that psychosis rates for Negroes, especially for schizophrenia and some organic psychosis, are higher than rates for whites."[17] Fried carries the analysis further and finds: "The weight of evidence continues to support the proposition that these high rates represent greater prevalence of severe psychiatric disorders among Negroes. It should be noted that a number of the studies comparing psychiatric hospitalization of Negroes and whites have used extensive controls and the finding is maintained when such factors as migration, education, and occupation are taken into account. Indeed, among all the factors considered in several studies, the Negro-white difference is the largest and most consistent."[18]

Using institutionalization rates as an indicator of the frequency and severity of mental illness in the Black population is extremely risky; mental hospitals and other public institutions may be convenient dumping grounds for individuals who have neither the family support nor social status to avoid incarceration.[19] Social and cultural forces may work a selective advantage for Anglos: individual Anglos who demonstrate behavior that would lead Blacks into psychiatric institutions may be protected and retained in their family or treated by general voluntary hospitals. This does not mean that Black families are less tolerant or protective; rather, proportionately more Black families are so poor that holding nonproductive individuals is impossible. Until income and socioeconomic status are controlled and the incidence of mental illness analyzed in comparable Black and Anglo populations, it is premature to assert that the former have an absolutely higher frequency of severe psychiatric disorders. And yet, it still remains a reasonable hypothesis that one of the consequences of being Black and living in American society is stress-induced mental health problems.[20]

This brief review of the frequency and rate of hypertension, mental illness, cancer, and infectious diseases suggests a pattern of disproportionately high morbidities in the Black community. However, except for the sophisticated methodology of several studies of hypertension, it is not clear that comparable samples of Blacks and Anglos have been analyzed. Nevertheless, a strong case can be made for the proposition that a set of special disadvantages adheres to the former that transcends aggregate socioeconomic inequality. Now we shall break apart the community and deal with specific cohorts. Here the effect of race independent of class becomes clearer; it is especially revealed in the health care problems of infants and the elderly.

Infant mortality

Aside from the outrage and indignation that infant mortality generates, a great deal about the overall conditions of a population is revealed by examining and comparing infant death rates. For instance, it is generally recognized that the mortality of infants from birth through the first month (neonatal mortality) is heavily influenced by biological factors such as the physical condition of the mother, her nutrition, the quality of prenatal medical care, and the delivery environment. On the other hand, death between the end of the first month of life and the first year (postneonatal mortality) is predominately sensitive to the baby's immediate environmental circumstances, such as diet, postdelivery medical care, sanitary conditions of its dwelling, dangers such as rats, lead paint, and violent and abusive attack by other human beings.

Table 5-1. Anglo and Black infant mortality, 1950-1973 (per 1,000 live births)*

	1950	1960	1965	1970	1971	1972	1973	Percentage rate of decrease from 1950 to 1973
Under 1 year								
Anglo	26.8	22.9	21.5	17.8	17.1	16.4	15.8	41
Black	44.5	43.2	40.3	30.9	28.5	27.7	26.2	41
Percentage of Black greater than Anglo	66	88	87	74	67	69	66	
Under 28 days								
Anglo	19.4	17.2	16.1	13.8	13.0	12.4	11.8	39
Black	27.5	26.9	25.4	21.4	19.6	19.2	17.9	34
Percentage of Black greater than Anglo	41	56	57	55	51	55	52	
28 days to 1 year								
Anglo	7.4	5.7	5.4	4.0	4.0	4.0	4.0	59
Black	16.9	16.4	14.9	9.5	8.9	8.5	8.3	49
Percentage of Black greater than Anglo	128	107	175	137	122	112	107	

Data from U.S. Bureau of the Census, *Current Population Reports, Special Studies, Series P-23, No. 54, The Social and Economic Status of the Black Population in the United States, 1974* (Washington, D.C.: U.S. Government Printing Office, 1975), p. 126.
*Data for "Black" includes other races; Blacks constitute approximately 90% of this group.

The national trends in Black/Anglo infant mortality are summarized in Table 5-1. Here we see a picture of consistent disadvantage. Indeed, while the death rates of both Anglos and Blacks show an absolute decline since 1950, the disparity of the racial differences has remained or grown greater. The ratio of Black over Anglo infant death rates has stayed the same (66%) for 2 1/2 decades; but during the same period, the relative disadvantage of the Black against the Anglo neonatal mortality has actually expanded—from 41% greater Black over Anglo in 1950 to 52% in 1973.

Another way of seeing the comparative situation of the Black mortality trends is to recognize that while both Black and Anglo trends are downward, the Black trends begin from a much higher absolute point than the Anglo; yet the Anglo trends show a steeper downward (favorable) slope. One might assume that just the opposite should be the case since there would seem to be a greater margin for improvement in the Black condition; if efforts were made in both communities, would not the Anglo's base situation reflect a hard core that would be less easily overcome? That is not the case; the relative disadvantage remains after 2 1/2 decades of effort—and in two out of three cases, the relative disadvantage of the Black community has increased.[21]

The national differences in infant death rates are paralleled by the disproportionately high rate of maternal death among Blacks. Table 5-2 indicates that Black women run nearly three times the risk of dying as a result of pregnancy: in 1970, the last year for which data are available, the level of Black maternal death over Anglo was 288%. As is the case with the

Table 5-2. Anglo and Black maternal mortality, 1950-1970 (per 100,000 births)*

	1950	1955	1960	1965	1970	Percentage rate of decrease from 1950 to 1970
Anglo	61.1	32.8	26.0	21.0	14.4	76
Black	221.6	130.3	97.9	83.7	55.9	74
Percentage of Black greater than Anglo	262	297	276	298	288	

Data from Bureau of the Census, *Statistical Abstract of the United States, 1974* (Washington, D.C.: U.S. Government Printing Office, 1975), p. 60.
*Data for "Black" includes other races; Blacks constitute approximately 90% of this group.

trend of infant death, while the Black community begins with a much higher absolute number of maternal deaths, its rate of decline over 2 decades is less than the Anglo's. In addition, the relative position of the Black, that is, the risk of dying compared with the Anglo's, has increased by 10% between 1950 and 1970; rather than the gap closing, greater inequality of risk remains.

Moving beyond these aggregate national figures, we shall find that both where one lives and one's social class bear on infant death rates. Jiobu reports that in cities of over 100,000 population, Blacks have 53% more neonatal and 142% greater postneonatal mortality than Anglos.[22] In 1964, poverty area Chicago Blacks reported 80% greater infant mortality than poverty area Anglos: 45.5 and 25.1 deaths per 1,000 live births, respectively.[23] In Hartford, Connecticut the 1970 infant mortality in its predominately Black North End was twice as high (30.7 per 1,000 live births) as in the rest of the city (16.3).[24] Los Angeles County reported a 1972 infant death rate of 27.5 for its largely Black southern health district compared with a countywide rate of 15.8.[25] In the state of North Carolina, the gross 1970-1972 infant death rates were 25.7 for Anglos and 41.0 for non-Anglos.[26]

Some observers argue that when close controls are applied to these crude Black/Anglo rates, differences in socioeconomic status explain the disparities; that is, if these factors were equally distributed in both populations, infant mortality differences would disappear.[27]

On the contrary, when such controls are used, the racial divergence remains. As Table 5-3 illustrates, Blacks from the national population who report over $10,000 annual income have a higher infant death rate than Anglos reporting less than $3,000. The offspring of Black physicians, executives, and engineers are only slightly less likely to die than the offspring of Anglo construction workers, domestic workers, and janitors.

The high rates among upper income, upper status Blacks suggest that we can discount (although certainly not exclude) inability to afford or reach health providers, ignorance of rudimentary hygienic and sanitary precautions, dramatically bad housing, and other such factors seen in the poor's environment. Rather, we can explore the notion that since part of the aggregate death rates stem from fetal (stillbirths) and neonatal mortality, the root rests in such biological factors as the mother's fitness to produce an infant sufficiently vital

Table 5-3. Effect of income and father's occupation on Anglo and Black infant mortality rates (per 1,000 live births)

	Anglo	Black
Father's occupation		
Perineonatal mortality, New York City, 1961-1963[*]		
Professional, managerial, technical	16.7	24.2
Clerical and sales	20.8	31.5
Craftspersons and operatives	20.9	32.9
Laborers and service workers	24.9	36.5
Income		
Infant mortality, United States, 1964-1966[†]		
Under $3,000	27.3	42.5
$ 3,000 to $ 4,999	22.1	46.8
$ 5,000 to $ 6,999	17.8	22.0
$ 7,000 to $ 9,999	19.2	37.6
$ 10,000 and over	19.4	31.5

[*]Data from Alonzo S. Yerby, "The Disadvantaged and Health Care," *American Journal of Public Health* **56** (Jan. 1966), p. 6.
[†]Data from Brian McMahon, Mary Grace Kovar, and Jacob J. Feldman, "Infant Mortality Rates: Socioeconomic Factors," *Vital and Health Statistics* **22** (March 1972), p. 13.

to survive its first month. The biological hypothesis, in turn, directs us to the impact on the present generation of Black mothers of historical nutrition patterns: conditions fostered by six or eight generations of inadequate nutrition certainly would not be remedied in one or even two generations of the type of improvement that is associated with middle or upper middle status. Fortunately, there are scattered studies of the diet patterns of southern Blacks that reveal what the mothers (and sometimes the grandmothers) of the present generation of childbearers themselves were eating when they bore their children. These studies document a persistent pattern of poor nutrition that may well stretch back into the slave period and beyond.[28]

Prior to World War II, Whitsitt found that the diets of Maryland Black patients of an antenatal clinic consisted mainly of pork, white bread, potatoes, corn syrup, cabbage, and dried beans and that their diets were strikingly deficient in dairy products, eggs, green vegetables, and fruit. Over 70% of the patients were anemic. Moore and associates reported that a sample of Louisiana Blacks had both lower caloric intake (1,546 compared with 2,041 for Anglo women) and poor nutrition; indeed, 36% were said to be meeting *none* of the dietary recommendations of the Food and Nutrition Board of the National Research Council. A post–World War II study by Ferguson and Keaton found that among pregnant Black Mississippians on the day prior to their survey, 46% had had no milk, 39% no lean meat, 57% no eggs, and 90% no other protein. Another study in New Orleans at about the same time found that 92% of the Black prenatal patients' diets ranked "poor" or "very poor." As in other research, this study found that Black women consumed daily just a little over half of the recommended 85 grams of protein.[29]

Current research reveals that traditional southern food preferences and habits are carried by migrants out of the South and are continued *in the absence of significant economic improvement.*[30] Thus, both historical and current nutritional deprivation is certainly associated with the high infant mortality rates among poor Blacks. Birch and Gussow conclude that while knowledge about nutrition is related to the eating habits of the poor, poverty is the basic factor that keeps poor women badly fed.[31]

Critics of the nation's infant death rates assert that too little has been or is being done, that massive new efforts such as free food for the needy, expanded pre- and postnatal outreach programs, new educational programs, and increased numbers of health care providers to serve infant and maternal needs could cut the rates. Such proposals lead to the question of why so relatively little has been done. Mechanic argues that the lack of attention to infant mortality reflects the class-conscious nature of the American political process: "In the [1960s], the concentrated efforts and attention devoted to attacking paralytic polio, in contrast to feeble efforts in closing gaps in infant mortality, must be understood within the context that the incidence of polio was higher in the middle classes than in the lower classes. The areas receiving official recognition and attention depend, in large part, on the ability of affected groups to make their needs known and to organize in order to stimulate official response."[32]

Although it is true that national health policy reflects the middle-class bias of the political system and that there are few if any powerful constituencies or interest groups pushing for massive initiatives against infant mortality, it is misleading, I think, to conclude that dramatic improvement in Black infant mortality would result from greater expenditures. The history of the 1960s and 1970s shows that eliminating poverty and making cities reasonably liveable cannot be accomplished by throwing a few billion dollars into the pot: poverty and its related pathologies are deeply rooted in the social, economic, and political institutions and traditions of American society. Their impact on the health of Black Americans falls with a little-understood cumulative weight—as illustrated by the mortality among upper income/status Blacks. It is folly to assume that generations and centuries can be expunged and their latent effects eliminated by new programs. Some improvement would arise from greater accessibility to providers, improved nutritional education, and greater availability and variety of foods; but it may take several generations to offset historical determinants of infant mortality.

The elderly Black

According to the 1970 census, there are approximately 1.6 million Blacks 65 years and older in the United States. Although most are under 75, almost 8% of the elderly are over 85 years of age. About 60% of the Black elderly live in the South. The sex ratio for the elderly Black is slightly higher than that of the Anglo—76 males per 100 females. Most Black females are widowed and report lower median incomes than Anglo females or Black males. Most Black aged have received no education beyond elementary school, and most are no longer gainfully employed. The majority are poor—poorer, typically, than Anglo or Spanish-surnamed aged. And the Black aged are becoming relatively worse off, because the income gap between the Anglo and Black aged has widened over the past decades. However, the mortality picture of the Black aged is not as depressing as we might expect because, generally, Black aged are a healthier population than their Anglo equivalent, perhaps reflecting the higher earlier mortality among Blacks—only the fittest survive and they then remain fit longer.[33]

There is very little definite information about the relative well-being and health care needs of Black aged. One project, however, that does present data from comparable samples of Black and Anglo aged is reported by Weeks and Darsky. In their 1964 study of 1,457 Detroit low income Anglos and 475 low income Blacks, over two fifths of the Black elderly but only one in seven of the Anglo elderly reported that they believed they had an unmet health need. Asked their reason for failing to obtain attention, 70% of the Blacks and 59% of the Anglos cited financial problems.

That poverty seems to bear more onerously on Blacks is suggested by the finding that somewhat more than one in five of the lowest income Blacks indicated that they had put off needed care, against only one in six of their Anglo peers. But Blacks reported more often putting off seeking care regardless of income level. Perhaps this reflects the disproportionately low number of Blacks holding health insurance: a majority of Anglos with under $1,000 incomes but only 15% of the Blacks; even in the highest income groups, no more than three quarters of the Black group compared with almost nine out of ten Anglos were policy holders.

Overall, among the Detroit Black aged there was a greater percentage who reported being ill, who indicated some type of eye and dental problems that had not been corrected, and who needed some medical care that had been postponed. "The generalizations hold even when Negroes and whites of similar income, age or living arrangements are compared."[34]

Utilization of providers

Factors associated with advanced age may have a special bearing on the underutilization of providers by elderly Blacks. Either earlier experiences with racist providers have rebuffed elderly Blacks, or they rely on folk medicine, or there is a general unavailability of physicians, dentists, and hospitals in the South, and the residential segregation of Blacks in Detroit further curtail them from seeking assistance. Other research indicates that nonelderly Blacks are as likely as their Anglo peers to seek health care. For instance, Cornely and Bigman report that when socioeconomic status is controlled, Blacks in Washington, D.C. actually report higher rates of checkups than Anglos.[35] In an Oakland, California poverty area, Blacks were found to be less likely to have had a dental checkup but more likely than Anglos to have received a medical examination.[36] The pattern of avoiding dentists was revealed in the results of a nationwide survey that reported that only 23% of the Blacks compared with 47% of the Anglos had seen a dentist during 1970. Below poverty Anglos were actually more likely than above poverty Blacks to have seen a dentist.[37] It should be noted that racial variation is seen in the type of treat-

Table 5-4. Percent of population reporting hospital-public clinics as usual source of care by race

	Anglo	Black
Boston	59	76
Bedford Stuyvesant, New York City	14	43
Red Hook, New York City	6	30
Philadelphia	9	53
Washington, D.C.	18	40
Atlanta	21	72
Charleston, S.C.	11	56
Kansas City	36	51
San Francisco	17	31
Palo Alto, Calif.	8	12

Data from Louise M. Okada and Gerald Sparer, "Access to Usual Source of Care by Race and Income," presented at the 1974 Annual Meeting of the American Public Health Association, New Orleans, La. Data from National Opinion Research Center surveys, 1968-1971.

ment received: Blacks much more often require serious care such as extraction and less often obtain purely preventive care.[38]

The type of health care provider contacted also varies by race. Blacks at any income or occupational level are, according to Robertson and his colleagues, less likely to have a continuing relationship with a physician.[39] Instead, Blacks disproportionately rely on public clinics and emergency rooms for service. A survey of New York City welfare families showed that 70% of the Black sample in contrast to 58% of the Anglo reported medical services from emergency rooms, and 73% of the former and 54% of the latter used outpatient clinics.[40] The pattern of selecting public providers is apparent in the recommendations of emergency rooms and outpatient clinics as places for treatment of common health problems made by Southern California Blacks. As we saw in Chapter 2, the sample of Black respondents said that they would recommend such a provider significantly more often than comparable samples of Anglos and Japanese (see Table 2-2). As Table 5-4 reveals, across the nation the percentage of Blacks reporting emergency rooms and public clinics as their "usual source of care" far exceeds that of the Anglos.

This preference for public providers crosses class lines. A study in Washington, D.C. reveals that Blacks of middle as well as lower classes literally bypass nearby private physicians and travel to the inner city for care.[41] In more quantitative terms, Berki reports from New York City that "for individuals in families with incomes between $3,000 and $6,999, 9.3% of the whites and 28.4% of non-whites receive primary care from hospital out-patient departments and emergency room facilities. Above $7,000 the percentages for both groups are decreased, but the differential, if anything, is increased: 6.3% whites, 18.8% nonwhites."[42] In St. Louis, Goering and Coe found that while use of a public facility declined sharply for Anglos with rising income, no such effect was seen among Blacks: under $3,000 Anglos reported 48.8% had used a public provider, only 18.8% of those earning over $6,000 had; among Blacks, the percentages were 67.4% and 47.0%, respectively.[43]

Why do Blacks rely so heavily on such public providers as outpatient clinics and emergency rooms? A ready answer is that there are few, if any alternatives, especially private physicians, available to most Blacks. Either providers are not located in their neighborhoods, or if they are, their fees are too high.

A growing body of evidence attests to the face validity of the scarcity hypothesis. Haynes and McGarvey report that across the country, the patient-to-physician ratio is twice or more as high in Black ghettos and other poverty neighborhoods as in nonpoverty neighborhoods. In addition, the available physicians tend to be generalists, not specialists, much older than the average physician, often from now extinct medical schools, lacking in board certification, and unavailable for house calls and for weekend and evening appointments.[44] Elesh and Schollaert report from Chicago that there are both fewer physicians and fewer hospital beds in Black neighborhoods[45]; in Houston, Fabrega and Roberts found nearly seven times as many general practitioners in Anglo as in Black areas[46]; and in Los Angeles County the ratio of physicians to population is 186:100,000 compared with 63:100,000 for Watts-Willowbrook.[47] Longitudinal studies reveal that present rates are related to demographic trends. For example, DeVise and associates document immigration of physicians as Blacks move into an area: "East Garfield Park had 212 physicians back in 1930, when the population was all white. Today, there are only 13 physicians serving 63,000 Negro residents. The near south side community of Oakland-Kenwood had 110 physicians serving a population of 28,000 whites back in 1930. Today there are but 5 physicians serving a population of 45,000 Negroes."[48]

Whether physicians leave Black areas out of fear for their own safety, because they can make more money treating suburbanites, to avoid losing social and professional status from being associated with Blacks, or simply because most upper-middle-class Anglos are latent racists, I need not discuss here.[49] The fact is that there are few physicians in private practice for Blacks to draw on. Yet, availability is only part of the answer to the question about disproportionately high public provider utilization. Some observers have suggested that Blacks who might otherwise use private providers, because they can afford them and have transportation to reach them, select public services. Robertson and his associates argue that there exists a conscious preference among Blacks for the impersonal clinic over the private physician because of the Black patient's desire to avoid an intimate contact with what will surely be an *Anglo* physician.[50] (That statistically the physician will be an Anglo is borne out by the proportion of 2.2% Blacks among practicing physicians—a ratio in 1975 of one Anglo physician to every 750 Anglo Americans, and one Black physician for every 5,000 Black Americans.[51]) Thus, choosing a public clinic where contact is casual, segmented, and usually nonrepetitive is actually a rational defense mechanism fostered by past discrimination and racist abuse.[52]

While the history of medical segregation throughout the nation provides ample reason to accept the fear-of-racism hypothesis,[53] there is substantial evidence of contemporary abuse. For instance, the National Advisory Commission on Civil Disorders concluded that "some private hospitals still refuse to admit Negro patients or to accept doctors with Negro patients. And many individual doctors still discriminate against Negro patients."[54] La Fargue studied possible prejudice among Anglo nurses and concludes that while it is difficult to document, minority patients might well perceive prejudice in the behavior and attitudes of the nurses.[55] Shaw discovered what he called "significant differences" in the hospital treatment accorded Blacks and Anglos.[56] Yamamoto, Dixon, and Bloombaum conclude that Anglo mental health therapists evidenced prejudice detectable by minority patients.[57]

But afterall, it is what patients feel about their experiences at the hands of Anglo health care providers that determines whether or not racism has been part of the treatment. Among the welfare families interviewed by Podell, 70% of the Blacks but only 35% of the Anglos agreed that doctors were sometimes rude; 72% and 46% respectively, agreed that doctors were prejudiced against people on welfare; and two out of three Blacks thought that doctors were prejudiced against them.[58]

The unavailability of private providers and the prevalence of prejudice can hide other reasons for selecting public providers. While the would-be patient often spends hours obtaining treatment, usually the bill is less than for equivalent services from private practitioners. Also, the emergency room is available after working hours and on weekends; when an individual finally gets there, there is almost always someone to help the person, sooner or later. And while Anglos may avoid the public facility because they associate it with "charity" and save status by utilizing private physicians, for millions of Blacks who grew up in the rigidly segregated South and had little or no access to private providers, a tradition of turning to emergency rooms and outpatient clinics was born of necessity and reinforced by societal attitudes that held it appropriate for "second-class human beings" to receive care from "second-class institutions." Thus, Black utilization of public providers may well reflect a complex set of economic, social, and even psychological forces that cannot easily be neutralized with the provision of alternative providers and the removal or easing of the present financial obstacles to private providers.

Meeting the need for providers

The complexity of meeting and overcoming the health needs of Black Americans is illustrated in selecting the proper responses to the call for more providers and expanded services for predominately Black areas. We have seen that there is an acute shortage of health care personnel in many ghettos and that there is at least inferential evidence that Blacks of the working and middle classes likewise find it difficult to secure care. It is perfectly reasonable, therefore, to call for more facilities and more physicians and medical specialists. Yet it may not be as simple as this to resolve the present shortcomings.

For instance, it is not clear that simply increasing the numbers of health care providers graduated from our colleges and professional schools will have any appreciable remedial impact on the shortage of practitioners. As long as fee-for-service is the prevailing device for allocating private providers, many will still avoid low income neighborhoods. Nor will the shortage disappear by recruiting more Blacks. While it seems a widely held if little-mentioned assumption that most Black health workers will turn to ghettos or other Black areas to establish their practices, this assumption may not only be empirically questionable, it is clearly discriminatory. Haynes underscored the double error of this line of reasoning when he wrote: "Many institutions are willing to train Black students for the ghetto but other students are expected to enjoy a free choice. It is true that Black physicians are providing much of the health care for the Black ghetto, but the health of the ghetto residents is everyone's responsibility . . . This obligation cannot be met by accepting a few Black students and hoping that they will practice only in the ghetto."[59]

Experiments during the late 1960s with decentralizing care by opening "storefront" health posts and neighborhood clinics often met with resistance from ghetto Blacks, especially when they found that some of the "doctors" were interns or third- and fourth-year medical students. Other complaints were heard about community medicine buffs who forsook conventional ties and white coats and bedside manners in order to project themselves as "one of the people." These efforts at being folksy were interpreted to mean that the doctors were inferior healers because they had not finished "becoming doctors." Informality was seen by many patients as laxness—as an additional "threat" to the patient's chances of surviving the encounter with modern medicine.

Similar unanticipated difficulties are encountered in establishing new facilities to help offset the dearth of private providers. A case in point is the Martin Luther King, Jr. General Hospital in Watts. Seen when it opened in 1972 as a means for improving the health of the region's Black and other residents while at the same time cutting unemployment, becoming a center for allied health career education, and a focus of pride for the community, its first 3 years of operation reveal how naïve these aspirations were. A 1975 review of the hospital's record included the following observations: it is not possible to document any real change in the health of the local community; the potential of King and its associate Charles R. Drew Postgraduate Medical School for uplifting the quality of care given by community physicians has not been realized; the planning of the facility proved to be inadequate for its walk-in load (the lobby had to be converted into a waiting room); there is no intensive care unit, in part because of King's inability to recruit and hold registered nurses; the hope of creating a 4-year medical school has all but vanished because of funding problems; few jobs were actually opened to the community largely because of the scarcity of required technical skills among local residents; and the Drew plan to supplement the region's deficit of nearly 700 physicians by training physicians' assistants has fallen far short.[60]

These negative comments should not obscure the fact that King-Drew has made an important contribution to the region, such as the unexpectedly large volume of walk-ins and the fact that thousands of residents are now spared the 5- or 6-hour trip to the region's pre-King facilities. The point is that making any real impact on the health needs and problems of a community such as Watts is vastly more complex a process than investing goodwill and spending $40 million to establish a medical center and another $35 million annually to maintain it.

Lifting the financial burden

Nevertheless, public policies may assist in cutting the provider shortage. In addition, government can act to reduce the financial barriers and burdens that inhibit and curtail treatment. Cost seems a likely target, because Blacks are concerned and critical about health care costs.[61] And as we shall see in Chapter 7, Blacks may be more willing than Anglos to support government actions designed to cut health care costs.

Would individuals, such as the elderly Blacks in the Detroit study, who have health care needs that they do not have treated seek care if costs were reduced or eliminated? Jiobu argues that "programs to reduce Black postneonatal mortality should be aimed at raising Black income levels rather than at altering residential patterns or increasing the Black percentage of hospital births."[62] Elesh and Schollaert conclude from their analysis of the factors affecting the distribution of physicians that increasing the buying power of Blacks will lead to more providers locating in Black areas. They argue that abolishing economic incentives (that is, the fee-for-service practice) would be counterproductive to bringing physicians into Black areas unless government also began to assign providers to specific areas.[63]

As previously discussed, the outcomes of reducing costs or increasing buying power, however, are more complicated than these two solutions suggest. McKinlay points out that economic considerations have been found not to be the only or necessarily even the primary determinant of utilization. He argues that the data indicate that utilization rates increase or remain constant as costs change depending on the type of complaint as well as the social class of population. For instance, Jiobu may be correct that cost may detour Blacks from seeking pre- and postnatal care and thus account for some part of the higher postneonatal death rate; that is, the death rate would decline because care would increase if costs were reduced. Another question is whether dental checkups, eye examinations, blood pressure tests, treatment of chronic but not incapacitating infirmities, and so forth would be affected by either national health insurance or government subsidies for treatment (such as Medicare and Medicaid). McKinlay questions it: "Certainly, from the studies that have appeared in Great Britain, there is no firm evidence that a nationalized, relatively efficient and free health and welfare service has been able to eradicate the variations by social class in the rate of use of certain 'freely available' facilities."[64]

Add to the influence of class the dimension of race and we have reason to explore more systematically the impact of variable cost on the rate of health care service utilization. While reducing health costs will free income for other discretionary use (such as food, recreation, clothing, and entertainment), it is not clear that such a step will have a direct bearing on Black morbidity and mortality.

Sickle-cell Anemia Control Act of 1972

Dollars are scarce, and in the national scheme of things there is little time and less interest in considering the problems of Blacks. Therefore, it is important that the target and the policy are worthwhile when the federal government takes notice and action because there is just so much that is going to be done: "You got your share, now it's someone else's turn." Therefore, the case of the government's sickle-cell anemia program is instructive for those advocating new public programs.

Sickle-cell anemia is a genetic trait that most often, though not exclusively, occurs in Blacks. Because of its association with the community, many Blacks have struggled to bring it to the broader public's attention and to secure federal assistance in screening, counseling, education, and research in order to control it. This association gave important symbolic overtones to the contest to gain government's attention. In 1972 Congress passed the Sickle-Cell Anemia Control Act and annually appropriates funds ($50 million in 1974) for a variety of programs.

Bristow concludes that the consequences of this initiative for the Black community have been that the act may actually have worked even a greater hardship than the disease itself. Sickle-cell trait occurs in perhaps 7% to 10% of the Black population; there is only a 25% chance that the child of two trait carriers will have anemia. Statistically, in the California population of a million and a half Blacks, less than 3,000 cases of sickle-cell anemia would be expected. Yet, in 1970 only 26 deaths in the entire state were attributed to sickle-cell.[65] Now that the Anglo community has learned of sickle-cell anemia, new forms of anti-Black discrimination have appeared: some employers reportedly reject all trait carriers; the New York State Health Commission reports that 13 major life insurance firms charge trait carriers additional premiums; the Air Force has declared trait carriers ineligible for pilot or copilot positions; several states have introduced compulsory screening laws.[66] Thus, not only are economic hardships being worked on Blacks, but serious civil liberties issues are raised by the nonvoluntary, racially directed blood testing.[67] Yet there is little or no evidence that being a trait carrier opens one to special risks: "Careful, controlled studies of carriers of the trait are few and far between, so the matter is clouded by a slew of impressions and erroneous notions."[68]

Moreover, the misinformation and distortion of the origins, symptoms, and dangers of sickle-cell anemia reinforce the notion of the inherent "genetic inferiority" of Blacks given academic respectability by Jensen, Shockley, and others. In the face of such massive problems over sickle-cell anemia, Bristow cautions that: "As genetic counseling becomes a bigger part of preventive medicine, failure to resolve them may worsen the unfortunate side effects of the sickle-cell program many times over."[69]

The legacy of being Black in America

All poor people share certain difficulties; not unexpectedly, we found that the Black poor have a level of health problems that surpasses those of their nonpoor brothers and sisters. But the preceding shows that race has an independent effect: that simply being Black confronts one with a greater likelihood of heart disease, infant mortality, mental illness, and disrespectful, discriminatory care. Many of the roots of these health problems are deeply set in the social, economic, and political foundations of our society, making it seem unduly optimistic to believe that the Blacks' disadvantageous morbidity and mortality profiles can be corrected by a few billion dollars here, a few billion there. Even if middle-class taxpayers could be convinced to shoulder the costs of building thousands of new facilities and training thousands of new health care providers, our analysis suggests that we could expect to see only marginal short-term reduction in Black infant mortality, mental illness, heart disease, and many other health problems. This is because most of the forces, both historical and current, that generate these problems stem from combined class and race prejudice, exploitation, and intolerance.

In the United States Blacks form a racial, not an ethnic community. That is, it is physical characteristic rather than culture (as for instance is the case with Chicanos, Asians, and native Americans) that principally distinguishes the Black from the majority population. Thus, even though Blacks may escape the objective conditions of poverty and attain a high level of economic security, they cannot escape the opprobrium of the dominant society: rich Blacks have a difficult time "buying" a reprieve from the latent effects of 3 centuries of nutrition deficiency or "educating" themselves out from under the stresses of what two Black psychiatrists describe as the inheritance of every Black child: "Black children from birth are exposed to heavily systematized hostility from the nation and for their own survival must reject the community's code of behavior, containing as it does the injunction that they themselves are to be the object of hatred."[70]

While other communities in the United States are both racially and ethnically distinctive, the legacy of 300 years in America bears with special force on the Black populace. One manifestation of this burden is their particular health care problems and needs.

Notes

1. Alonzso S. Yerby, "The Disadvantaged and Health Care," *American Journal of Public Health* **56** (Jan. 1966), p. 6.
2. William Ryan, *Blaming the Victim* (New York: Pantheon Books, Inc., 1971), p. 78.
3. For historical perspective, see Mary Gover, "Physical Defects of White and Negro Families Examined by the Farm Security Administration, 1940," *Journal of Negro Education* **18** (Summer 1949), pp. 251-265; Marcus S. Goldstein, "Longevity and Health Status of Whites and Non-Whites in the United States," *Journal of the National Medical Association* **46** (March 1954), pp. 83-104; Richard F. Tomasson, "Patterns in Negro-White Differential Mortality, 1930-1957," *Milbank Memorial Fund Quarterly* **38** (Oct. 1960), pp. 362-386; Symposium "Health Status and Health Education of Negroes in the United States," *Journal of Negro Education* **18** (Summer 1949), pp. 197-443; Evelyn M. Kitagawa and Philip M. Hauser, *Differential Mortality in the United States: A Study in Socioeconomic Epidemiology* (Cambridge: Harvard University Press, 1973); Marcus S. Goldstein, "Longevity and Health Status of the Negro American," *Journal of Negro Education* **32** (Fall 1963), pp. 337-348; Paul B. Cornely, "The Health Status of the Negro Today and in the Future," *American Journal of Public Health* **58** (April 1968), pp. 647-654; Whitney M. Young, Jr., *Poor Health in the Richest Nation* (New York: McGraw-Hill Book Co., 1964), pp. 182-211; Ann H. Pettigrew, "Negro American Health," in Thomas Pettigrew, *Profiles of the American Negro* (New York: D. Van Nostrand Co., 1965), pp. 72-79, 202-235; Ralph H. Hines, "The Health Status of Black Americans: Changing Perspectives," in E. Gartly Jaco (editor), *Patients, Physicians and Illness*, ed. 2 (New York: The Free Press, 1972), pp. 40-50.

4. Compare with James F. Bates, Harry H. Lieberman, and Rodney N. Powell, "Provisions for Health Care in the Ghetto: The Family Health Team," *American Journal of Public Health* **60** (Jan. 1970), pp. 1222-1224; John L. S. Holloman, Jr., "Medical Care and Black Community," *Archives of Internal Medicine* **127** (Jan. 1971), pp. 51-56; E. T. Johnson, "The Delivery of Health Care in the Ghetto," *Journal of the National Medical Association* **61** (May 1969), pp. 263-270; John C. Norman (editor), *Medicine in the Ghetto* (New York: Appleton-Century-Crofts, 1969); Milton I. Roemer, "Health Resources and Services in the Watts Area of Los Angeles," *California's Health* **23** (Feb.-March 1966), pp. 123-143; Peter DeVise and others, *Slum Medicine: Chicago's Apartheid Health System* (Chicago: Illinois Regional Medical Program, Report #6, 1969).

5. Herbert C. Birch and Joan D. Gussow, *Disadvantaged Children: Health, Nutrition and School Failure* (New York: Harcourt Brace Jovanovich, Inc., 1970), p. 243.

6. Jack Slater, "The Rise of Cancer in Black Men," *Ebony* **29** (July 1974), p. 92.

7. George W. Comstock, "An Epidemiologic Study of Blood Pressure Levels in a Biracial Community in the Southern United States," *American Journal of Hygiene* **65** (May 1957), pp. 271-315; J. R. McDonough, G. E. Garrison, and C. G. Hames, "Blood Pressure and Hypertensive Disease Among Negroes and Whites: A Study in Evans County, Georgia," *Annals of Internal Medicine* **61** (Aug. 1964), pp. 208-228; J. H. Phillips and G. E. Burch, "Cardiovascular Diseases in the White and Negro Races," *American Journal of the Medical Sciences* **238** (July 1959), pp. 97-124; Geoffrey Rose, "Cardiovascular Mortality Among American Negroes," *Archives of Environmental Health* **5** (Nov. 1962), pp. 412-414.

8. "17 Million Americans with Hypertension," *Public Health Reports* **81** (March 1966), p. 262.

9. Margaret M. Kilcoyne, "Hypertension and Heart Disease in the Urban Community," *Bulletin of the New York Academy of Medicine* **49** (June 1973), pp. 501-509.

10. F. Gilbert McMahon, Phillip A. Cole, and Jerome R. Ryan, "A Study of Hypertension in the Inner City. A Student Hypertension Survey," *American Heart Journal* **85** (Jan. 1973), pp. 69-70; also see L. A. Solberg and P. A. McGarry, "Cerebral Atherosclerosis in Negroes and Caucasians," *Atherosclerosis* **16** (Sept.-Oct. 1972), pp. 141-154; Margaret C. Oalmann, Henry C. McGill, Jr., and Jack P. Strong, "Cardiovascular Mortality in a Community: Results of a Survey in New Orleans," *American Journal of Epidemiology* **94** (Dec. 1971), pp. 546-555.

11. S. Leonard Syme and others, "Social Class and Racial Differences in Blood Pressure," *American Journal of Public Health* **64** (June 1974), p. 619; also see Thomas W. Oakes and others, "Social Factors in Newly Discovered Elevated Blood Pressure," *Journal of Health and Social Behavior* **14** (Sept. 1973), pp. 198-204.

12. Ernst Harburg and others, "Socioecological Stress, Suppressed Hostility, Skin Color and Black-White Male Blood Pressure: Detroit," *Psychosomatic Medicine* **35** (July-Aug. 1973), pp. 276-296; Ernst Harburg and others, "Socioecological Stressor Areas and Black-White Blood Pressure: Detroit," *Journal of Chronic Diseases* **26** (Sept. 1973), pp. 595-611.

13. Edwin Boyle, Jr., "Biological Patterns in Hypertension by Race, Sex, Body Weight, and Skin Color," *Journal of the American Medical Association* **213** (7 Sept. 1970), pp. 1637-1643.

14. On sociopsychological stress, also see James P. Henry and John C. Cassell, "Psychosocial Factors in Essential Hypertension: Recent Epidemiologic and Animal Experimental Evidence," *American Journal of Epidemiology* **90** (Sept. 1969), pp. 171-200; Stanislav V. Kasl and Sidney Cobb, "Blood Pressure Changes in Men Undergoing Job Loss: Preliminary Report," *Psychosomatic Medicine* **32** (Jan.-Feb. 1970), pp. 19-38.

15. Judith R. Kramer, *The American Minority Community* (New York: Thomas Y. Crowell Co., Inc., 1970), p. 18.

16. Alvin Poussaint, psychiatrist at Harvard Medical School, points out that explaining "victim-precipitated" homicides as stemming from rage—and therefore as a form of suicide—implies that Blacks who rise up and rebel against an unjust system are "crazy" rather than courageous, "insane" rather than incensed. Accordingly, the policeman who kills is morally absolved of homicide; the victim is held responsible, and the dominant society is free of any guilt or blame for the action of its agents. See "Black Suicide," unpublished manuscript.

17. Ann H. and Thomas F. Pettigrew, "Race, Disease and Desegregation: A New Look," *Phylon* **24** (Winter 1963), pp. 317-318.

18. Marc Fried, "Social Differences in Mental Health," in John Kosa, Aaron Antonovsky, and

Irving K. Zola (editors), *Poverty and Health: A Sociological Analysis* (Cambridge: Harvard University Press, 1969), p. 136.

19. See A. B. Hollingshead and F. C. Redlich, *Social Class and Mental Illness* (New York: John Wiley & Sons, Inc., 1958).

20. Compare with L. Scrole and others, *Mental Health in the Metropolis: The Midtown Manhattan Study,* I (New York: McGraw-Hill Book Co., 1962); Seymour Parker and Robert J. Kleiner, *Mental Illness in the Urban Negro Community* (New York: The Free Press, 1966); William H. Grier and Price M. Cobbs, *The Jesus Bag* (New York: Bantam Books, 1971).

21. For a longitudinal analysis, see Helen C. Chase, "A Study of Infant Mortality from Linked Records: Comparison of Neonatal Mortality from Two Cohort Studies: United States, January-March 1950 and 1960," *Vital and Health Statistics* Series 20, #13 (June 1972).

22. Robert M. Jiobu, "Urban Determinants of Racial Differentiation in Infant Mortality," *Demography* 9 (Nov. 1972), p. 608.

23. Monroe Lerner, "Social Differences in Physical Health," in Kosa, Antonovsky, and Zola (editors), *Poverty and Health*, p. 95.

24. Ray H. Elling and Russell F. Martin, *Health and Health Care for the Urban Poor* (North Haven, Conn.: Connecticut Health Services Research Series, 1974), p. 49.

25. Los Angeles County Health Department, *Provisional Vital Statistics, 1972* (1974).

26. Gary S. Berger, J. Richard Udry, and Charles H. Hendricks, "Control of Excess Perinatal Mortality Among Nonwhites in North Carolina," paper presented at the 1974 annual meeting of the American Public Health Association, New Orleans, La.

27. Charles V. Willie and William B. Rothney, "Racial, Ethnic and Income Factors in the Epidemiology of Neonatal Mortality," *American Sociological Review* 27 (Aug. 1962), pp. 522-526.

28. The following is drawn from Birch and Gussow, *Disadvantaged Children*, pp. 144-153, 232-233.

29. Also see E. Payton, E. P. Crump, and C. P. Horton, "Growth and Development, VII: Dietary Habits of 571 Pregnant Southern Negro Women," *Journal of the American Dietetic Association* 37 (Aug. 1960), pp. 129-136; Faye W. Grant and Dale Groom, "A Dietary Study Among A Group of Southern Negroes," *Journal of the American Dietetic Association* 35 (Sept. 1959), pp. 910-918.

30. Harold H. Sandstead and others, "Nutritional Deficiencies in Disadvantaged Preschool Children," *American Journal of Diseases of Children* 121 (June 1971), pp. 455-463; Cecilla Schuck and June B. Taritt, "Food Consumption of Low-Income Rural Negro Households in Mississippi," *Journal of the American Dietetic Association* 62 (Feb. 1973), pp. 151-155; Festus O. Adebonojo and Susan Strans, "The State of Nutrition of Urban Black Children in the U.S.A. The Role of Day Care Services in the Prevention of Nutritional Anemia," *Clinic Pediatrics* 12 (Sept. 1973), pp. 563-570.

31. Birch and Gussow, *Disadvantaged Children*, pp. 149-151.

32. David Mechanic, *Public Expectations and Health Care* (New York: John Wiley & Sons, Inc., 1972), p. 84.

33. Jacquelyne J. Jackson, "NCBA, Black Aged and Politics," *The Annals* 415 (Sept. 1974), pp. 143-150. A comprehensive bibliography is included in the piece. Also see Gayle B. Thompson, "Blacks and Social Security Benefits: Trends, 1960-73," *Social Security Bulletin* 38 (April 1974), pp. 30-40.

34. Herbert A. Weeks and Benjamin J. Darsky, *The Urban Aged: Race and Medical Care* (Ann Arbor: University of Michigan, School of Public Health, 1968), p. 39.

35. Paul B. Cornely and S. K. Bigman, "Cultural Considerations in Changing Health Attitudes," *Medical Annals of the District of Columbia* 30 (April 1961), pp. 191-199.

36. Joseph R. Hochstim, D. A. Athanasopoulos, and John H. Larkins, "Poverty Area Under the Microscope," *American Journal of Public Health* 58 (Oct. 1968), pp. 1815-1827.

37. Joanna Kravits, "Attitudes Toward and Use of Discretionary Physician and Dental Services by Race Controlling for Income," paper presented at the 1974 annual meeting of the American Public Health Association., New Orleans, La., p. 16.

38. *Ibid.*, pp. 18, 20; also see Jane Moosbruker and Anthony Jong, "Racial Similarities and Differences in Family Dental Patterns," *Public Health Reports* 84 (Aug. 1969), pp. 721-727.

39. Leon S. Robertson and others, "Race, Status and Medical Care," *Phylon* **28** (Winter 1967), pp. 353-360.
40. Lawrence Podell, *Studies in the Use of Health Services by Families on Welfare* (Springfield, Va.: National Technical Information Service, PS 190 391, 1 April 1970).
41. G. W. Shannon, R. L. Bashshur, and C. W. Spurlock, "Variations in Health Care Opportunities and Behavior Among Middle and Low Socioeconomic Status Blacks," paper presented at the 1974 annual meeting of the American Public Health Association, New Orleans, La.
42. Sylvester E. Berki, *Hospital Economics* (Lexington, Mass.: Lexington Books, 1972), p. 201.
43. John M. Goering and Rodney Coe, "Cultural Versus Situational Explanations of the Medical Behavior of the Poor," *Social Science Quarterly* **51** (Sept. 1970), p. 318.
44. M. Alfred Haynes and Michael R. McGarvey, "Physicians, Hospitals, and Patients in the Inner City," in Norman (editor), *Medicine in the Ghetto*, pp. 117-124.
45. David Elesh and Paul T. Schollaert, "Race and Urban Medicine: Factors Affecting the Distribution of Physicians in Chicago," *Journal of Health and Social Behavior* **13** (Sept. 1972), pp. 241.
46. Horacio Fabrego, Jr., and Robert E. Roberts, "Ethnic Differences in the Outpatient Use of a Public Charity Hospital," *American Journal of Public Health* **62** (July 1972), p. 936.
47. Bonnie Bullough, "Poverty, Ethnic Identity and Preventive Health Care," *Journal of Health and Social Behavior* **13** (Dec. 1972), p. 351.
48. DeVise and others, *Slum Medicine*, p. 20.
49. See Elesh and Schollaert, "Race and Urban Medicine"; Robert E. Coker, Jr., John Kosa, and Kurt W. Back, "Medical Student's Attitudes Toward Public Health," *Milbank Memorial Fund Quarterly* **44** (April 1966), pp. 155-180. Wendy G. Brooks, "Health Care and Poor People," in Barry A. Passett and Edgar S. Cahn (editors), *Citizen Participation: Effecting Community Change* (New York: Praeger Publishers, Inc., 1971), p. 113, argues that the prevailing practice of financially exploiting interns and residents by employing them at low wages to serve in emergency rooms and clinics has not only direct negative consequences for their immediate patients, but also plays a major part in conditioning physicians to avoid future practice in these areas. "During his post-graduate period of internship, residency and military service, the physician usually works very long hours for low pay . . . Small wonder that, when they finish their training, so few elect to work on county hospital staffs, in ghetto practices or rural solo practice."
50. Robertson and others, "Race, Status and Medical Care." It is at least arguable that many Blacks are not concerned about the race of providers. A 1968 study in Cleveland found that 80% of the 353 Blacks interviewed expressed no preference between Anglo and Black nurses and physicians. Ten percent "very strongly" preferred Blacks, five percent Anglo physicians. From Sumati N. Dubey, "Blacks Preference for Black Professionals, Businessmen, and Religious Leaders," *Public Opinion Quarterly* **34** (Spring 1970), pp. 113-116.
51. Data reported by Dr. Jasper Williams, President of National Medical Association, in *Los Angeles Times*, 14 Aug. 1975; also see James L. Curtis, *Blacks, Medical Schools, and Society* (Ann Arbor: University of Michigan Press, 1971), p. 36; Max Seham, *Blacks and American Medical Care* (Minneapolis: University of Minnesota Press, 1973), p. 63.
52. "The Negro at any income level may feel more distant from the white, upper-class physician than the white of the same income level; hence, the Negro tends to eschew the offices of private-practice physicians and instead prefers the public clinics where the institutional setting works to protect against the feeling of social distance." From Julius A. Rith, "The Treatment of the Sick," in Kosa, Antonovsky, and Zola (editors), *Poverty and Health*, p. 218.
53. For an excellent review of racism in medicine, see Paul B. Cornely, "Segregation and Discrimination in Medical Care in the United States," *American Journal of Public Health* **46** (Sept. 1958), pp. 1074-1081.
54. Quoted by David M. Gordon (editor), *Problems in Political Economy: An Urban Perspective* (Lexington, Mass.: D. C. Heath & Co., 1971), p. 328; also see James D. Snyder, "Race Bias in Hospitals: What the Civil Rights Commission Found," *Hospital Management* **96** (Nov. 1963), pp. 52-54.
55. Jane P. LaFargue, "Role of Prejudice in Rejection of Health Care," *Nursing Research* **21** (Jan.-Feb. 1972), pp. 53-58.

56. Clayton T. Shaw, "A Detailed Examination of Treatment Procedures of Whites and Blacks in Hospitals," *Social Science and Medicine* 5 (June 1971), pp. 251-256.

57. Joe Yamamoto, Frieda Dixon, and Milton Bloombaum, "White Therapists and Negro Patients," *Journal of the National Medical Association* 64 (July 1972), pp. 312-316.

58. Podell, *Studies in the Use of Health Services by Families on Welfare,* p. 41.

59. Alfred Haynes, "Problems Facing the Negro in Medicine Today," *Journal of the American Medical Association* 209 (18 Aug. 1969), p. 1068.

60. Harry Nelson, "King Hospital: Optimism Amid the Headaches," *Los Angeles Times,* part 2 (23 March 1975), p. 1.

61. In a 1971 national survey, nonpoor Blacks more often indicated dissatisfaction with out-of-pocket medical costs than *poor* Anglos. See Ronald Andersen, JoAnna Kravits, and Odin W. Anderson, "The Public's View of the Crisis in Medical Care: An Impetus for Changing Delivery Systems?" *Economic and Business Bulletin* 24 (Fall 1974), pp. 44-52. The present analysis suggests that this higher rate of Black dissatisfaction should be viewed as a reaction to a network of social and psychological factors as well as the purely economic ones.

62. Jiobu, "Urban Determinants," p. 610.

63. Elesh and Schollaett, "Race and Urban Medicine," p. 249.

64. John B. McKinlay, "Some Approaches and Problems in the Study of the Use of Services—An Overview," *Journal of Health and Social Behavior* 13 (June 1972), p. 120.

65. Lonnie R. Bristow, "Sickle-Cell Program: Worse than Problem?" *Los Angeles Times,* part 3 (6 March 1975), p. 3.

66. *Ibid.,* p. 3.

67. Irwin Feinberg, "Ethical and Social Issues in Screening for Genetic Disease—A Group Report," *New England Journal of Medicine* 286 (25 May 1972), pp. 1129-1132.

68. Barbara Culliton, "Sickle-Cell Anemia: The Route from Obscurity to Prominence," *Science* 178 (13 Oct. 1972), p. 142.

69. Bristow, "Sickle-Cell Program," p. 3.

70. Grier and Cobbs, *The Jesus Bag,* p. 1.

CHAPTER 6 Women and the health industry

As between the sexes, the male is by nature superior and the female inferior, the male rules and the female subjects.

Aristotle[1]

What, oh Lord, do women want?

Sigmund Freud[2]

Though it is hard work, the minds of women students can be forced out of their conventionality and made to cope with even abstractions.

Jacques Barzun[3]

The difficulty that confronts the [medical] industry is that it employs many women. Women are not as career-oriented as men. . . . The industry should take steps to attract more men. . . .

Eli Ginzberg[4]

Women in American society may be said to constitute a minority community because they are deprived of their proportional share of the social, economic, and political values of American society. For instance, women number 37% of the nation's holders of $60,000 or more in real estate, bonds, corporate stock, and other economic goods, and own as much as 18% of the country's stock. However, these figures are misleading because women have only nominal possession of many accounts since their "ownership" is a male device to avoid taxes. Women comprise just 3% or 4% of the armed forces and about the same percentage of police, lawyers, and judges, and 3% of the clergy. In the work force, women account for 71% of the secretarial and clerical positions but only 17% of the managerial and executive strata.[5] In 1974, state legislatures contained 94% males, the U.S. House of Representatives 96%. While women are invariably seen as responsible for their children's upbringing, women number only about 15% of the members of school boards. When women are as equally qualified and experienced as male workers, there is an average salary discrepancy of 42%, with dollar gaps ranging from $3,000 to $6,000 annually.[6]

There are similar gender inequalities in the health field. While women account for 60% of the contacts with physicians, they are treated by a male-dominated system in which men physicians outnumber women physicians ten to one. The gender difference between patients and providers is only one aspect of distinct disadvantages suffered by women. Reproduction, child rearing, susceptibility to certain diseases and disorders, and societal-reinforced gender behavior such as the wearing of cosmetics create for women a whole range of androcentric health interests and needs. It is not surprising, then, that reforming the health delivery industry to eliminate barriers and to improve service to women has always been of concern to many women; since the reemergence of feminist political activism in the late 1960s, the health industry has been a major target. Thus, looking at the involvement of women with the health industry reveals a wide range of social and political relationships generally missed when ethnicity, race, or class cleavages are studied. In this chapter health care needs and problems that confront women will be analyzed and the role of government as both a contributing factor and as a potential agent for change will be discussed.

Gender role and gaining admission to practice medicine

Ehrenreich and English argue that the health industry is not simply a service industry: "It is a powerful instrument of social control, replacing organized religion as a prime source of sexist ideology and an enforcer of sex roles."[7]

Krauss[8] explains that "gender," a more precise concept than "sex," consists of two aspects, gender identity and gender role. Gender identity is a biological fact determined for us at birth and subject to constant reinforcement throughout our lives: most people accept being either a "boy" or a "girl" and exhibit the expected social traits.

Gender role is the constellation of traits and behaviors that are defined by the prevailing culture as "feminine" and "masculine." Gender roles often vary from social class to social class and from time to time. For instance, lower-class males are taught (that is, socialized) to be physically aggressive in protecting their "honor" but to be politically passive. For middle-class males just the reverse is true. Lower-class women may be sexually aggressive and take on heavy physical labor; "nice" middle-class girls are conditioned to be demure and to pretend that even opening a car door or carrying a small bag of groceries a few feet is beyond their capacity.

Throughout American society, women are socialized to accept a gender role that includes the appropriateness of receiving unequal pay, of doing menial work, and of eschewing leadership positions to males. Gender segregation, stratification, and discrimination are reinforced constantly by the mass media, within the family, and, as Ehrenreich and English point out, in the health as well as other industries. The process is based on the assertion that the male is the primary and dominant figure, the "significant other," for the female. Once the notion is formed that the male is the more powerful, the female is vulnerable to all sorts of social manipulations.[9] Thus, boys have presented to them the possibility of becoming a doctor; girls the possibility of becoming a nurse.

This role playing is captured, perhaps unintentionally, by Wessen in an example from a nurses' training program. In an exercise designed to indoctrinate the student nurse into the mores of the hospital (that is, demonstrate proper gender role behavior), a senior nurse is asked by a student why she has instructed the student to stand aside at doorways and allow the physician to enter first. The young lady asks if this is not a reversal of customary protocol. The instructor replies that it is but that it is done to signify the respect paid the physician by the nurse because "they contribute more to the community" than does the nurse and thus are due this act of respect.[10]

When we find that women constitute 1% of dentists, 2% of optometrists, 6% of physicians, and 12% of pharmacists, but 97% of registered nurses,[11] we are seeing the extent to which female entry into a male-dominated profession is regarded as inappropriate behavior. It is not that thousands of willing applicants are turned away, although unquestionably admissions discrimination is a part of the segregation process; rather, gender role playing effectively channels male and female applicants to "appropriate" occupations. As Dube and associates have pointed out, admission of males and females to medical schools over a 40-year period has been roughly equal to the numbers applying.[12] The recruitment pools for medicine, nursing, or health care administration are simply very largely predetermined by the society's gender roles.

Woman's place is in the basement of a public hospital
Physicians

Within the health care industry, women are denied equal pay, equal status, and equal representation among decision makers. At the top of the health delivery hierarchy again more than half as many male physicians as female physicians are engaged in office-based, self-employed practice; women on the other hand, are twice as likely to be found in hospitals and public health departments.[13] Carpenter and Walker speculate that this dualism reflects gender socialization: the role of private practitioner involves risk-taking and competitive (with males) behavior, traits women are taught to avoid. Moreover, financial success in private practice is often linked to the charismatic qualities of the practitioner—qualities that in our society are usually ascribed to males, not females.[14]

Gender role appears to extend from where one practices to one's medical specialization. A national review of the 1970 distribution found women physicians in pediatrics, psychiatrics, child psychiatry, allergy, and anesthesiology; almost no women were seen in surgery, radiology, or internal medicine.[15] Lopate points out that in the postgraduate hospital departments of neurological surgery, ophthalmology, orthopedic surgery, otolaryngology, and plastic surgery over 90% of the residents are occupied—an indication of popularity and status within the profession. Conversely, in areas where women are more often encountered, as many as 25% to 50% of the available residences go unfilled. Thus, where competition is keen, (male) department heads seem to select disproportionately more male applicants. Women are "allowed" into the less desirable specialities that are "appropriate" expressions of female concerns, such as child rearing, community service, the provision of compassion and understanding.[16]

Reflecting their exclusion from the "elite" specialties and entrepreneurial forms of care, women physicians report a substantially lower median income than their male counterparts: between one-third and one-half less income for equal hours on the job.[17] Along with lower financial reward, women are rarely encountered in professional leadership positions. In medical schools there are virtually no female heads of departments or full professors[18]; in the Ameri-

Table 6-1. Distribution of female administrators by type of facility and occupational category

	Percentage of category	N
Type		
Proprietary	27.2	6
Nonprofit	27.7	15
Government	17.1	6
Occupation		
Convalescent hospital administrator	35.3	6
Chief administrator short-term and extended-care hospitals	13.6	3
Department Administrator	37.2	16
Administrative assistant	4.3	1
Outpatient clinic administrator	16.6	1

Adapted from Jerry L. Weaver, *Conflict and Control in Health Care Administration* (Beverly Hills: Sage Publications, Inc., 1975).

can Medical Association and its state chapters, there is a similar underrepresentation of women among elected policy makers.

Health care administrators

Nationally, women hold roughly half of the positions classified as health administration.[19] This finding is misleading, however, because it fails to reflect the distribution of women within the administrative hierarchy and across the spectrum of types of institutions. A closer look by Dolson found that women are disproportionately administrating in small, rural, proprietary facilities, and in lesser, low-paying positions.[20]

In a 1973 survey of 70 health care facilities (acute-care short-term, convalescent, state mental, Veterans Administration, health maintenance organizations, outpatient clinics) in southern California, women amounted to only 24% of the middle- and upper-administrative cadre. These female administrators were located in such traditional "women's" departments as housekeeping, dietetics, and nursing; only a small fraction were found in institutionwide policy-making positions[21] (Table 6-1).

Nurses

During the early 1970s the American Nurses' Association became much more aggressive in negotiations and challenged management over wages, job insecurity, and lack of control over the working conditions that rank-and-file nurses suffer.[22] The California Nurses' Association (CNA) and several other state-level organizations have begun collective bargaining with facility administrators, and they seem to be fully committed to traditional labor negotiations procedures—including strikes.[23] In many California hospitals the CNA has signed contracts establishing professional performance committees that are analogous to shop grievance committees in other industries. These committees not only bring nurses' representatives and management together to discuss the firing, promoting, and scheduling of nurses, they also deal with matters associated with the quality and procedures of patient care.[24]

Table 6-2. Comparison of median income of health workers by sex and by race, 1970

	Male	Female	Sex differentials
Health technologists and technicians			
Anglo	$7,368	$5,182	−$2,186
Black	6,932	5,252	−1,680
Race differentials	−436	+70	
Health service workers			
Anglo	$4,425	$3,265	−$1,160
Black	4,595	3,682	−913
Race differentials	+170	+417	

Data from U.S. Bureau of the Census, *Statistical Abstract of the U.S.* (Washington, D.C.: U.S. Government Printing Office, 1973), Table 375.

Demands by nurses and other occupational groups in hospitals for increased pay, better working conditions, and formalization of personnel procedures often have at their root the belief that the facility is victimizing and exploiting its employees.[25] Writing to this point, Cleland calls sex discrimination the nurse's most pervasive problem.[26] Roberts and Group compare the plight of women in the health industry to that of Blacks in American society.[27]

Technologists, technicians, and service workers

As we move down the occupational hierarchy through the skilled and semi-skilled levels of the medical technologist and laboratory technicians to the cooks and cleaners of the service work stratum, the percentage of women increases: from 70% to 88%. At the same time, the percentage of the category that is Black increases: from 9% to 22%. Here, in these subprofessional occupations, we have the potential double jeopardy of gender *and* race discrimination.

Sometimes it is difficult to distinguish which is the greater of the two forces; in the case of hospital employees, however, it is clear that within similar occupational categories, there is far greater economic discrimination associated with sex than with race.

Table 6-2 reveals that in the more well-paying technological and technician jobs, the salary differential between Anglo and Black males is $436 against the latter; among females, Blacks actually average a little higher salaries than the Anglo. But male/female comparisons of Anglos show that the female salary disadvantage is over $2,000; between male and female Blacks, the latter is disadvantaged by $1,680. In the lower-paying service-worker positions, Blacks report a higher annual wage than Anglos. Sex differences remain, however, for both racial groups: male Anglo salaries exceed female by $1,160, while the average Black male salary advantage over the Black female is $913.

Reemergence of the women's rights movement

The effort of women to secure political rights and social and economic justice dates from the founding of the Republic.[28] Its trail across American history is marked by brief highs of extensive action followed by a long period of dormancy. The publication of *The Second Sex* in the United States (1953) and *The Feminine Mystique* (1963), and the creation by John F. Kennedy of a presidential commission on the status of women provided the impetus for the contemporary women's liberation movement. Concerned with legal discrimination and oppression of women throughout the society, the movement early focused on abortion reform.

Within the movement there are specific organizations and individuals whose principal concerns include establishing women's clinics, raising the consciousness of women about their physical and psychological well-being, and providing alternative sources of health care information written by and for women—the widely read *Our Bodies, Ourselves*[29] being an outstanding example of a feminist effort to complement, some would say replace, dependence on gynecologists, 97% of whom are men.[30]

Levitt summarizes nicely the scope and diversity of feminist concern with reforming the health industry:

> Women have been using different approaches to change the present delivery of health care for women. Ideological differences within the women's health movement and the Women's Liberation Movement lead reformers and radicals to struggle on different issues. Some women are fighting for a greater access to institutions and quantitatively more service within the present health system; some are fighting for a qualitatively and structurally different type of health care. Some women are fighting for a "larger piece of the pie" as the pie looks today, i.e., more women doctors; some want to change the nature of the pie altogether, i.e., change the nature of professionalism and the role of the physician. For some, the goal is better health care for women regardless of who provides it—men or women; others believe that only women can truly understand the needs of women and should be the sole providers of women's health care. For some women the goal is comprehensive health care for all; others want to perpetuate specialized women's health care. Some women want to glorify and institutionalize their biological identity by fighting for better care around reproduction alone; others want to attack the general health care system. Some women feel setting up alternative clinics takes the pressure off changing existing health care institutions; others feel it is the way to force those institutions to change.[31]

One of the factors that has brought attention to problems of personal health care is apparent ability of government to affect them. For example, the struggle between the individual woman's rights to control her own body and government's regulation of abortion has become over the centuries a classic struggle.[32] Another issue of concern is the battle to gain government's authority to compel proportional admission of women to medical schools, or equal pay for equal work for women in the health industry. In the following section several contemporary controversies that illustrate this mixture of gender, medicine, and politics will be reviewed.

Controversy of contraceptives

In its 1973 *Jane Roe* v. *Henry Wade* decision, the Supreme Court of the United States struck down many state laws restricting therapeutic abortions. This decision appears as a major step in a redefinition of what Levitt calls ". . . one of the oldest state-individual conflicts: who has the right to determine who, how, when, where, and if a woman can have a child."[33] In fact, however,

there remains a host of unresolved and controversial issues concerning government's role in regulating family-planning methods.

The pill

An oral contraceptive, popularly known as "the pill," was developed in
the late 1950s and approved for general use in 1960 by the Food and Drug
Administration (FDA). Since its introduction, the pill has been used worldwide by 150 million women; currently by about 50 million women, with
10 million of those in the U.S. When used properly, the pill is virtually 100%
effective; this effectiveness has led to very widespread acceptance among
young women who reached fertility after its introduction.

Yet, as Silverman and Lee point out, the pill created, apart from its social
and ethical impacts, a highly unusual health issue:

> While most drugs (the vitamins and most hormones are notable exceptions) are used
> for relatively brief periods, a contraceptive pill would be used by millions of women
> during most or all of their childbearing years. . . . While most drugs are used on patients
> who are ill—or who think they are ill—contraceptives would be used by women who
> presumably are in good health. Under these conditions, with the possibility that women
> might be taking the Pill regularly, month after month, for twenty or thirty years, the
> problem of long-term safety was destined to build up a storm of controversy.[34]

And build a storm it has. Almost as soon as the pill came into general
use, reports began to appear in medical journals of deaths or severe risks
to users. Over the years congressional committees have examined and reexam-
ined questions of consumer risks. While the tone of some hearings has been
critical and occasionally alarmist, the response of the pharmaceutical industry
and most of the spokesmen for the medical profession has been repeatedly to
reassure users and to attack critics for "interfering with the doctor-patient
relationship."[35]

In a 1975 review of worldwide research on oral contraceptives, Connell
summarizes the following major points: (1) There is an increased association
between use and the frequency of cerebral thrombosis: pill users run about
nine times the risk of thrombotic stroke as nonusers; the risk of hemorrhagic
stroke is twice as great for users. Nevertheless, the absolute risk to the individual appears to be very small. (2) There is evidence of an increased risk of
gallbladder disease associated with pill use: the rate is twice that among nonusers. (3) Oral contraceptives apparently produce a slight elevation in blood
pressure in some women, and the incidence of hypertension increases with
duration of use. (4) There is an increase in urinary tract infections among
users, apparently associated with the estrogen hormone in the pill. The increase is on the order of 20% to 50%. But Connell goes on to make the point
that while the frequency as a percentage of reported cases of all these pathologies is higher among pill takers, the absolute risk as a percentage of every
100,000 women remains tiny. Moreover, much of the published research is
based on investigations of earlier versions of the pill, which had higher than
currently used dosages of active hormones. She concludes: "The benefits con-
ferred generally outweigh the risks if women are adequately informed and
effectively instructed, and if supportive backup is available to deal with emergencies."[36]

It is precisely on these two "ifs" that critics make their case: they argue for stricter controls, more research, and greater education of the population to the dangers of the pill and alternatives to it because they believe that physicians do not take adequate time to instruct women to watch for contraindications. From what we have previously seen of the health care services available to and used by millions of low income women, there can but remain grave doubts that "supportive backup" is even remotely available for emergencies.

Basically, the issue of taking or not taking the pill, as with all medication, is one of informed consent: does the consumer know enough, is there enough knowledge available, to make a rational decision? To argue, as many do, that there is a small risk—30 chances in a million of a pill-related blood clot killing a woman[37]—misses the point: the consumer is not a statistic; rather, she is an intelligent creature fully capable of self-determination.

Intrauterine devices

An alternative to the pill is the intrauterine device (IUD). These devices, while designed to be placed inside the body, do not fall under the control of the FDA; consequently, they are not subject to federal standards of premarket proof of safety and efficacy. Nor must IUD manufacturers notify the FDA if they recall a product, even if it has been associated with a fatality.

Spurred by the reports of as many as 60,000 painful and dangerous pelvic diseases as well as fatalities and septic abortions (miscarriages spontaneously induced by uterine infections caused by an IUD) among the 4 million American women who use IUDs, women's rights groups represented by the Center for Law and Social Policy and Ralph Nader's Health Research Group began a campaign in 1975 to have the FDA change the designation of IUDs to the "new drug" classification so that manufacturers would have to demonstrate the safety of the contraceptive before marketing it. In addition, the petitioners seek to require that a written information sheet be provided each would-be user outlining the risks of IUDs and comparing them with other methods of contraception. Proposed physician labeling would include details on patient examination before insertion, insertion and removal techniques, and indications of adverse reactions.[38] Legislation incorporating many of these reforms cleared Congress in June 1976. It remains to be seen how the FDA will implement it.

Morning-after pill

Many women prefer not to take hormone-based contraceptives during the time that they are not sexually active, and a postcoital drug is widely seen as simpler and more reliable since it does not depend for its effectiveness on prior planning. Scientists have developed a nearly 100% reliable "morning-after" pill whose major active ingredient is the synthetic hormone, diethylstilbestrol (DES). This drug has been released for limited use (in such situations as after a rape, incest, or where the patient's life would, in the judgment of a physician, be endangered by pregnancy). But FDA specifically warns against routine or frequent use of DES, and some critics demand the complete prohibition of it.[39]

The clamor over DES arose because DES is linked to 220 known cases of vaginal and cervical cancer in the daughters of women who took medicatio containing DES while they were pregnant during the 1950s and 1960s when it was routinely given to prevent spontaneous miscarriage. In one of those bizarre twists of fate not uncommon in the pharmaceutical industry, DES has come under fire in its role as a stimulant to the fattening of cattle. While the U.S. government refused to outlaw its use, some 20 countries have banned importation of beef fed DES because of its association with cancer. Dr. Frank J. Rauscher, Jr., Director of the National Cancer Institute, testified in February 1975 that pregnant women should not eat beef liver, because it may contain residues. He further testified that although DES proved an effective postcoital contraceptive, DES should be banned because of the threat posed by its uncontrolled use.[40]

The threat of DES is critical to women—especially for the daughters of women who took DES—and compounded by the fact that neither control over use of the morning-after pill nor the effect of DES passed to humans through beef has been established by the FDA. [41] The rate with which hallucinogenics such as LSD escaped from carefully controlled clinical use into the youth counterculture of the 1960s gives rise to concern by those who see how carelessly DES is prescribed to college coeds.

Sterilization

Between 1967 and 1973 the federal government increased its support for family-planning services by almost 1,500%—from $1 million to $149 million. While a sizeable proportion of this outlay went to support birth control efforts in our foreign aid programs, a growing volume of dollars is being allocated to pay for sterilizations of 100,000 to 150,000 women. (The Health, Education, and Welfare Department will pay 90% of sterilization costs for welfare recipients but nothing for abortions.) The government's policy of supporting sterilization is part of a definite and widespread trend: according to the Association for Voluntary Sterilization, there has been a threefold increase in female sterilization between 1970 and 1974, with 548,000 reported in the latter year.

Critics of sterilization raise two considerations: Are women given sufficient information about the consequences, physical and psychological, of sterilization? And are there adequate safeguards to ensure that sterilization is truly voluntary? Caress has answered the first question negatively: "Sterilization abuse is not the exception but the rule. It is systematic and widespread. Women are often misled about the dangers of surgery, misinformed about its permanence and coerced while under the stress of labor or abortion."[42]

Westoff cites figures from a 1970 National Fertility Study that suggest a decided racial bias in selection of sterilization as a method of family planning. Among college-educated Anglos and Blacks surveyed, 5.6% of the former and 9.7% of the latter had been sterilized; among women interviewed with less than a high school diploma, the sterilization rate was 14.5% for Anglos compared with 31.6% for Blacks. The high rate of sterilization among Black women should be seen in the context of a survey of doctors from Detroit, Grand Rapids, West Virginia, and Memphis that indicated that sterilization of private patients was a family-planning method of choice in only 6% of the sample; but 14% of the physicians chose sterilization as the first method that they would push with welfare patients.

Caress quotes the acting director of obstetrics and gynecology at a municipal hospital in New York City as reporting: "In most major teaching hospitals, in New York City, it is the unwritten policy to do elective hysterectomies on poor Black and Puerto Rican women, with minimal indications, to train residents. . . . At least 10% of gynecological surgery in New York City is done on this basis. About 99% of this is done on Blacks and Puerto Rican women." And a staff doctor at Los Angeles County Hospital commented: "Let's face it, we've all talked women into hysterectomies who didn't need them during residency training."

Sterilization represents a decided threat to the lives of women: mortality from tubal ligation is variously estimated to be from 14 to 30 per 100,000, mortality from hysterectomy between 10% to 34% of the recipients. Aside from death, outcomes include infection, bleeding, pain during menstruation, and increased menstrual flow. Agitated depression lasting more than 6 months is reported among 40% of one sample of women studied. Among women under 30 years of age, a regret rate (wishing to become pregnant) of 32% was reported. Most women who regret sterilization, Caress reports, subsequently become frigid.

In all, sterilization and other birth control procedures are unadvertised, yet definite, aspects of national health policy. Along with the use of pills and devices, sterilization is growing in acceptance; yet there is growing concern and criticism of government's role in protecting the rights and interests of consumers. The reaction (or inaction) of the government to reform-minded inquiries and demands for tighter control is paralleled in another health area of special concern to women: the safety of cosmetics.

"Does she, or doesn't she?"

So began the sales pitch that is credited with popularizing the use of hair dyes. By 1975, some 20 million Americans, mostly women, spent $250,000,000 annually on hair dyes. This river of dyes, however, is only a drop in the cosmetic ocean—an ocean built by 210 million users of one or more products, pouring an estimated $7 billion into the economy. Annually, hundreds are maimed, tens of thousands are seriously injured, and hundreds of thousands suffer painful reactions from cosmetic poisoning. The FDA, the government's watchdog, spends approximately 1/6,000 of the cosmetic dollar volume on its cosmetic-control budget.[43] Yet the potential hazard to consumers is far beyond this symbolic ratio.

Hair dyes

Dyes, and their bathroom companion home permanents, cause chemical burns, conjunctivitis (inflammation of the eyeball covering and the eyelid lining), nausea, blisters, and deterioration of the cornea's epithelial layer. Ana-line, an intermediate in the manufacture of hair dyes, is linked to inflammation of the scalp, scalp sores, and serious facial swelling.

Recently, researchers have suggested a link between hair dyes and cancer and birth defects. Dr. Bruce N. Ames reports that 150 of 169 commercial hair dyes produce changes in the genetic structure of bacterial test systems that are used for screening potentially dangerous substances in food additives, drugs, and cosmetics. His findings also raise the possibility that dyes are carcinogenic.[44] A spokesman for the Cosmetic, Toiletry, and Fragrance Association responded that experiments on "180 New Zealand rabbits, 600 female rats, 600 male rats . . ." show no evidence that hair dyes are unsafe.[45]

Eye cosmetics

A 1973 report of 1,031 eye cosmetics in use by 460 women shows that 50% were contaminated by bacteria and 10% by fungi.[46] A potentially dangerous form of contamination, *Pseudomonas,* has been found in recalled eye makeup. *Pseudomonas aeruginosa* can cause blindness without prior warning within 48 hours of contact.

Chemicals that are considered toxic substances are routinely encountered in unexpectedly high levels in eye cosmetics: according to a 1973 FDA ruling,[47] the mercury level in all types of cosmetics, except eye makeup, must not exceed one part per million. Eye cosmetics are permitted up to 35 parts mercury per million—despite the fact that mercury accumulates in the body and may cause permanent neurological damage.

Vaginal deodorants

Vaginal deodorants pose a double threat to women: physical and psychological. Irritations and infections are caused by the propellant, alcohol, perfume, and talc; hexachlorophene, which was used before 1972 in most of the thirty-odd brands and is still found in several, is absorbed into the blood and causes damage to the white matter of the brain.[48] Allergic reactions to these chemicals are reported in the medical press. A much more harmful consequence of deodorant marketing, however, is that women who detect a vaginal odor assume from the deodorant advertising that this is because of their "natural foul smell"; consequently, minor infections as well as vaginal cancers go untreated until they reach advanced—possibly lethal—stages.[49]

So much for their threat to a woman's physical well-being. What is the effect on a woman's self-image of an advertising campaign that tells her that without the use of a deodorant she is foul-smelling or unclean, that she must, in order to escape the stigma of her unpure genitals, spray chemicals into her vagina? There are no advertisements that tell us that male genitals must be wiped, douched, or sprayed because they "smell funny." Are women, therefore, naturally inferior, naturally repulsive? Vaginal deodorant makers and the mass media certainly strive to create this impression; in 1971, 24 million women must have thought so when their purchases of deodorants generated an estimated $53 million profit for the cosmetic industry.[50]

Magnitude of consumer hazards

The full impact of cosmetic contamination and inadequate testing is unknown; one study reports that one out of ten cosmetics sold is contaminated before sale.[51] Aside from the products just reviewed, other commonly encountered beauty and grooming aids produce irritations and injuries: a 1975 survey showed 40.5 injuries per 10,000 deodorants and antiperspirants used, 40.2 per 10,000 depilatories and hair removers used, and 14.6 per 10,000 hair sprays and lacquers used.[52] In 1970, the National Committee on Product Safety reported that 60,000 people are injured each year "so seriously to restrict activity for one day or require medical attention." Beauty aids alone ranked second among products reported as causing these injuries.[53]

Part of the problem with cosmetic safety arises from the Food, Drug, and Cosmetic Act of 1938. Under this law, the FDA may move only against "adulterated" or "misbranded" cosmetics. The law does not require safety testing, ingredient labeling, registration of manufacturers, or reporting of consumer injuries. Moreover, the FDA is handicapped by the lack of subpoena authority to compel manufacturers to turn over records. FDA officials plead lack of staff, particularly lack of investigators and scientists. In any event, the consequence of these factors is clear: the low priority given cosmetics is reflected by 1973 figures showing that although the FDA "took 2,075 legal actions against firms and products, only 17 of them were related to cosmetics."[54]

The politics of protection

What is not seen in the legislation, regulations, and budget and staff limitations with which the FDA must operate is the magnitude of the political forces bearing on the regulatory process. We have noted the interest and efforts of feminist and consumer groups to shape and control the process. But these actors pale into insignificance in comparison with the resources of the industrial interests involved: the cosmetic industry, the drug industry, and the food industry—all of which have excellent and compelling reason to watch the FDA: their profitability.

Dollars and votes

The cosmetic industry is a $7 billion-a-year proposition with more than 1,000 manufacturers and thousands of jobbers, wholesalers, and retailers distributing over 25,000 products. Sales in the industry have doubled since 1965, and 1975 projections call for a 15% annual growth. "And, like beer, cosmetic sales don't seem to suffer the ravages of hard times."[55] The political muscle of this booming industry is applied in Washington by the Cosmetic, Toiletry, and Fragrance Association.

The drug industry recorded over $5 billion in U.S. sales for a net profit in 1972 of $734 million. Compared with the national profit rate of 10.6%, the drug industry's 18.3% is an enviable accomplishment.[56] The Pharmaceutical Manufacturers' Association is often joined in its lobbying activities by the American Medical Association and by representatives of the individual corporations and multinationals.

Because of their common concern with the regulatory activity of the FDA, the cosmetic and drug industries often collaborate. Combined, the two not only have the resources of their individual companies and their trade associations but enjoy the public image carefully developed by extensive advertising campaigns—campaigns that not only sell particular products and corporate logos, but also reinforce the general benefits ("sex appeal," "good health," "freedom from sleeplessness," and so forth) the public derives from the industries. The combined advertising expenditures of the cosmetic and drug companies in 1972 was over $1.13 billion. As a consequence of these promotional budgets,[57] large chunks of both the mass media and the advertising industries have a significant investment in the well-being and continued prosperity of their colleagues in cosmetics and drugs.

When regulation or proconsumer legislation is under consideration, the $125-billion food industry's various interest groups often join their cosmetic- and drug-making colleagues. The potential campaign contributions and the presence of representatives of the three industries in nearly every congressional district give the three industries massive power in Congress and at the White House.

Inside the FDA

Over and above the tremendous power of industrial interest groups and the influence of their political allies is the issue of the very independence of the FDA from proindustry, anticonsumer influence from within. Critics have charged that there are altogether too many top industry representatives temporarily holding policy-making and investigative positions in the Administration. These top-level people come over from a drug, cosmetic, food, or related firm for a few years (top posts in the FDA are politically appointed) and then return to private employment—often to firms that they were temporarily regulating or watching.[58] At the lower levels, scientific, medical, and technical personnel resign or retire and accept positions with industries related to their FDA work. "The top ranks of FDA are thoroughly peppered with employees who had once labored long and hard for food and drug companies. Twenty-two of the fifty-two top officials have worked for regulated industries or organizations that cater to those industries."[59] Examples include:

A *general counsel* who previously represented such clients as Continental Baking, the Cosmetic, Toiletry, and Fragrance Association, Carnation Company, and the Institute of Shortening and Edible Oils

A *director* of the Bureau of Foods who previously spent 8 years with Ralston Purina, 3 years with Libby, McNeill, & Libby and came to his post from the vice-presidency of Hunt-Wesson

A *deputy director* of the Bureau of Drugs who was recruited after 5 years with Merck Sharp & Dohme, a major pharmaceutical house

A *commissioner* who came from a vice-presidency of Booz, Allen, and Hamilton, a major management consulting firm with drug and food accounts, and who had also previously worked for the American Medical Association

A *director* of the Cosmetics Division who was formerly an executive of a cosmetic company

As of 1973, not one FDA official had previous experience with Consumers Union, Consumer Federation of America, Common Cause, or any of the women's health groups.[60]

Having previously worked in private industry does not blind one to the public interest; the recent history of the FDA contains notable cases of individuals from such backgrounds who at great personal hardship pressed investigations that resulted in major victories for consumer interests. But the record is certainly not top heavy with such victories.

There are different reasons for this. Science tends to be slow and conservative; scientists may be cautious, unwilling to take risks. When millions of dollars of research and development are involved, when powerful political actors are watching, and when one's professional peers are being judged, researchers and their superiors can be expected to pay less attention to the clamor of "outsiders."

Yet the fact remains that the incentive system within the FDA and the broader society is not balanced between consumer and industry interests. "An inescapable truth is that industry will pay many of their salaries when they leave FDA. The psychological implication is obvious: don't bite the hand that will feed you. The deferred bribe is one of industry's mightiest weapons for subverting regulatory officials."[61] One need not even be consciously striving to pave a way into lucrative private employment: psychological pressures to conform to the expectations of what earlier we called "significant others" are no less powerful determinants of behavior for their being unconscious.

Community or caste?

Some very substantial parts of the health problems that have been reviewed arise from the socialization and gender role of American women. This is particularly true of the hazards and hardships caused by cosmetics and the occupational segregation and discrimination within the health care delivery industry. But to throw up one's hands and become resigned to accepting these problems because social change is such a slow process is certainly uncalled for. We have seen that a relatively narrow range of public policy reforms, such as bringing cosmetics and IUDs under effective governmental control or the rigorous application of equal employment opportunity and nondiscriminatory legislation, could have important remedial effects. Indeed, when we see how much of the health situation of women is intimately connected with government action or inaction, it becomes all the more clear that an active political response rather than passive resignation is the correct course. Politicians and bureaucrats, not socialization and gender role, keep DES on the market.

Aside from revealing the extent to which the androcentric health problems of women have a political base, the preceding analysis also suggests the nature of women's condition in American society. The analysis was begun by the argument that women form a community, a disadvantaged community, that is denied access to social, economic, and political values. Conceptualizing the condition of women in this manner has important implications for their political response to female health needs and problems. This conceptualization takes us into a significant, often polemical, controversy.

Some feminist ideologues, either from a desire to form a foundation for broad-based attacks or out of a commitment to collectivist principles, argue that women form a *caste*. The distinguishing features of a caste system are status positions based on inherited attributes such as color, parents' occupation, or gender identity; very rigidly maintained boundaries between caste lines such that marriage or contact between members of different castes cannot lead to the inferior achieving the rank of the superior; generalization of the worth of an individual on the basis of caste membership rather than on individual achievement; and nearly uniform socialization into prescribed roles with little or no deviance tolerated. On the basis of her analysis of women's situation in the American labor force, Almquist concluded that women do in fact form an inferior caste and that this caste oppression works a sex-based discrimination equally against all women.[62]

But when women are viewed from their situation in the health industry, they do not form a caste; rather, there are clearly major differences in the quantity and quality of treatment that they receive according to their position in the American class system. For instance, we have seen that infant and maternal mortality varies with socioeconomic status: the higher the class, the fewer the deaths.[63] When we look at male/female competition for high-status health occupations, we find that upper- and middle-class women are more frequently encountered in medical school classes than are working-class and poverty males.[64] And throughout recent history, a class bias is recognizable in the vision of what is "good" for women: in the late nineteenth and early twentieth centuries, middle-class women were told by their physicians that they were too fragile to work and that they required prolonged bed rest after childbirth; and working-class females were employed in the most back-breaking labor, with no outcry from the medical profession. Currently, middle-class women are warned that their children will suffer psychological damage if the mother leaves them in a nursery in order to take a job; working-class and poverty mothers, on the other hand, are urged to place their children in day-care centers so that they can go to work and get off welfare.[65]

To manipulate the meaning of caste to incorporate this diversity of gender role behavior and fluidity of sex boundaries is to compromise the definition so extensively as to make caste a useless analytical tool.

This caveat, however, does not invalidate the observation that sex difference in the health delivery industry and the broader society *should be* a major focus for attention. On the contrary, by concentrating on their androcentric problems and priorities, feminists raise important and compelling demands for change.

In responding to these demands and becoming more sensitive to other areas of exploitation suffered by women, we must be equally alert to the fact that difficulties are felt with varying weight. This variation is related to and perhaps reflects the other social attributes of the individual woman—age, education, ethnicity, race, social class, and so forth. For instance, the upper middle-class woman in the examining room of her private physician faces nowhere near the same threat of "voluntary" sterilization as her impoverished sister confronts in being treated at a public maternity hospital.

Nor will the perception of issues be unaffected by demographic differences. A woman who cannot find a doctor for her sick child simply is not going to react to the warning of potential poisoning through cosmetic contamination in the same manner as a female lawyer who has just experienced a painful scalp rash after using a hair rinse. And to point out that female physicians average "only" about $16,000 compared with $25,000 for male colleagues seems to be less a commentary on our social and economic system than the $4,500 average income of health service workers, male as well as female.

The appropriate conclusion to be drawn from this review of women and health is that women do in fact have special disadvantages but that many or most of these problems either stem from or are exacerbated by the relative power that women possess in our society. In working to overcome that basic inequality in the distribution of power, we must understand that a potential for action exists in the wide sharing of experiences and needs. Yet a community consciousness of the strength and pervasiveness presently seen among Blacks is not close to realization among women. In working to build a collective recognition of shared problems and a widespread loyalty to sisterhood, feminist reformers must meet the challenging interaction of gender, economic, racial, and ethnic forces that are mirrored in the attitudes and behavior of women in the arena of personal health care.

Notes

1. Aristotle, *Politics* (H. Rockham, translator) (Cambridge: Harvard University Press, 1944), 1254b, 13-15 quoted by Barbara Tovey and George Tovey, "Women's Philosophical Friends and Enemies," *Social Science Quarterly* **55** (Dec. 1974), p. 586.
2. Patricia S. Kruppa, "The American Woman and the Male Historian," *Social Science Quarterly* **55** (Dec. 1974). p. 611.
3. *Ibid.*, p. 607. The reference is to Jacques Barzun, *Teacher in America* (New York: Anchor Books, 1955), p. 221.
4. Eli Ginzberg, *Men, Money, and Medicine* (New York: Columbia University Press, 1969), p. 97.
5. Elizabeth M. Almquist, "Untangling the Effects of Race and Sex: The Disadvantaged Status of Black Women," *Social Science Quarterly* **56** (June 1975), p. 134.
6. Wilma R. Krauss, "Political Implications of Gender Roles: A Review of the Literature," *American Political Science Review* **58** (Dec. 1974), pp. 1708, 1711. This is an invaluable guide to the basic social science literature through 1974.
7. Barbara Ehrenreich and Deirdre English, *Complaints and Disorders: The Sexual Politics of Sickness* (Old Westbury, N.Y.: The Feminist Press, 1973), p. 83.
8. Krauss, "Political Implications," p. 1707.
9. The notion of "significant other" is developed in George H. Mead, *Mind, Self and Society* (Chicago: University of Chicago Press, 1943).
10. Albert F. Wessen, "Hospital Ideology and Communication between Ward Personnel," in E. Gartly Jaco (editor), *Patients, Physicians, and Illness*, ed. 2 (New York: The Free Press, 1972), p. 331.
11. Eugenia S. Carpenter and Scott Walker, "Women in Male-Dominated Health Professions," paper presented at the 1974 annual meeting of the American Public Health Association, New Orleans, La.
12. W. F. Dube and others, "Study of U.S. Medical School Applicants, 1970-71," *Journal of Medical Education* **46** (Oct. 1971), pp. 837-857.
13. Carpenter and Walker, "Women in Male-Dominated Health Professions."
14. *Ibid.*
15. Maryland Y. Pennel and Josephine E. Renshaw, "Distribution of Women Physicians, 1970," *Journal of the American Medical Women's Association* **27** (April 1972), pp. 197-200. A similar distribution is reported by Carpenter and Walker, "Women in Male-Dominated Health Professions."

16. Carol Lopate, *Women in Medicine* (Baltimore: The Johns Hopkins University Press, 1968), pp. 127-128; also see Geoffrey Marks and William K. Beatty, *Women in White* (New York: Charles Scribner's Sons, 1972).

17. Lopate, *Women in Medicine*, p. 185. Figures are for 1964.

18. *Ibid.*

19. U.S. Bureau of the Census, *Census of Population: 1970, Subject Reports, Occupational Characteristics, Final Report PC (2)-7A* (Washington, D.C.: U.S. Government Printing Office, 1970).

20. Miriam Dolson, "Where Women Stand in Administration," *Modern Hospital* **108** (May 1967), pp. 100-105; "Womanpower in Hospital Administration," *FAH Review* **5** (Aug. 1972), topical issue; Robert Pecarchik and William G. Mather, "Lack of Business Skills Threatens Women Administrators," *Modern Nursing Home* **24** (May 1970), p. 58. Vicente Navarro reports that women make up 6% of the boards of trustees of private medical teaching institutions and 12% of the boards of voluntary community hospitals, from Vicente Navarro, "Women in Health Care," *New England Journal of Medicine* **292** (20 Feb. 1975), pp. 398-402.

21. Jerry L. Weaver, *Conflict and Control in Health Care Administration* (Beverly Hills: Sage Publications, Inc., 1975).

22. Bonnie Bullough, "New Militancy in Nursing: Collective Bargaining Activities by Nurses in Perspective," *Nursing Forum* **10** (1971), pp. 273-288.

23. Norma K. Grand, "Nursing Ideologies and Collective Bargaining," *Journal of Nursing Administration* **3** (March-April 1973), pp. 29-32.

24. Eva H. Erickson, "Collective Bargaining: An Inappropriate Technique for Professionals," *Nursing Forum* **10** (1971), pp. 300-311.

25. Health Policy Advisory Center, "Health Workers," a packet of the Health/PAC *Bulletin* (March 1970; July-Aug. 1970; April 1972; Nov. 1972); John Ehrenreich and Barbara Ehrenreich, "Hospital Workers: A Case Study in the 'New Working Class,'" *Monthly Review* **24** (Jan. 1973), pp. 12-27; Elinor Langer, "Inside the Hospital Workers: The Best Contract Anywhere," *New York Review of Books* **16** (20 May, 3 June 1971), pp. 25-33, 30-37.

26. Virginia Cleland, "Sex Discrimination: Nursing's Most Pervasive Problem," *American Journal of Nursing* **71** (Aug. 1971), pp. 1542-1543.

27. Joan I. Roberts and Thetis M. Group, "The Women's Movement and Nursing," *Nursing Forum* **12** (1973), pp. 303-322.

28. See Miriam Schneider (editor), *Feminism: The Essential Historical Writing* (New York: Vintage Books, 1972); Eleanor Flexner, *Century of Struggle: The Women's Rights Movement in the United States* (New York: Atheneum Publishers, 1970); William L. O'Neill, *Everyone Was Brave: A History of Feminism in America* (Chicago: Quadrangle/The New York Times Book Co., 1969).

29. Boston Women's Health Book Collective, *Our Bodies, Ourselves* (New York: Simon & Schuster, Inc., 1973).

30. The figure is taken from Ellen Frankfort, *Vaginal Politics* (New York: Bantam Books, Inc., 1973), p. xxviii. Women are 5.5% of office-based OB/GYN practitioners; from Pennel and Renshaw, "Distribution of Women Physicians," p. 199.

31. Jane Levitt, "The Women's Health Movement as a Critical Approach to the Delivery of Health Care," *Health Politics: A Quarterly Bulletin* **4** (Feb. 1974), p. 9. For a useful bibliography, see Jane B. Sprague, "Women and Health Bookshelf," *American Journal of Public Health* **65** (July 1975), pp. 741-746.

32. See Frankfort, *Vaginal Politics*, pp. 51-89; "Abortion," *American Journal of Public Health* **61** (March 1971), topical issue.

33. Levitt, "Women's Health Movement," p. 8.

34. Milton Silverman and Philip R. Lee, *Pills, Profits and Politics* (Berkeley: University of California Press, 1974), p. 98.

35. See the hearings of the U.S. Senate, Select Committee on Small Business, Subcommittee on Monopoly, Ninety-first Congress, Second Session, *Present Status of Competition in the Pharmaceutical Industry* (Washington, D.C.: U.S. Government Printing Office, 1970), known as the "Nelson Hearings" after the Subcommittee's chairman, Sen. Gaylord Nelson.

36. Elizabeth B. Connell, "The Pill Revisited," *Family Planning Perspectives* **7** (March/April 1975), pp. 62-71.

37. U.S. Senate, *Present Status of Competition*, **16**, p. 6800.
38. Marlene Cimons, "Government, Activists Dispute IUDs," *Los Angeles Times*, part 4 (18 July 1975), pp. lff; *Los Angeles Times*, part 1 (1 August 1975), p. 2. Data on diseases reported by Dr. King K. Holmes of the University of Washington.
39. Marlene Cimons, "Sen. Kennedy Spearheads Anti-DES Drive," *Los Angeles Times*, part 4 (17 April 1975), pp. lff; "Health Research Group Report on the Morning-after Pill" (Washington, D.C.: Health Research Group, 8 Dec. 1972).
40. Cimons, "Sen. Kennedy Spearheads Anti-DES Drive," p. 5.
41. Given the severity of the consequences of vaginal cancer, many feminists find the lethargy of the government further evidence of misogyny: "The standard treatment for vaginal cancer is surgical removal of the vagina. A woman can live without a vagina; she can even have a new one constructed. But I wonder: if DES had been shown to cause cancer of the penis in young male adolescents and the standard treatment was removal of the penis, would the all-male set of authorities who delayed action on stopping the drug's use have been so sluggish in their response?" in Frankfort, *Vaginal Politics*, p. 103.
42. Barbara Caress, "Sterilization: Women Fit to be Tied," Health/Pac *Bulletin*, 62 (Jan.-Feb. 1975), pp. 1-6, 10-13; Charles F. Westoff, "The Modernization of U.S. Contraceptive Practice," *Family Planning Perspectives* 4 (July 1972), pp. 9-12; Bernard Rosenfeld, Sidney M. Wolfe, and Robert E. McGarrah, Jr., *A Health Research Group Study on Surgical Sterilization: Present Abuses and Proposed Regulations* (Washington, D.C.: Health Research Group, 29 Oct. 1973); Robert E. McGarrah, Jr., "Sterilization Without Consent: Teaching Hospital Violations of HEW Regulations" (Washington, D.C.: Health Research Group, 21 Jan. 1975).
43. John G. Fuller, *200,000,000 Guinea Pigs: New Dangers in Everyday Foods, Drugs, and Cosmetics* (New York: G. P. Putnam's Sons, 1972), p. 247; also see S. S. Epstein and R. R. Grundy (editors), *Consumer Health and Product Hazards: Cosmetics and Drugs, Pesticides, Food Additives*, 2 vols. (Cambridge: MIT Press, 1974).
44. Bruce N. Ames, H. O. Kammen, and Edith Yamasaki, "Hair Dyes are Mutagenic: Identification of a Variety of Mutagenic Ingredients," *Proceedings of the National Academy of Sciences* **72** (June 1975), pp. 2423-2437.
45. Betty Liddick, "Hair-Dye Hazard a Debatable Issue," *Los Angeles Times*, part 4 (31 March 1975), p. 6.
46. Samuel J. Taub, "Contaminated Cosmetics as Cause of Eye Infection," *Eye, Ear, Nose and Throat Monthly* **52** (June 1973), pp. 227-228.
47. "Mercury Use in Cosmetics Now Restricted by FDA," *Wall Street Journal* (9 Jan. 1973), p. 3.
48. "FDA Warnings on Hexachlorophene," *New York Times*, part 4 (12 Dec. 1971), p. 12. On the dangers from absorption of these ingredients, see "Testimony of Dr. Sidney M. Wolfe before the Senate Health Subcommittee Hearings on Cosmetic Safety, February 21, 1974" (Washington, D.C.: Health Research Group); also see Margaret Morrison, "The Great Feminine Spray Explosion," *FDA Consumer* (Oct. 1973), pp. 1-2.
49. Bernard Davis, "Deodorant Vulvitis," *Obstetrics and Gynecology* **26** (Nov. 1970), p. 812; "Feminine Hygiene Deodorant Sprays," *The Medical Letter* **12** (16 Oct. 1970), p. 88; Alexander A. Fisher, "Allergic Reactions to Feminine Hygiene Sprays," *Archives of Dermatology* **108** (Dec. 1973), pp. 801-802.
50. Frankfort, *Vaginal Politics*, p. 97.
51. Taub, "Contaminated Cosmetics," p. 228.
52. *Los Angeles Times* (29 June 1975), p. 14.
53. *New York Times* (14 April 1971), p. 56.
54. Jourdan Houston, "The Great Cosmetic Safety Debate," *Saturday Review* (26 July 1975), p. 48; also see Thomas P. Southwick, "FDA: Efficiency Drive Stumbles over the Issue of Drug Efficacy," *Science* **169** (18 Sept. 1970), pp. 1188-1189; Nicholas Wade, "Drug Regulation: FDA Replies to Charges by Economists and Industry," *Science* **179** (23 Feb. 1973), pp. 775-777; National Academy of Sciences, *How Safe Is Safe? The Design of Policy on Drugs and Food Additives* (Washington, D.C.: U.S. Government Printing Office, 1974).
55. Houston, "The Great Cosmetic Safety Debate," p. 47.
56. Silverman and Lee, *Pills*, pp. 327-328.

57. *Ibid.*, p. 340.
58. Records obtained under new "freedom-of-information" legislation disclose that the FDA leads the nation's regulatory agencies in industrial ties with at least 115 employees who came directly or indirectly from industries it regulates. From *Los Angeles Times*, part 4 (7 Sept. 1975), p. 1.
59. Michael Jacobson and Robert White, "Company Town at FDA," *The Progressive*, April 1973, p. 49.
60. *Ibid.*, pp. 49-52. For a discussion of industry's ties with the National Academy of Science, see Robert Gillette, "Academy Food Committees: New Criticism of Industry Ties," *Science* **177** (29 Sept. 1972), pp. 1172-1175.
61. Jacobson and White, "Company Town at FDA," p. 49.
62. Almquist, "Untangling the Effects," p. 141.
63. Dixon shows class-based variations in reproductive behavior across the world, in Ruth B. Dixon, "Women's Rights and Fertility," *Population/Family Planning* **17** (Jan. 1975), pp. 1-20.
64. Renee C. Fox writes: "Despite the efforts being made to recruit young persons into medical school from minority groups and nonprivileged social class backgrounds, the new medical student is still likely to be a white, middle-class man." From "Is there a 'New' Medical Student?" in Laurence R. Tancredi (editor), *Ethics of Health Care* (Washington, D.C.: National Academy of Sciences, 1974), p. 216.
65. Ehrenreich and English, *Complaints and Disorders*, p. 81.

CHAPTER 7 The elderly as a minority community

Between 1950 and 1970 the over-65 population increased at more than twice the rate of the increase for those under 45. One out of every ten Americans is now 65 or older; at the present rate of increase, by the year 2000 roughly half of the population will be over 50 years of age. Aside from its dramatic increase in size, the over-65 population is undergoing important sociological changes. Because of social security and private retirement funds, because of the rural-to-urban trend, and because of improved medical procedures, more and more older people are living apart from their families and the younger society. This is exemplified in the planned retirement communities where only persons over 55 or 60 are eligible to reside. For the lower end of the income continuum, there is residential isolation in the geriatric ghettos of the inner cities where the impoverished elderly live in fleabag hotels, spend their time sitting alone, and get their food at greasy-spoon cafeterias that specialize in feeding the indigent.

Rose[1] concludes that millions of old Americans, once holding different political attitudes and affiliations, are, because of poverty and isolation, being shaped into a coherent, self-conscious community. Men and women who recently identified themselves as liberal/moderate/conservative, Republican/Democrat/independent, are ignoring old alliances and loyalties and are beginning to ask: "What's in it for us old folks?" Their community identity and consciousness are growing, as witnessed by the climbing memberships of such interest groups as the American Association of Retired Persons and the National Council of Senior Citizens.

While there is no denying the gravity of the economic circumstances of many elderly (the over-65 population is the only group in the society whose number of poor is rising), other analysts argue that there is little likelihood that differences that developed during youth and middle age will be overcome at 65. Campbell, for example, concludes that there is little or no chance of an elderly political bloc emerging.[2]

We might seek a clue to community consciousness among the elderly by analyzing current election data. With the exception of the apparent referendum-type voting on former President Nixon in a handful of 1974 congressional elections, however, there is little clear-cut issue difference in the typical electoral campaign. As Binstock notes, the elderly are not offered foci for political action. "While most politicians wish to avoid offending the aged, and many favor proposals to provide incremental benefits to older persons, few are disposed to develop special appeals to the aged among the central issues of their campaigns."[3] Therefore, merely comparing young and old voting or opinions on candidates is not a useful means for revealing the presence or absence of intragroup solidarity among the elderly.

In order to locate community consciousness, I will analyze the position of older citizens on a particular issue. Issue-orientation is an especially useful technique for examining the effects of aging on political participation, because many studies have found that unlike voting or other active forms of involvement that may be circumscribed and curtailed by infirmity or the absence of transportation, the elderly give great attention to political campaigns and are more likely than nonelderly to follow public affairs in the media. It has been found that persons over 60 consistently show the highest interest in politics, and the elderly are strongly issue-oriented in making their preferences among competing positions and candidates.[4] Thus, *if* the isolation and separation that characterize millions of elderly presage a political community, the opinions and preferences of elderly people on an issue salient to them should remain consistent regardless of socioeconomic variations.

Political sociology of the elderly

Contrary to Rose's assertion, the literature on the political behavior of the elderly suggests that no bloc behavior is likely. Age is not considered a powerful predictor of political behavior. Campbell writes that "there is no instance in modern history in which a major political movement has grown out of the interests of a particular age group and it seems improbable that any such development will occur soon."[5] Now, if we are willing to accept this assertion in the face of the Townsend movement of the 1930s,[6] the McCarthy "children's crusade," and the antiwar, antidraft movement of 1965-1968, we may ask why the elderly are unlikely to overcome class, socioeconomic, partisan, and other political cleavages and vote their objective interests.

Binstock notes that the elderly have not had powerful organizational representatives. He sees interest groups such as the American Association of Retired Persons and the National Council of Senior Citizens that claim to represent the elderly as lacking programs and appeals that are broad and basic enough to establish a cohesive identity among the elderly. And these interest groups, he argues, have little power in Washington to cause legislation for new programs capable of redressing the abuses suffered by the poor and disadvantaged among the old.[7]

Moving from the organizational level, we find a number of studies that point to behavior and motivational features that curtail the political strength of the old.

Schmidhauser suggests that old persons rank lowest in sense of political efficacy (defined as the feeling that individual political action does have, or could have, an impact upon the political process). Also, a significant proportion of elderly persons rank at the bottom of the citizen duty scale (defined as the feeling that one ought to participate in politics). These findings are interpreted to mean that many old people have virtually withdrawn into a state of complete political indifference.[8]

Their withdrawal and disinterest are taken as a reflection of the so-called disengagement syndrome. This notion contends that the transition from middle age to old age is characterized by a progressive withdrawal from other members of society. Gergen and Back suggest a political consequence of disengagement in their assertion that the old become less attuned to the issues that are of central importance in the overall society.[9] Conceivably this leads to ignoring the appeals of parties and candidates.

Data drawn from three presidential election studies, however, reveal that political participation, comprehensively defined, does not drop off in the older cohorts. Campbell reports that there is only a very slight decline in voting of the over-65 group and notes that this segment still surpasses the youngest in turnout at the polls.

The disengagement/low-interest and low-efficacy hypotheses are further challenged by observers who report that political interest actually increases with age. For example, after reviewing 23 national opinion surveys, Glenn and Grimes conclude that the data do not support the disengagement hypothesis, at least the version that says that elderly people become less attuned to the central issues of the society.[10] After analyzing the results of the 1960 presidential election study, Campbell and his associates argue that the sense of political efficacy and sense of citizen duty fail to show any systematic pattern of age differences whatever.[11] In fact, interest in politics may *increase* to replace waning family, recreational, and occupational interests and involvements.[12]

But in order to transform political interest into a voting bloc, the power of existing partisan affiliations would have to be broken. Campbell suggests that this is very unlikely to happen because the old have the highest level of partisan identification. Old people are more likely than young to identify themselves as either Democrat or Republican, and these identifiers demonstrate a record of party loyalty. "Older people, having had more time to develop a strong partisan self-image, are notably more stable in their voting than younger people and less likely to be moved by the political winds of the time."[13]

If the old are resistant to change, does this mean that they are, as a group, more conservative than the rest of society? The answer appears to be "yes, but. . . ." As Campbell points out, among those surveyed in the national presidential election studies of 1960, 1964, and 1968, the older a person is the more likely that person is to call himself or herself a Republican. Thus, insofar as Republican is synonymous with conservative,[14] the older cohort is more conservative. (I must hasten to add that a number of factors are related to the prevalence of Republicans among the older voters, including the disproportionate high mortality among working class, minority, or other segments usually registered as Democrats, the preponderance of the GOP in the 1910s and 1920s, and the continuing strength of party identification.)

However, lest credibility be lent to the myth that people *become* more conservative as they grow older, it should be noted that students of cohort behavior have found that if the same relative measures of liberal/conservative that were prevalent in the era of primary socialization (that is, the years between 15 and 25 when one's political philosophy and party identification that continue throughout life are formed) are used at various points along the cohort's lifespan, then there is little or no trend toward conservatism. When cross-sectional analysis is employed, responses that may have earned a "liberal" rating for the 65-year-old in 1940 may, in 1975, be scored as "conservative." In fact, what is reported as growing conservatism in the cohort may well be a result of the changing issues, not the changing values of the older individuals.[15]

Schmidhauser places another dimension of the conservatism issue in perspective when he writes: "Psychological testing provides evidence that older people are frequently more careful and deliberate than younger ones. Consequently, it has been argued that what is commonly referred to as the conservatism of the aged may be related to their tendency to be more deliberate rather than to inherent inflexibility."[16]

How, then, can the elderly be expected to respond to a political issue of concern to the general population but of extraordinary significance to them? From the preceding we can speculate that socioeconomic class, education, income, and religion, all factors that correlate with party preference, will be related strongly to the responses of the elderly as they are to the responses of the nonelderly. And we seem justified in hypothesizing that older persons will be less willing to take a radical position on the proferred issue. That is, the old more often than the young will refuse to see the issue as especially critical—after all, the former have lived through two or three major wars, an international depression, a stock market crash, and so forth. And the old will be less willing to support radical or nontraditional approaches to solving the problem.[17]

Health care as a political issue

An issue of particular salience to the elderly, one that may reasonably test the bloc behavior, emerging community thesis, is the cost of personal health care services. Depending on what indicators are used, as many as one third or more older Americans are afflicted by at least one chronic disease or health-related impairment causing a limitation of activity.[18] In addition, in the overall American population, the old seek hospital care more often and must receive it for longer periods than any other group. The per capita 1971 health expenditure of those under 65 was $250; for those over 65, $861.[19] And Medicare, designed to lift much of the burden of health costs from the impoverished elderly, actually covers only about 42% of their total health bill.[20]

Here in the issue of health care costs and ways of controlling them lie the classic ingredients for community political behavior: an issue that is well established throughout the society but that bears with special rigor on an identifiable population that possesses demographic, cultural, and structural particularities. How do the elderly react to the rising costs of health care? Do proposals to reduce or control costs find a broad base in the elderly population? Or does the elderly community, true to prevailing theory, ignore the issue and reject nontraditional approaches to mounting costs?

Comparisons of elderly and young

Data from three recent national surveys provide a basis for assessing the position of elderly Americans toward proposals to reduce or control health care costs. In 1968, researchers from the Survey Research Center (SRC) of the University of Michigan asked their presidential election study respondents whether or not the federal government should "help" people get low-cost medical care. Among Anglo respondents, almost two thirds of the 65-and-older compared with half of the 35-and-younger approved government assistance.[21] Thus, a significantly greater proportion of the elderly support an ambiguous yet nontraditional form of meeting health care charges.[22]

In 1970 and 1972 the SRC asked its national samples if they thought that the government should provide health insurance to cover all medical and hospital expenses. The respondents were told to indicate their preference on a continuum from "government insurance" through "private insurance." Among Anglos in the two samples, the elderly selected the government health insurance option well over 50% more frequently than did their younger neighbors: 39% versus 21% in 1970, 40% versus 24% in 1972.

Within the two cohorts we find only minor variation in support for help or government insurance associated with socioeconomic characteristics. That is, there is little difference in the per cent of the sample who select an alternative according to whether the respondents are urban or rural, well educated or poorly educated, upper income or impoverished. Coefficients of association between individual independent variables and preference for insurance alternatives (that is, dependent variables) are in the neighborhood of plus or minus .100/.150.

It is possible, however, that some of the variation between the elderly and young samples is a consequence of the disproportional representation of one or more of the variables found to be associated with minor differences in opinion. For example, perhaps a disparity representation of women, not age in itself, is responsible for the profile differences.

In order to determine what the profiles of the three pairs of national samples would have been if there were no differences in their socioeconomic characteristics, three independent variables found to be associated with minor response variation (sex, income, and length of residence in the community or neighborhood) were submitted to the Rosenberg "test factor standardization" procedure. This procedure involves standardizing across all categories (sex, income, and length of residence) by obtaining a weighted average of the proportions of each sample within the cells of a three-dimensional correlation matrix. In effect, this technique removes the consequences of unequal distribution of selected independent variables.[23]

Table 7-1 convincingly supports the notion that there is a significant difference in the position on national health issues between the old and nonold. This finding, based on three national samples at three points in time, also indicates strong support for those who argue that when an issue that bears directly on the elderly's self-interest is presented to them, they are quite likely to take a nontraditional, innovative—even "radical"—position. Moreover, the data show that socioeconomic factors that are associated with attitude and

Table 7-1. Distribution of young and old samples' ranking on proposals to control health care costs*

	Cohort	
Proposal	**35 years or less (percent)**	**65 years or more (percent)**
1968 Presidential election sample		
Support for:		
Government help get low-cost care	55.0	64.6
No preference	7.2	3.5
Government stay out	37.8	31.9
1970 Congressional election sample		
Prefer:		
Government insurance	23.0	34.3
2	9.8	8.2
3	9.2	8.7
4	13.8	16.4
5	8.6	4.7
6	13.9	4.8
Private insurance	21.7	23.0
1972 Presidential election sample		
Prefer:		
Government insurance	26.2	40.5
2	8.0	4.9
3	9.9	7.4
4	16.1	21.3
5	9.7	3.2
6	4.6	.9
Private insurance	25.6	21.8

*Standardized for sex, income, and length of residence. No response, "don't know" omitted. The data utilized in this table were made available by the Inter-University Consortium for Political Research. Neither the Consortium nor the original collectors of the data bear any responsibility for the analysis or interpretation presented here.

opinion cleavages in the younger group are not nearly as important among the elderly; this lack of variation reinforces Rose's hypothesis about the blurring of previous loyalties and ideological dispositions and the emergence of bloclike solidarity among the elderly.

Detailed study of age-related health policy attitudes

While the SRC data offer support for the hypothesis that those people who are over 65 are both more progressive and more uniform in their attitudes and preferences in health policy, the data are not conclusive. Other national samples have returned contradictory results. For instance, results from a 1971 survey of 11,800 individuals' opinions of various aspects of "the nation's health crisis" (costs, courtesy of treatment, access, overall quality of care) suggest that the elderly are not more willing to support the expansion of Medicare to everyone; nor are they more critical of costs, quality, and so forth.[24]

In order to more clearly establish the relationship between age and position on health policy, we shall turn to the results of the 1973-1974 southern California study discussed in Chapter 2.

The interviewers collected the usual biographic information plus the respondents' choices of providers for a series of different events or problems requiring treatment, the respondents' attitudes toward the cost of health care ("too high, reasonable, a bargain"), and their support or disapproval of several approaches alleged to result in reduced charges for personal health care ("government pay all doctors' bills, reduce wages of hospital employees, reduce medical research, regulate doctors' and hospitals' charges, base charges on ability to pay, and compulsory government health insurance").

The independent effect of ethnicity, sex, education, and occupation (socioeconomic status) is controlled by standardizing the response profiles. The answers of the elderly are compared with those of the 35-and-younger respondents in order to get a standard for determining the significance of age. The 65-and-older sample contains a few more individuals with less than eighth grade education and whose customary occupation was unskilled or semi-skilled. However, given the evolution of indicators of socioeconomic status in the past 2 or 3 decades, I believe the two groups are very symmetrical: that is, the old people who come out with low socioeconomic status because their former occupation and limited educational attainment are being judged by current standards. In their time they would have ranked higher since the overall profile was lower (more farmers, unskilled laborers, less-than-eighth-grade educations). Thus, relative self-perceptions and societal acceptance of the old and younger samples are nearly equal when the inflation of socioeconomic status introduced by post-Depression mass education and the replacement of muscle by technology are controlled out.

Attitudes toward health care costs

Table 7-2 indicates that there is a consistent difference between the willingness of the old and young samples to declare health care costs "too high." Hospital rates come in for near unanimous characterization as being too high; two thirds of both samples agree on the same designation for the cost of medicine and dentists' and physicians' fees. But on three of the four issues, the elderly are more critical.

Table 7-2. Percentage of samples reporting selected health care costs "too high"*

Budget item	Cohort	
	35 years or less	65 years or more
Hospital costs	84.8	85.5
Dentist bills	69.3	76.9
Physician fees	70.1	74.4
Cost of medicine	68.0	77.8
Total number of cases	267	152

*Standardized for SES, sex, and ethnicity.

In order to determine whether personal experiences with the health industry might be related to the respondent's evaluation, the interviewers asked each respondent if a member of the household had visited a physician or dentist or had been a patient in a hospital during the 6 months before the interview. It was found in both samples that there was no difference in likelihood of citing each item too high between those with and without contact.

These responses, however, did reveal that among the low income southern Californians only 19% of the old compared with 34% of the younger sample had had a contact with a hospital; moreover, 14% fewer of the old group reported that a member of the family had visited a physician (92% of the younger, 78% of the 65-and-older). Similarly, 13% fewer of the elderly sample reported contact with a dentist. When the relationship between income and contact was examined, a positive association was found: that is, frequency of contact increases with increased family income. This suggests that for the low income elderly, cost is an effective barrier to utilization. Given the number of chronically ill old people, there must be millions of individuals who are kept from obtaining care and treatment by prices that they cannot afford to pay.

Support for cost-cutting proposals

Table 7-3 demonstrates that more than half of each group approves of the idea of government paying physicians' fees, a proposal that can be seen—and was seen by many individuals—as "socialized medicine." Apparently the bugaboo so aggressively propagandized during the 1940s and 1950s by the American Medical Association and others opposed to government intervention in the medical industry is less a fright term than it was a decade or so ago.

Two other cost-cutting proposals that indicate direct roles for government (regulation and mandatory national health insurance through social security) won approval of a very large majority of elderly persons. This approval indicates that far from being rigidly committed to outdated or traditional ideas and rejecting expansion of governmental control as "conservatives" presumably are, a large percent of older Americans are willing, at least in theory,

Table 7-3. Percentage of samples agreeing with proposal*

Cost-cutting proposal	Cohort	
	35 years or less	65 years or more
Government pay physicians' fees	53.8	60.7
Reduce wages of hospital employees	10.4	26.6
Reduce medical research	14.2	25.0
Regulate medical costs	86.1	79.8
Base charges on ability to pay	59.0	71.1
National health insurance for everyone	81.0	80.0
Total number of cases	267	152

*Standardized for SES, sex, and ethnicity.

Table 7-4. Response profiles of young and old to the reform scale[*]

	Cohort	
Six-item reform scale	**35 years or less (percent)**	**65 years or more (percent)**
1 (general disapproval)	13.0	14.9
2	43.4	11.5
3	27.3	40.9
4 (general approval)	16.3	32.7

[*]Standardized for SES, sex, and ethnicity. Combined scores based on approval or disapproval of six proposals for reducing health care costs (summarized in Table 7-3).

to support expanding public authority. Indeed, the attitudes of the elderly sample confirm the judgment of Campbell that the "retired person is likely to be favorably inclined to proposals of federal underwriting of his medical costs despite the fact that such programs are regarded as rampant communism in some sections of the population."[25]

The degree of reformist inclination in the two samples was measured by the construction of a "reform scale" that combined the individual's scores on the six items summarized in Table 7-3. (An approve scored 2; disapprove scored 1.) Once more, standardization, as indicated by Table 7-4, does not eliminate the divergence between the young and old samples. As was the case with the three national comparisons, the southern California elderly sample presents a more reformist, more unified position than an equivalent younger group.

Health policy: a focus for action

The evidence found in recent survey data is consonant with Rose's interpretation of the effects of poverty and isolation on millions of elderly Americans. At least as far as national health policy is concerned, the elderly apparently offer a coherent, self-conscious response that transcends previous ideological and partisan attitudes, opinions, and loyalties. For instance, in the 1970 survey, party identification was associated more strongly with support for one or the other insurance alternative among the young (gamma = .236) than among the elderly (gamma = .169). Since a high coefficient indicates that as one moves from strong Democrat to strong Republican there is a commensurate trend away from government to favoring private insurance, the figures indicate a greater ideological/partisan consistency among the younger respondents. This is confirmed in the 1972 study. Here the 35-and-younger respondents more often retained an ideological consistency than was the case among the over-65. The associations of liberal/conservative predilection and position on insurance was .249 for the younger sample, .189 for the older, indicating that otherwise conservative elderly supported the "liberal" government plan.

But the reader must quickly be cautioned that this bloclike posture is not found in areas removed from direct economic interest. The elderly react to campus unrest, busing to achieve racial integration, abortion reform, Vietnam involvement, and other issues of the late 1960s and early 1970s much as their younger neighbors. Here fragmentation is seen along traditional socio-economic, partisan, and ideological lines.

Overall, the SRC and southern California data appear to support the contention that the elderly are becoming more group conscious and, because this consciousness has not led to bloc behavior in areas other than health, that there is little likelihood of an elderly political community. But before the latter conclusion is accepted, it should be noted that the past to which Campbell turns is a poor indicator of present and future trends. In the past those who became incapacitated or retired remained in the extended family. Now, however, more individuals survive to retire, and many live outside the family, alone or in geriatric ghettos. Most of these individuals have only government to turn to for assistance. This dependence stimulates self-consciousness; witness the booming growth of interest groups. In 1974, the American Association of Retired Persons claimed 6.5 million members and a growth rate of 60,000 new members each month; the National Council of Senior Citizens, an organization of 3,700 affiliated groups, had grown from 1.7 million in 1972 to 3.5 million in 1974; the National Council on Aging reports 1,400 organizational affiliates. *And,* as was seen in the chapter's opening paragraph, the proportion of the American population that is elderly is annually increasing—particularly in politically important metropolitan regions along both coasts.

Thus, the political significance of the elderly will increase as their proportion of the total population rises, in large part because there will be more individuals in the pool from which membership in special interest groups is drawn.

Size alone, however, is not the key to the rise of geriatric politics. I believe that Rose is essentially correct in picturing the development of a new identity among millions of elderly persons as stemming from other experiences that have befallen them simply because they are old. One consequence of this has a parallel in the Black community. That is, just as the Black population came to realize that to be nonwhite is not to be inferior, the elderly realize that to be no longer young is not cause to be cast aside as obsolete. In other words, the elderly, like other minority communities, are beginning to stake a claim on society and on government to be accepted as full-fledged citizens—citizens who demand to be treated with the same respect, consideration, and dignity accorded the majority. It is this recognition of their self-worth and the rejection of traditional stereotypes of their inferiority that are the key aspects of the rise of Black, Chicano, Asian, native American, and now elderly community spokespersons and organizations.

Health policy is a natural focus for this emerging collective concern among the elderly because their rising morbidity and approaching mortality direct their consciousness to their bodies and to those designated to maintain and repair them. But as more and more elderly people must cope with the inadequacies and exploitation in housing, transportation, employment opportunity and security, nutrition, recreation, and so forth, we can expect their demands for fair and dignified treatment (often meaning drastic reform or massive innovation) increasingly to be taken to government. As American politics becomes more and more a competition among different life-styles for recognition, legitimacy, and public resources, the elderly will become a more clearly discernible community of interests and demands.

Notes

1. Arnold M. Rose, *Older People and Their Social World* (Philadelphia: F. A. Davis Co., 1965), p. 14.
2. Angus Campbell, "Politics Through the Life Cycle," *Gerontologist* 11 (Summer 1971), p. 113.
3. Robert H. Binstock, "Interest-group Liberalism and the Politics of Aging," *Gerontologist* 12 (Aug. 1972), p. 266.
4. Norval D. Glenn and Michael Grimes, "Aging, Voting, and Political Interest," *American Sociological Review* 33 (1968), pp. 553-575; Matilda W. Riley and Ann Foner, *Aging and Society, Vol. I. An Inventory of Research Findings* (New York: Russell Sage Foundation, 1968), p. 368.
5. Campbell, "Politics," p. 117.
6. If we take "major political movement" to include a political force in a major state, then we probably would reject Campbell's assertion. See Frank A. Pinner, Paul Jacobs, and Philip Selznick, *Old Age and Political Behavior: A Case Study* (Berkeley: University of California Press, 1959), a study of the California Institute of Social Welfare, a pressure group composed chiefly of recipients of Old Age Assistance; Jackson K. Putnam, *Old-Age Politics in California: From Richardson to Reagan* (Stanford: Stanford University Press, 1970), which includes a detailed account of the Townsend movement.
7. Binstock, "Interest-group Liberalism," p. 267; Robert C. Atchley, *The Social Forces in Later Life* (Belmont, Calif.: Wadsworth Publishing Co. Inc., 1972), p. 254.
8. John R. Schmidhauser, "The Elderly and Politics," in Adeline M. Hoffman (editor), *The Daily Needs and Interests of Older People* (Springfield, Ill.: Charles C Thomas, Publisher, 1970), p. 74.
9. Kenneth J. Gergen and Kurt W. Back, "Communication in the Interview and the Disengaged Respondent," *Public Opinion Quarterly* 30 (Fall 1966), pp. 385-398.
10. Glenn and Grimes, "Aging," pp. 563-575.
11. Angus Campbell and others, *The American Voter: An Abridgement* (New York: John Wiley, 1964), pp. 263-264.
12. Glenn and Grimes, "Aging," pp. 572-574; Jaber F. Gubrium, "Continuity in Social Support, Political Interest, and Voting in Old Age," *Gerontologist* 12 (Winter 1972), pp. 421-423; G. A. Steiner, *The People Look at Television* (New York: Alfred A. Knopf, Inc., 1963); Bernard R. Berelson, Paul F. Lazarsfeld, and William N. McPhee, *Voting* (Chicago: University of Chicago Press, 1954).
13. Campbell, "Politics," p. 113; "Aging seems to induce greater consistency in partisan political orientations." From John Crittenden, "Aging and Political Participation," *Western Political Quarterly* 16 (June 1963), p. 330. Note that Crittenden attributes *causality* to aging itself; Campbell, on the other hand, argues that aging is *associated* with a stronger partisan self-image. Neither offers the controls necessary to substantiate his assertion.
14. Which, of course, it is not. Schmidhauser, "The Elderly," correctly points out the fallacy of ascribing a blanket philosophical label to partisans of either the Republican or Democratic parties. Also see Seymour Martin Lipset, *Political Man: The Social Bases of Politics* (New York: Anchor Books, 1963), pp. 279-286.
15. See, for example, the work of Neal Cutler, "Generation, Maturation, and Party Affiliation: A Cohort Analysis," *Public Opinion Quarterly* 33 (Winter 1969), pp. 583-590; "Generational Succession as a Source of Foreign Policy Attitudes," *Journal of Peace Research* 1 (1970), pp. 33-48.
16. Schmidhauser, "The Elderly," p. 81.

17. Campbell, "Politics,"; Crittenden, "Aging,"; Abraham Holtzman, "Analysis of Old-Age Politics in the United States," *Journal of Gerontology* 9 (Winter 1954), pp. 56-66; and several contributors to Wilma Donahue and Clark Tibbits (editors), *Politics of Age* (Ann Arbor: University of Michigan, Division of Gerontology, 1962).

18. Herbert H. Marks, "Prevalence of Disease in Older Persons: Nature and Interpretation of Statistics," *Geriatrics* **20** (Aug. 1965), pp. 688-690.

19. U.S. Senate, *Developments in Aging: 1971 and January-March 1972. A Report of the Special Committee on Aging* (Washington, D.C.: U.S. Government Printing Office, May 1972), p. 23.

20. *Ibid.*, p. 24.

21. Blacks, who compose nearly all of the SRC's non-Anglo subsample, support government intervention almost twice as frequently as Anglos: 83% to 48%, respectively. Because there is no variation among Black samples in level of support for intervention (and government-sponsored health insurance), they have been eliminated from the present analysis. The attitudes of Blacks and other minorities regarding national health insurance are examined in the following chapter.

22. Government-sponsored national health insurance has been a recurring issue since 1935. For a review of earlier public attitudes toward it, see Hadley Cantril, *Public Opinion: 1935-1946* (Princeton: Princeton University Press, 1952); Clarence A. Peters (editor), *Free Medical Care* (Bronx, N Y · The H. W. Wilson Co., 1964), p. 38. Between 1943 and 1965 a relatively stable two-thirds majority of Americans favored some government assistance in the financing of personal health services. From Theodore R. Marmor, *The Politics of Medicare* (Chicago: Aldine Publishing Co., 1973), p. 3.

23. Morris Rosenberg, "Test Factor Standardization as a Method of Interpretation," *Social Forces* **41** (Oct. 1962), pp. 53-61; also see Hubert M. Blalock, Jr., *Social Statistics*, ed. 2, (New York: McGraw-Hill Book Co., 1972), pp. 310-311.

24. Ronald Andersen, Joanna Kravits, and Odin W. Anderson, "The Public's View of the Crisis in Medical Care: An Impetus for Changing Delivery Systems?" *Economics and Business Bulletin* **24** (Fall 1971), pp. 44-52.

25. Campbell, "Politics," p. 117.

CHAPTER 8

The public's opinion of national health insurance

In 1965 the federal government took its first major step in the regulation and control of health care costs by enacting Medicare. But Medicare ushered in an unprecedented rise in health care costs; in the following decade, real health costs rose by 12% to 20% per year. Rising costs and other alleged shortcomings have stimulated an outpouring of books, editorials, and condemnations of the health industry. In 1969 the President of the United States officially proclaimed a "crisis in American medicine."

A number of opinion leaders have presented approaches to controlling costs. During the 1972 presidential campaign, both major candidates discussed curtailing the rising cost of health services; between Nixon's second inaugural and his resignation, a number of proposals for establishing a national health insurance were submitted to Congress—including one from the American Medical Association. I believe it may reasonably be inferred that the political and medical elites are generally concerned about rising costs and the political and economic fallout from the upward spiral. But what has been the response of the public? More specifically, is there broad-based concern about health costs, and is there any appreciable support for one or another of the profered cost-control programs?

In this chapter the responses of the American population to various questions concerning health care costs will be reviewed. The following analysis reveals that responses depend heavily on how the proposal is stated and to whom it is presented and that there is widespread concern about costs but not uncritical support for any proposal that allegedly would control or reduce personal health care costs. The question of support for cost control will be treated as an evolving issue and analyzed longitudinally by following the changing pattern of public opinion over the period 1968 to 1974.

Should government help?

As part of its 1968 study of partisan preference and participation in the 1968 presidential election, the Survey Research Center (SRC) of the University of Michigan asked its national sample of 1,957 voters whether they supported the notion of the federal government "helping" people obtain low cost physician and hospital care. This vague question, unrelated to an actual partisan

Some of the data used in this chapter were made available by the Inter-University Consortium for Political Research. Neither the Consortium nor the original collectors bear any responsibility for the analysis or interpretations presented here.

position at the time and reflecting little issue formulation beyond general concern about costs, drew the approval of 52% of the sample.

While this sample contained a cross section of the American population, it is noteworthy that support for government intervention did not vary significantly according to socioeconomic characteristics. Being high or low income, urban or rural dwelling, or from a large or small family made little difference in the frequency of approval. A list of ten independent variables (including sex, age, income, religion, education, and place of residence) was run through a regression procedure in order to locate any possible hidden associations. After the effects of the variables were separated, it was discovered that only education was even moderately related to direction of preference: the higher the level of education the more likely the "government-should-stay-out" response ($r = .177$). And perhaps of greatest interest to students of public opinion, *all* of the independent variables in the regression equation accounted for only 4.5% of the response variation. (Being over 65 years, as we saw in the preceding chapter, but not age alone, is of course associated with a particular response profile.) Variables not collected, such as level of satisfaction with one's previous medical care or percent of income going to health care costs, may be the key elements in determining one's position on the 1968 question.

One variable did, however, separate the 1968 sample: race. While 48% of the Anglos approved of government intervention, the figure leaped to 83% in the Black subsample. Fortunately the sample contained enough Blacks ($n = 149$) to show if race itself was independent (Do all Blacks regardless of socioeconomic characteristics support intervention?).

It appears that race was independent because there was no significant variation in the Black sample in support for government help by income, education, age, or any of the other demographic variables used. Because demographic variables accounted for practically none of the difference within the Black sample, it can be inferred that the difference in level of support between the Black and Anglo samples is not attributable to unequal representation of these factors in the two samples. The fact that the Black sample contains more low income, less-educated respondents would be significant in explaining the intersample difference only if Blacks of different characteristics responded differently to the question. But this was not the case; therefore, an explanation of the dramatically higher level of Black support for government intervention must be sought elsewhere.

Health costs are too high

The racial difference found in the 1968 sample was repeated in a southern California study of Anglos and Chicanos. In 1969, 484 low and middle income respondents were asked their opinion of the costliness of several personal health care items and whether or not they supported a number of cost-cutting schemes.[1] In response to direct questioning, over 50% of all respondents characterized the cost of physicians' fees, dentists' bills, and hospital charges as "too high." There was little significant difference in characterizing costs between the Anglo and Chicano samples.

But in level of approval of cost-cutting proposals there was a major variation

Table 8-1. Combined affirmative responses to five cost-reduction proposals with selected socioeconomic variables controlled (1969) (in percent)

	Anglo	Chicano
Total family income		
Less than $4,000	37	44
$4,000 to $5,999	36	44
$6,000 to $7,999	35	32
$8,000 to $9,999	29	40
$10,000 to $12,000	30	42
More than $12,000	24	40
Number of children 17 years of age and younger		
None	31	29
One	27	50
Two	27	36
Three	28	36
Four	37	47
Five or more	30	44
Educational attainment		
Eighth grade or less	37	38
Ninth to twelfth grade	31	38
High school diploma	30	41
College	28	36

Adapted from Jerry L. Weaver, "Health Care Costs as a Political Issue: Comparative Responses of Chicanos and Anglos," *Social Science Quarterly* 53 (March 1973), p. 850.

between the two ethnic groups. As Table 8-1 reveals, once family size, income, and education were controlled for, the Chicano sample was more willing than the Anglo to support all forms of cost cutting—particularly government intervention in the forms of direct payment of physicians' fees and regulation of medical costs.[2]

1972: The issue is insurance

By the 1972 presidential campaign, partisan alternatives to protection from health care costs had appeared in Congress. The Republican leadership and its conservative congressional allies talked about "voluntarism" and strengthening the traditional physician/patient relationship. Programatically, this meant noncompulsory individual health insurance financed by employers and employees, with the government paying private carriers the premiums for indigent and elderly people. Commercial insurance companies would provide coverage. Most Democrats, leaders of organized labor, and those interested in rationalizing health insurance coverage argued for a comprehensive, compulsory plan under which the government would administer a Social Security–type program.

One half of the SRCs 1972 national sample (n = 1372) was asked: "There is much concern about the rapid rise in medical and hospital costs. Some feel there should be a government insurance plan which would cover all medical and hospital expenses. Others feel that medical expenses should be paid by individuals, and through private insurance like Blue Cross. Where would you place yourself on this scale, or haven't you thought much about

Table 8-2. Support for national health insurance (1972) by ethnic group

Insurance plan preference scale	Anglo	Black
1 (government)	28.0%	54.9%
2	6.8	9.7
3	7.7	7.1
4	15.2	7.1
5	7.1	.9
6	6.5	.9
7 (private)	28.7	19.5
Total number of cases	988	113

this?" Evidently, either the question or the issue was too complex for many individuals, because 19% of those asked were unable to respond or said that they had not thought about national health insurance (NHI).

While there was not variation in the percent of no-opinion responses between the Anglo and Black samples, there was a decided difference between them in preference for government insurance. Table 8-2 shows that the Black sample twice as often selected the government option (55% versus 28% of the Anglo sample). In addition, the Black sample was more polarized than the Anglo: only half the percent of Blacks selected the middle (undecided) position on the public/private continuum.

Aside from the polarity associated with race, no other demographic variable was related to a significant response variation. It is noteworthy that while rising health care costs bear especially hard on the under-$8,000 respondents, their preference profile parallelled their middle and upper income cousins. Apparently support for public or private insurance was independent of income.

Within the Anglo sample, only religion was even moderately associated with insurance preference ($r = -.155$). That is, support for private insurance was higher among Presbyterians, Lutherans, and Methodists, while the government option found greater support from neofundamentalist and nontraditional Christians, Catholics, and Jews.

Among Blacks, there was rather substantial variation in support for public insurance according to increase in age ($r = -.231$) and family size ($r = -.239$) and to status of religious affiliation ($r = -.150$). And the closer the respondent lived to the central core of a large city, the more likely the selection of the public alternative ($r = .144$).[3] These figures suggest that the strongest support for government health insurance in the Black community was found among ghetto dwellers who presumably had low per capita incomes. These are the families who often turn for health care to emergency rooms, outpatient clinics, and public hospitals. Perhaps they see NHI as offering the wherewithal to "better" (that is, fee-for-service) health care.

With partisan position on NHI fairly well established by 1972, it seems reasonable to assume that those who identified themselves as strong Democrats would support the government option (comparable to the Kennedy-Griffiths bill) and those who selected the strong Republican label would support the private approach (similar to the Nixon administration's proposal). But such was hardly the case. Among Anglos who positioned themselves on a continuum of strong Democrat to strong Republican, choice of insurance plan correlated modestly (r = .172); among Blacks, the relationship between insurance and party identification was even weaker (r = −.010). (A high positive score would mean that strong Republicans selected the private, strong Democrats the government, option.)

Let us turn to another indicator of the association between political identity and issue position: the relationship between self-identified ideological persuasion and the insurance proposal. Here the correlations for both racial samples were stronger and in the predicted direction: self-professed liberals selected the government option while conservatives selected the private (the Anglo sample, r = .253; the Black, r = .321). Yet these figures hardly suggest ideological cleavages in the electorate.

When the coefficients of party and ideological identifications are considered together, it is clear that preference for NHI alternatives and partisan/philosophical persuasion was largely independent. Why? Perhaps the advocates of either one or the other approach to NHI failed to develop a clear-cut understanding of and identification with their proposal in the minds of their customary constituencies. Alternatively, the partisan and ideological constituencies had not made up their minds or had already selected an alternative not in keeping with that of their liberal or Republican national leadership. Or information simply was not adequate to allow many citizens to make up their minds.

Ethnicity as an independent factor

We have seen in the southern California and national data evidence that attitudes toward government intervention in the area of health care costs vary with ethnicity: Anglo, Black, and Chicano samples manifested different levels of approval/disapproval for regulation, compulsory insurance, direct payment of physicians' fees, and so forth. But there remains a level of uncertainty about the significance of ethnicity. In the three preceding surveys, the number on non-Anglos was small and very thinly spread over demographic and socioeconomic categories. The argument about the independent effect of ethnicity would be more convincing if intersample inequalities in the representation of other variables could be controlled for.

Table 8-3 presents the responses of southern Californians interviewed in 1973-1974 to cost-cutting proposals. For comparative purposes, the profiles of the 1969 Anglo and Chicano samples are included. The chronological comparison revealed that support for direct payment of physicians' fees had increased appreciably: two and a half times more Anglos supported the proposal in 1973-1974 than in 1969.

Few in any ethnic group supported cutting medical research or reducing wages of hospital employees, and there was widespread approval of regulating medical costs. But on direct government payment, basing charges on ability

Table 8-3. Effect of ethnicity on responses to proposals to reduce costs (1973-1974)

Support for cost reduction proposals	Percent of group agreeing					
	Anglo	Black	Japanese	Pilipino	Anglo (1969)	Chicano (1969)
Government pay physicians' fees	41.3	55.0	59.3	62.9	11.7	29.9
Reduce wages of hospital employees	14.4	3.7	16.4	12.4	3.8	15.6
Reduce medical research	15.3	14.2	15.7	21.5	5.4	18.1
Regulate medical costs	81.2	85.8	85.7	81.7	74.6	91.4
Base charges on recipient's ability to pay	47.6	58.3	67.1	65.1	56.0	58.0
Government health insurance for everyone	67.8	75.0	77.1	79.6	(na)	(na)
Total number of cases	208	120	141	189	381	75

to pay, and government health insurance, non-Anglos consistently gave greater approval.

Aside from the controls incorporated in the survey design, selected demographic variables were statistically equalized in order to isolate ethnicity. This was done by submitting the intersample response variations to questions about costliness and support for cost-cutting proposals to the "test factor standardization" procedure.

The samples were standardized according to age, sex, education, income, occupation, religion, length of residence in present dwelling, family size, and socioeconomic status. Because of space considerations, the consequence of the combined standardizing of three variables previously identified in the analysis as associated with distinctive attitudes—sex, age, and socioeconomic status—will be examined. A cumulative "costliness scale" was created from the four costliness items (physicians' fees, dentists' bills, hospital charges, and the cost of medicine). Responses were scored ("a bargain" = 1, "reasonable" = 2, "too high" = 3). The reform scale discussed in the preceding chapter is used here to ascertain ethnic variations in support for change. In Table 8-4 the two scales are condensed to reflect the basic distribution of the four groups. After standardizing for SES, sex, and age, we find that there is a higher frequency of general approval of reform among non-Anglos and that the non-Anglo samples are more dissatisfied with overall health care costs.

Why is ethnicity such a powerful independent factor? It may be that to be a non-Anglo in the United States is to harbor a pervasive skepticism about or even alienation from the institutions of the dominant society. Thus, when offered opportunities to support reforms of these institutions, non-Anglos are more willing to support reforms because preserving the status quo is less valuable to many minorities. Being less psychologically satisfied with their

Table 8-4. Responses to reform and costliness scales*

	Anglo (percent)	Black (percent)	Japanese (percent)	Pilipino (percent)
Six-item reform scale				
1 (general disapproval)	18.0	10.8	9.4	8.1
2	23.8	26.6	22.5	21.6
3	32.9	26.7	24.6	26.6
4 (general approval)	25.3	36.0	43.5	43.7
Four-item costliness scale				
1 (a bargain)	9.3	13.7	16.3	16.9
2	17.7	24.0	14.8	17.3
3	27.0	12.9	24.2	17.8
4 (too high)	45.9	49.4	44.7	48.0

*Standardized for sex, age, and SES.

treatment at the hands of the dominant society's institutions makes accepting change easier or more desirable.

Alternatively, it may be that regardless of their own income or social status, members of minority communities are aware of the economic burden that health care costs impose on other members of their community. This greater sense of communal identity, reinforced by contacts with family members and friends of varying circumstances, may foster a set of cooperative humanitarian values. Supporting proposals, even those that have little direct payoff to oneself but may help less fortunate "brothers and sisters," would be a reflection of such a value system.

Male/female attitudes

In Chapter 6 the fact that women have a range of particular health care needs and problems was shown; here the impact of gender difference on attitudes toward the health industry will be examined. The saliency for women of health and health care allows us to test the hypothesis that women as a group typically manifest what is characterized as more conservative, less innovative responses to social issues.[4] The response profiles of men and women from the 1973-1974 southern California study have been compared with the personal health care budget items and with the proposals for reducing costs. The effects of independent variables that have already been found to be significant were isolated by standardizing the two profiles by age, SES, and ethnicity. Table 8-5 shows the results.

There is no difference in the frequency with which men and women characterized items as too high or expressed approval of the cost reduction proposals. Contrary to the hypothesized direction of female attitudes, women are no more or less conservative than men. While it may be that health is of such a major concern to women that they set aside their normal conservatism, it is more likely that when the standardization technique is introduced, spurious associations that have previously remained and have given rise to the "female conservatism" notion are removed. That is, when samples of men and women

Table 8-5. Comparison of male/female responses to health care costs and proposals to reduce costs*

	Percent of group agreeing	
	Male	**Female**
Health care costs too high		
Hospital costs	89.7	87.8
Dentist bills	72.1	77.0
Physician fees	69.7	70.5
Cost of medicine	76.0	71.3
Support for cost reduction proposals		
Government pay physicians' fees	59.3	53.0
Reduce wages of hospital employees	14.2	14.1
Reduce medical research	16.5	17.0
Regulate medical costs	86.6	86.0
Base charges on recipient's ability to pay	62.1	61.2
Government health insurance for everyone	82.8	78.9
Total number of cases	268	443

*Standardized for age, SES, and ethnicity.

are equally constituted of age, SES, and ethnic characteristics, the bases of divergence are eliminated. Even controlling for a single variable, such as age, might not offset the combined effects of other factors. Here, however, *four* major independent variables were equalized simultaneously (SES is a combination of occupation plus education), and there were no significant male/female differences to report.

Is support for NHI crystalizing?

Before leaving the 1973-1974 survey data, we should note that this sample was presented basically the same question about national health insurance as the one used in 1972. The southern Californians were asked: "Do you approve or disapprove of a national health insurance for everyone paid for through withholding tax (like Social Security) for the employed and by the federal government for the unemployed?" Only 7% of the overall sample was unable or unwilling to respond. Does this indicate a firming of support and a clarification of the issues surrounding national health insurance since the 1972 survey?

I think not; rather, it suggests the ability of individuals to comprehend fundamental social issues and to form a response when they are offered structured alternatives and when interviewers are willing to take some time to explain the question while not pressing the respondents or creating an impression of impatience. The question in the national survey is set among several hundred items in an instrument requiring more than an hour to administer. When the reliability and validity of the 1972 and 1973-1974 responses are estimated, the possibility of considerable respondent fatigue in the former case should not be minimized.

Citizen impact on national health policy

The survey data summarized above indicate that there is a widespread belief that the costs of personal health care are exhorbitant. The 1968 SRC poll, which revealed that a majority of the electorate favor government helping people get health care at low costs, points to a central feature of the public's concern: *something* should be done but there is not clear-cut preference. Currently there is no widespread acceptance of "radical," nontraditional approaches to cost cutting. This is evident in the limited, though growing, support for direct payment of physicians' fees, a proposal that may be seen as tantamount to supporting governmental control of the health industry. On the other hand, "regulation" is widely accepted, perhaps because the concept is familiar to most Americans. But pressure for action seems to be mounting: comparison of essentially similar samples of southern Californians interviewed in 1969 and 1973-1974 reveals that criticism of prices is growing and support for direct intervention to control charges is now much more extensive.

Although the 1972 SRC results reveal little support for any form of national health insurance, another interpretation of these data, one that I believe is more insightful, is that there has been little crystalization of the issues and implications of the various insurance proposals. Put somewhat differently, the 1972 survey reveals that health insurance is an issue about which few individuals, other than political and health elites and what Almond[5] calls the "attentive public," are informed. Why are so few Americans able to articulate a programmatic preference?

Rainwater[6] suggests that social problems progress through stages of ever broadening public awareness: one or a few *detached scholars* or a "voice in the wilderness," such as Rachel Carson's book, *Silent Spring* calling our attention to the environmental threat posed by pesticides, initiate concern. Next, *pressure groups* begin to assert the existence of the problem against what they see as an indifferent or resistant society. These pressure groups advance their solutions and recommend them to the public. Rainwater says that the most significant stage is *pervasive elite concern.* Here the issue comes to be defined as important by individuals who see themselves as opinion leaders, as "knowledgeable persons." For example, civil rights in America was more the province of pressure groups until the early 1960s, when it was transformed by the nation's opinion leaders into an issue that could no longer be ignored by any individual who wished to claim to be knowledgeable, judicious, and constructive minded. More recently, "Watergate" evolved in much the same manner. Now, elite concern does not mean that no racists exist or that no American continues to see nothing criminal in Nixon's handling of Watergate; quite the contrary is the case. But elite concern paves the way for the broadest level of involvement: *societywide concern.* Here the average person is talking about an issue and has rather definite opinions about it—opinions, however, that may bear little resemblance to the elite's views.

If we take this evolution of concern about social problems as fairly indicative of how the real world works, we may conclude that health care costs have become a subject of societywide concern; yet the various alternatives for policy action to remedy the situation remain the concern of pressure groups and their allies among the elite. The relevant pressure groups are organized medicine, the insurance industry, organized labor—especially the United Automobile Workers—and associations of the elderly.[7] Agents of these organized interests grab headlines, intellectuals ruminate proposals and trends, and individuals wishing to confirm their standing among "the informed" argue about plans, priorities, and personalities. But the general public remains largely uninformed, passive spectators. Why?

An adequate explanation of the public's role requires far fuller treatment than that just given. But studies of other cases of health policy making may point to the beginning of an explanation. For example, Strickland suggests that the handful of physicians and scientists, federal bureaucrats, interest group representatives, and legislators who shape cancer research policy act to restrict public involvement. Issues are couched in complex scientific jargon. Government decision makers, who lack technical expertise and seemingly are unaware of independent advisers, rely on the testimony of representatives of competing established industrial and professional interest groups. Compromising and bargaining for political advantage dictate that only brief *pro forma* public hearings are held. Indeed, legislators clearly resent attempts to involve the general public in the decision process. Strickland recounts the example of an attempt by the American Cancer Society to inform the public about key policy changes being contemplated by Congress that led to an explicit threat by the public's representatives to withdraw the Society's tax-exempt status as a result of its educational efforts. "If the advertisement created greater awareness of the issue among the people, it created sharp indignation among the members of the House [Health] subcommittee."[8]

One need not assume a massive conspiracy to subvert democracy by the ruling elite and its lackeys among the governing class to accept the aforementioned explanation of the public's ignorance or lack of concern about specific policy alternatives. It is convenient and profitable for the medical/industrial complex and its agents to restrict and control the decision-making process. After all, only losers are eager to increase the number of players. Winners are quite content with the smallest successful coalition; losers risk nothing by being willing to gamble smaller shares from potential victories for larger individual shares of defeat. And there are few incentives for voluntarily sharing one's access to the game with nonplayers since there may be secrets revealed in the decision arena better kept among the initiated. Barring new and sustained efforts at educating the public, little likelihood exists for genuine citizen participation in charting the course for national health policy. Pressures on pension plans, protection of professional privilege, and pragmatic politics will continue to be the dominant forces in the politics of health.

Notes

1. Jerry L. Weaver, "Reducing Health Care Costs: Responses of a Multiethnic Population," *Inquiry* **9** (Dec. 1972), pp. 20-27.

2. Jerry L. Weaver, "Health Care Costs as a Political Issue: Comparative Responses of Chicanos and Anglos," *Social Science Quarterly* 53 (March 1973), pp. 846-854.

3. The elderly Black, among all minority groups, may have the most complex yet little understood or recognized health care problems. Compare with Jacquelyn J. Jackson, "NCBA, Black Aged and Politics," *Annals of the American Academy of Political and Social Science* 415 (Sept. 1974), pp. 138-159.

4. Seymour Martin Lipset, *Political Man: The Social Bases of Politics* (New York: Anchor Books, 1963), p.242 and *passim.*

5. Gabriel Almond, *The American People and Foreign Policy* (New York: Praeger Publishers, Inc., 1960).

6. Lee Rainwater (editor), *Social Problems: Inequality and Justice* (Chicago: Aldine Publishing Co., 1974), pp. 8-9.

7. On national health insurance, see Odin W. Anderson, "The Politics of Universal Health Insurance in the United States: An Interpretation," *International Journal of Health Services* 2 (1972), pp. 577-582; Roger M. Battistella, "National Health Insurance: An Examination of Leading Proposals in the Light of Contemporary Policy Issues," *Inquiry* 8 (June 1971), pp. 20-34; Roger M. Battistella, "Rationalization of Health Services: Political and Social Assumptions," *International Journal of Health Services* 2 (1972), pp. 331-348; Lee Goldman, "Doctors' Attitudes Toward National Health Insurance," *Medical Care* 12 (May 1974), pp. 413-423; Godfrey Hodgson, "The Politics of American Health Care," *The Atlantic* 232 (Oct. 1973), pp. 45-61; Richard Margalis, "America's Medical Crisis and the Politics of Health Reform," *New Leader* (15 April 1974), pp. 3-35; Nancy Milio, "Dimensions of Consumer Participation and National Health Legislation," *American Journal of Public Health* 64 (April 1974), pp. 357-363; Vicente Navarro, "National Health Insurance and the Strategy for Change," *Milbank Memorial Fund Quarterly* (Spring 1973), pp. 223-251; Joseph Newhouse and others, "Policy Options and the Impact of N.H.I.," *New England Journal of Medicine* 290 (13 June 1974), pp. 1345-1359; K. L. White and J. H. Murnaghan, "Health Care Policy Formulation: Analysis, Information and Research," *International Journal of Health Services* 3 (1973), pp. 82-90.

8. Stephen P. Strickland, *Politics, Science, and Dread Disease* (Cambridge: Harvard University Press, 1972), p. 283.

CHAPTER 9

Health policy making

In the following analysis of health policy formulation, the word power is used to describe the potential that one party has to control another. This potential to constrain the alternatives of another derives from one's possession of or ability to manipulate commodities that are desired by others. These commodities, here called resources, are valued because they are scarce and may be converted to other desired goals. When party "A" recognizes that "B" values something and is willing to exchange something that A desires (such as a government contract for a campaign contribution, or a neighborhood park in return for electoral support), then party A may be said to have power relative to party B. Thus, in order to establish a power relationship, one must possess one or more resources *and* be able to find a trading partner willing to make an exchange.[1]

By conceptualizing power relations as voluntary, conscious exchanges of resources, we bring into focus not only the necessity of possessing resources but also the central role of would-be trading partners. For students of public policy, viewed from the perspective of social equity and justice, a central trading partner is the federal government.

Government is in the business of making allocations—grants, programs, facilities, jobs, the absence of force and coercion at the hands of law enforcement agencies—even increased community status through the appointment of individuals to prestigious offices (the Supreme Court or the President's cabinet, for example). These resources cannot be obtained *if* government refuses or fails to see a community's request as legitimate. The separate disadvantaged communities simply lack the resources to compel a recalcitrant agency or doubtful decision maker to accept the community's or organization's definition of the problem and solutions. We see this clearly in the reaction of the Nixon administration to the rebellions of America's ghettos: rather than improving existing programs and policies and creating new ones in line with the demands of the ghetto dwellers, the Nixon administration reduced and eliminated programs, especially those involving allocations of income in kind (such as housing, health, education, and social service subsidies, and federally supported programs).

This does not mean that efforts at building community-based political organizations, correcting racist images and negative characterizations of minorities, and developing a comprehensive understanding of the disadvantaged's heritage and reality through ethnic studies, consciousness-raising rap groups, and other educational efforts should be abandoned or written off as of little or no practical value—just the opposite. These efforts are investments that will yield significant new political resources in the years to come. Already such activities have won important reforms such as the Civil Rights Commission's recent call for special attention to the educational needs of the bilingual, bicultural child, the Census Bureau's drastic upward reestimation of the size of the Chicano population in the United States, and the election of Asians, Blacks, Chicanos, and women to local, state, and federal offices. But these successes must be weighed against the magnitude of the minorities' disadvantages.

To illustrate the nature of the obstacles that the disadvantaged minorities face in gaining meaningful exchanges from government in obtaining health care services, I shall use as a case study the health situation of millions of low income Chicanos. I shall focus on the behavior of government policy makers in formulating responses to the Chicanos' health problems, then ask why the policy makers have reacted as they have. In answering the "why" question, my central focus will be the decision rules or *official doctrine* that the federal government has employed over the past decade or two in dealing with the persistent problems of poverty, one of which is the absence of health care services. My aim is to reveal that gaining government's resources in the form of health and other poverty programs is largely a problem of changing the prevailing definitions of the causes and consequences of poverty. Changing official doctrine is as important to reform as mobilizing the community for electoral politics.

Health in the barrio

The qualitative and quantitative reports of the health care provided Chicanos reveal a picture of serious inadequacies. In many areas of high Chicano concentration, there are few providers and facilities; those that are available are either drastically overloaded or inferior (or both). Many health care personnel are either ignorant of the preferences, medical problems, and interpersonal style of hundreds of thousands of Chicanos or consciously choose to disregard the social and psychological needs and expectations of their Chicano patients. As a result of unavailability, inhuman and disrespectful treatment, and lack of information about what is available to them, millions of Chicanos are inadequately served by physicians, public clinics, hospitals, and other components of the health care delivery system.

The comparative morbidity and mortality statistics of the Chicano community illustrate the failure of the health system. Chicanos are twice as likely as Anglos to die of the results of accidents, influenza, or pneumonia. Infant mortality is 33% higher among Chicanos. Chicanos die younger than Anglos (56.7 years compared with 67.5 years), a figure that in part reflects the higher rate of death among Chicano school-age children. Chicanos have a lower average physician-visitation rate per person per year (2.3) than Blacks (3.7) or Anglos (5.6). And health care costs are a greater burden on the Chicano community (and thus a deterrent to both early diagnosis and continued treatment) because Chicanos are more likely not to hold an insurance policy: the percent of a sample of Chicano, Black, and Anglo populations reported to be insured is 39.7, 45.8, and 58.1, respectively.[2]

Although these data are drawn from different studies, basically they reflect the conditions of the lower economic strata of the Chicano community. Indeed, there is some evidence that the health conditions and behavior of middle- and upper-class Chicanos are comparable with those of their Anglo peers.[3]

When the health care problems of lower-class Chicanos are considered, it is important to determine how poverty and ethnicity are interrelated. That is, it might be that the grim mortality and morbidity profiles reported reflect the disproportionate percent of barrio residents living in poverty. If this is the case, there is little or no reason to treat the Chicano's health care problems differently from those of other low income groups. But if being Chicano, in addition to being poor, is responsible for some or much of the barrio's poor health, then programs designed to meet the needs of poor Anglos, Blacks, and other low income groups will not, unless they are directed to the unique dimensions of the Chicano situation, greatly improve the Chicano's health profile.

While it has not been established conclusively that ethnicity is independently related to the Chicano's problems, there is a good deal of evidence and some powerful implications that it is. Some support for this conclusion is found in the work of anthropologists and sociologists who have examined Chicano health care attitudes and behavior. As mentioned in Chapter 4, their findings suggest that some Chicanos have ethnocentric dietary and curative practices, beliefs in the magical origins and treatment of disease, and negative, even hostile, attitudes toward scientific providers; all these traits combine to form a "Chicano health care subculture" that blocks its adherents from both preventive and remedial services while contributing to the neglect of conditions that later incapacitate or even kill them. According to its investigators, this Chicano subculture is unique and sets its members apart.[4]

It cannot be denied that some Chicanos, especially those in isolated rural areas and recent arrivals from rural Mexico, believe in the magical origins (and cures) of illness, that they prefer folk healers to scientific providers, and that they eat foods not conducive to optimal resistance to disease. Consequently, in addition to being poor, these Chicanos have very particular health problems and needs stemming from their beliefs and life-style.

However, these individuals are by no means the majority of the disadvantaged among the Chicano population. There are many thousands of urban-dwelling, third- and fourth-generation Chicanos who are poor, who do not hold the folk health subculture, and yet have severe problems. One indicator of this much larger population is the preference of Spanish over English in informal conversation. Such individuals may be able to communicate with Anglos, but they are not confrontable or fluent in English. Consequently, some Chicanos are embarrassed when confronting the formality and jargon of modern medical care facilities. They do not want to be made to appear ridiculous in their inadequate English; they may be unable to understand the directions given them or to explain their symptoms accurately, yet pride or fear or lack of comprehension inhibits the exchange of medically relevant information.

In the broader social context, the marginally acculturated Chicanos tend also to be marginally assimilated in the economic system. Put more directly, lower-class Chicanos are poor because they are exploited. Working as agricultural laborers, garment assemblers in sweatshop conditions, domestics, menial service workers, or as hourly laborers, marginal Chicanos are exposed to disproportionately high risks of industrial accidents and diseases (such as pesticide poisoning or chronic backache from stoop labor in the fields), communicable diseases, and respiratory tract infections. Most are without union protection, are often forced to change jobs and even residence in search of work, and are paid at a subsistence level or below. These factors in turn deny them access to private health insurance plans, public services (because they cannot establish residence or citizenship requirements), assure interrupted care for serious or chronic conditions, and work against their being able to gain information about the types and locations of local health care services. So the circle is endlessly redrawn: Poor Chicanos remain unhealthy because they are exploited, exploited because they are poor, poor because they are economically unassimilated, unassimilated because they are exploited . . .

From the combination of language, cultural, economic, and legal barriers comes a set of circumstances that magnifies the inherent problems of poverty and isolation for lower-class Chicanos.

Determinants of government's role

Improving the health of poor Chicanos and other low income populations requires comprehensive action in many areas: education, employment, housing, nutrition, and public transportation as well as health facility construction and expansion, increase of health and allied health care personnel, comprehensive health insurance, regulation of the pharmaceutical industry, and so forth. The federal government has acted in all of these areas and billions of dollars and other resources have been expended. Yet, from what we have seen in the preceding analyses, critical problems remain largely unaffected by governmental efforts. Several aspects of the policy-making process are related to this shortfall.

Established interests

In general terms, those who attempt to broaden government's role to provide high quality health care have been blocked by the power of status quo forces. For example, the American Medical Association successfully prevented the passage of comprehensive government-sponsored health insurance from 1935 until 1965. Although a modest first step was taken with the enactment of Medicare and the AMA is no longer the veto group it was, it and other vested interests such as the health insurance companies have succeeded in vitiating measures designed to remove the financial burdens of health care through comprehensive compulsory coverage.

Again, at the general level, the elites who rule America have been unconcerned about the health of the poor. Monies have gone into highways, education, and such social welfare programs as aid to remedial education and food stamps—that is, programs that provide huge payoffs to established interests (the education lobby, or the farm block) while generating jobs for middle-class college graduates. Rather than reforming existing social and economic institutions, these programs have strengthened them. The fears of the established health interests that compulsory insurance, neighborhood clinics, paramedical providers, and other reforms would disrupt the prevailing institutions have been sufficient to discourage major government allocations. The Nixon administration, for instance, talked much about the "health care crisis" in the United States but did nothing to reform the institutions that have created the so-called crisis. Moreover, the Nixon administration dismantled the decentralized consumer-sensitive neighborhood health center program while allocating millions of dollars for the development of prepaid health maintenance organizations that have an economic incentive to reduce treatment and that see as many patients as possible—features that have been severely criticized by those attempting to gain better care for the low income population.

Advocates for the disadvantaged

Much of the power of the established health policy elites and the resultant timidity of politicians and bureaucrats stem from the absence of what Galbraith calls "countervailing power."[5] That is, there are no organizations well endowed with resources advancing the interests and needs of the disadvantaged. In the case of the Chicano community, there are neither spokespersons nor organizations that are able to reinforce their demands with expenditures of resources relevant to the decision makers.

At a somewhat different level of abstraction, there is no location in the decision-making or policy-implementing bureaucracies to focus the needs and demands of Chicano and other minority communities; thus the needs of these populations go unrecognized. For instance, there is nothing in Washington, D.C., that serves the Chicano, Black, or Asian populations as the Veterans Administration, Department of Labor, or even Bureau of Indian Affairs do in acting as foci and lobbies for their particular constituents. (These agencies certainly do not return to their constituents anything like an optimal output of government resources. And they are not models for the organization and articulation of demands. But laborers, veterans, and native Americans would be even less well treated if they did not have organized brokers and spokespersons at the seat of government.)

The lack of well-endowed advocates representing the demands of minority communities must be seen as responsible for much of the disadvantage suffered by millions. But concentration on elites, interest groups, and administrative practices and procedures does not provide a comprehensive picture of the policy-making process. After all is said about these structural features, the fact remains that choices from among alternative claims for action are made by human beings. Presidents, cabinet secretaries, middle-range bureaucrats, congresspersons, and welfare caseworkers are all part of the process, and their decisions contribute to the availability and quality of health care.

Official doctrine

Demands for new programs and changes in existing ones are constantly being made. For example, the neighborhood health center program was supported by many local community boards and consumer organizations. Why did the decision makers not see fit to expand the program in line with the requests of many local groups of consumers? This question suggests that decision makers have a range of choice, of discretion, so that they are not straight-jacketed by omnipotent agents of the vested interests. I take this as given and make the point only because of the prevalence of conspiracy theories that hold that all official acts are controlled by the "establishment," "the system," or "the military (medical)–industrial complex."[6] In rejecting this contemporary version of the "devil" theory, we need not conclude that decision makers have free will; in fact just the opposite is true. Decision makers are drastically circumscribed in the range of alternatives they consider and even further in the types of demands they satisfy. One of the sets of forces that constrains the decision maker is found in the structural features of the political system; but another, and the one I am going to discuss here, arises from the definitions, assumptions, and normative preferences that constitute official doctrine.

Role of official doctrine

Official doctrine is the set of rules that guide the decision maker in making allocations. These rules define the nature of the problem, what the government considers the legitimate scope of its action, and sets forth the relative value of resources. Official doctrine acts for the decision maker as the paradigm of the scientists, the root metaphor of the philosopher, or the dogma of the theologian—it helps the decision maker create a priority list from demands to be dealt with, to place a request in the overall scheme of things, and to evaluate the merits of alternative courses of action. Doctrine reveals not only what is sought, but how it is to be achieved.

In some societies, doctrine is comprehensively developed and intensively acclaimed—the condition implied by the term "indoctrinated." In the United States, the recent governments have developed little partisan doctrine. The guidelines for solving health care and other social problems of the poor have changed through the Kennedy, Johnson, Nixon, and Ford administrations, but only in terms of concentrating on one or another program (Model Cities versus Revenue Sharing) rather than major redefinitions of the causes and cures of disadvantage.

Sources of doctrine

In the 1960s and 1970s the foundations of official antipoverty doctrine have been supplied by the research and theories of academicians and intellectuals. The works of Michael Harrington, Kenneth Clark, Daniel Moynihan, Oscar Lewis, S. M. Miller, and Edward Banfield, to mention some prominent individuals, very largely establish the decision rules within which politicians and administrators operate. It is the thrust of this analysis that only after changing the prevailing doctrine of causes and responses to poverty will disadvantaged groups be able to enter into meaningful exchanges with government. I shall look for support for this hypothesis among the evidence, theories, and assumptions of prevailing social welfare doctrine.

In examining official doctrine, I find that it is clearly beyond the scope of this analysis to place the individual works of Harrington, Clark, and others in their proper place. Even to suggest that one or another writer has a "place" is to imply a consistent or static quality that doctrine lacks. For example, Moynihan's theories and recommendations provided a beacon during the first 2 years of the Nixon administration, even succeeding in gaining Nixon's support for a progressive family income maintenance program. But by 1970, Moynihan's conceptualization of social problems and solutions faded, and the luminary himself shortly departed Washington. In much the same fashion Harrington briefly flashed and quickly dimmed during the Kennedy administration.

It is useful to look at the general contours of antipoverty doctrine rather than specific observers and theorists because I find that there is much commonality as well as difference among the several major contributors. In this manner, I shall examine the works of Oscar Lewis and Edward Banfield. Each has had an individual impact on official doctrine; yet each is representative of other writers (Lewis of Harrington; Banfield of Moynihan) Lewis's work is illustrated in the doctrine of the Kennedy-Johnson era and is still reflected in the liberal view. Banfield was chairman of the Nixon administration's Model Cities Task Force, and his research and theory, as we shall see below, offers intellectual justification for the continued "benign neglect" approach of the Ford White House.

While Banfield's conceptualization of the causes and consequences of poverty is directed to urban environments, his concern with the lower class and its pathologies inscribes a very large proportion of Chicanos because the community is urban dwelling at about the same proportion as the Anglo. Moreover, many of the problems of the lower-class Chicano are a consequence of the high rate of urbanization during the 1960s. Oscar Lewis explicitly includes much of the Chicano population among those he characterizes as possessing the "culture of poverty." In addition, since Lewis's theory is largely derived from research among Spanish-speaking communities and families (in Mexico, Puerto Rico, and New York City, none of whom are Chicano), his work has an *a priori* attraction for decision makers dealing with Chicanos.

In the following summary of the major tenets of the works of Lewis and Banfield, I am principally concerned with the consequences for the Chicano and other disadvantaged communities of the formulation and execution of health and other social policies on the bases of the assumptions and prescriptions of either Lewis's culture of poverty or Banfield's lower-class culture.

Culture of poverty

As presented by Lewis,[7] the culture of poverty originates in an adaptation and reaction of the poor to their marginal position in society. It is a local solution to problems not met by existing institutions and agencies, but it becomes institutionalized and is perpetuated from generation to generation: "By the time slum children are six or seven they have usually absorbed the basic values and attitudes of their subculture and are not psychologically geared to take full advantage of changing conditions or increased opportunities which may occur in their life-times." Social conditions that sustain the culture of poverty are: (1) a cash economy, wage labor, and production for profit; (2) a persistently high rate of unemployment and underemployment of unskilled labor; (3) low wages; (4) the failure to provide social, political, and economic organization, either on a voluntary basis or by government imposition, for the low income population; (5) the existence of a bilateral kinship system rather than a unilateral one; and (6) the existence of a set of values in the dominant class that stresses the accumulation of wealth and property, the possibility of upward mobility and thrift, and explains low economic status as the result of personal inadequacy or inferiority.

Community participation

Although in the United States it may be simpler to eliminate poverty itself than to eliminate the culture of poverty (Lewis seems to rule out the possibility of basic structural changes in the society, changes he sees as having eliminated the culture of poverty in Cuba), Lewis suggests a public policy providing welfare payments to raise the standard of living supplemented by social workers and psychiatrists who assist the rising population to divest itself of the traits associated with its former poverty. As a concomitant of this effort to do something *to* the lower class, Lewis argues that something must be done *with* these individuals: the poor must be brought to effective participation in the major institutions of the larger society. It is their lack of participation, or involvement, that Lewis singles out as the crucial characteristic of the culture of poverty. Get the people into active relationships with schools, museums, art galleries, hospitals, welfare agencies, and government, and there is a presumption that the culture of poverty will be displaced.

Lewis's hand is seen in the War on Poverty's approach to the poor. Children are reached through Head Start, a variety of remedial programs such as English as a second language, familiarization with the dominant culture through trips to museums and concerts, and a host of other efforts aimed at the "culturally deprived." Meanwhile, their parents are brought into federally funded programs that require community participation on planning councils at the neighborhood and higher levels as a condition of funding.

In the health field, the philosophy of community participation is embodied in Public Law 89-749, the Comprehensive Health Planning Act of 1966. This act established as national policy that representatives of the consuming public (as well as health care providers) should be incorporated in local, regional, and state agencies that develop comprehensive programs of health delivery systems. Yet, in many cases "consumer representation" is a myth. For example, the legislation establishing the guidelines of Orange County, California's local planning agency set forth that consumer representatives will be selected "taking into consideration," which presumably means "inclusion of," ethnic and socioeconomic characteristics.[8] But among the 78-member Orange County Health Planning Council in 1972 there was only one member with a Spanish surname, an executive of a national retailing firm. On the important executive board, this man was joined by the wife of a baseball executive, an owner of a locally prominent insurance agency, a judge, and a city councilman, among ten consumer representatives.[9] Examining the regional medical planning councils throughout California's multiethnic counties reveals similar class/ethnic composition.

Negative consequences

Implementing Lewis's model may generate profoundly negative ramifications. What are the consequences for the viability of the Chicano family of an official policy that *assumes* that children are unhealthy because of their parents' beliefs and behavior? Can children be expected to develop or retain any sense of self-respect when they are told their "culture" is counterproductive to their own health and safety? The ego-destroying forces let loose by programs aimed at the "culturally deprived" seem to have social and psychological implications that call for serious consideration. The implications of biculturalism are not eliminated by trips to museums or schoolyard celebrations of Cinco de Mayo.[10]

The tactic of insisting on community participation may be either a crafty means of securing legitimation for programs supported by the existing power structure or it may lead to greater sensitivity and accommodation to the perspectives of the Chicano. However, placing consumer representatives on health-planning agencies, to take one common programmatic example, raises the question of who is capable of representing the Chicano community: upper middle-class businessmen, young activists, rural laborers who speak Spanish only, or recent migrants to the cities? This question raises the issue of whether there is one Chicano or many—whether there is a Chicano culture that is widely shared and that makes all Chicanos brothers and sisters in the sense of mutual recognition of collective problems. The representative's sensitivity and understanding of the realities of the different peoples who are Chicanos is crucial since the more economically disadvantaged and the more isolated spacially and psychologically from existing delivery systems a Chicano is, the more acute the health care problems. How do we obtain the perspectives of the rural, the poor, the non-English speaking? As long as membership on planning bodies and other community-participation agencies is composed of individuals nominated by mayors, county supervisors, medical associations, and other "establishment" institutions, the barrio resident has only a slight chance of gaining a place at the table and no chance at all of obtaining major structural reforms in systems supported by the massive political power of the health care professionals and the political strength of their supporters in state and federal governments.

Community representation and participation are complex problems that affect the success of remedial efforts. Since participation is a cardinal tenet of Lewis's model of the cause and cure of the culture of poverty, a thorough exploration of the implications of participation is in order. One consequence of efforts to gain the participation of Chicano representatives on planning bodies has been the exacerbation of factionalism within the community as various organizations, philosophies, and socioeconomic groups vie for recognition. From the vantage point of many committed to building a broadly based communitywide movement, officially sponsored and encouraged participation smacks of co-optation and divide-and-continue-to-rule tactics engineered by the Anglo-dominated power structure.

Lower-class culture

Banfield draws on a wide range of social science scholarship to find examples of lower-class behavior and its consequences for the broader society. He sees the problems of America's cities in a combined historical (things are not nearly as bad as they used to be) and Social Darwinian (the lower class is responsible) perspective. He argues that the lower class is the *cause,* not the result, of poverty and the social problems associated with poverty. It is lower-class culture that is learned in youth and passed along from generation to generation that is responsible for the city's problems.

"The defining characteristic of a class subculture is . . . one primary factor; namely, psychological orientation toward providing for the future."[11] "At the present-oriented end of the scale, the lower-class individual lives from moment to moment. If he has any awareness of a future, it is of something fixed, fated, beyond his control . . . his bodily needs, (especially for sex) and his taste for 'action' take precedence over everything else—and certainly over any work routine. He works only as he must stay alive . . . he suffers from feelings of self-contempt and inadequacy . . . in his relations with others he is suspicious and hostile, aggressive yet dependent . . . he is a nonparticipant . . . [p. 53]." "The stress on 'action,' risk-taking, conquest, fighting, and 'smartness' makes lower-class life extraordinarily violent [p. 54]." "The lower-class individual lives in the slum and sees little or no reason to complain. He does not care how dirty and dilapidated his housing is either inside or outside, nor does he mind the inadequacy of such public facilities as schools, parks, and libraries: indeed, where such things exist he destroys them by acts of vandalism if he can [p. 62]."

Class and race

The lower-class culture is not necessarily an attribute of any particular segment of the population, but Banfield concedes that "the present lower class is mostly black [p. 212]." He attempts to head off the accusation that his denunciation of the "lower class" is nothing more than a racist attack on Blacks by arguing that it is their culture and not their pigmentation that makes lower-class Blacks undesirable neighbors [p. 69]. Because of the pervasiveness of the lower-class culture in the Black population, "the situation of most Negroes would not be fundamentally different even if there were no racial prejudice at all [p. 85]."

How completely Banfield is committed to the cultural interpretation of the Black's situation in American society is summarized in the following: "If, overnight, [lower class] Negroes turned white, most of them would go on living under much the same handicaps for a long time to come [p. 73]." Banfield sees no conceptual or operational difficulty in separating *race* from *culture* from *social reality.* Those thoughtless or malicious people who blame poverty on Anglo racism, thereby failing to place the rightful responsibility on the improvident behavior of the Blacks themselves, are creating and perpetuating a "reign of error" (Merton's term) about the prevalence of racism, thus creating a self-fulfilling prophesy. (See Banfield's chapter "Race: Thinking May Make It So.")

Quarantine

Banfield has no faith in the social work, psychiatric approach to the lower class; indeed, he doubts that anything can be done to eliminate the psychological and sociological disorders associated with the lower class. He offers several provocative schemes (such as, "It would seem that the problems posed by the lower class can be resolved fundamentally only if the children of that class are removed from their parents' culture [p. 229]") but concludes that none of the basic remedies he sees as feasible is politically acceptable [p. 246]. The range of responses that are acceptable will not affect the problem: job opportunities will be scorned, new curricula will be ignored, law and order will be baffled, welfare checks will be squandered, new housing will be defaced and neglected [pp. 210-211]. "Social workers, teachers, and law-enforcement officials . . . cannot achieve their goals because they can neither change nor circumvent this cultural obstacle [p. 211]." All attempts fail: "The conclusion is unavoidable that for at least several decades there will be a lower class . . . [p. 235]."

Banfield's prescription is to work to the upper boundaries of the lower class and to go no further since there is little or no likelihood that prevailing lower-class norms and life-style can be changed; hence there is an equal improbability that lower-class health profiles can be improved. His heroic pessimism suggests that insofar as the policy maker can determine the overlap of the lower class and the Chicano population, this identity should detour resources elsewhere. Present mortality and morbidity will continue regardless of efforts, so why waste government's resources on lower-class Chicanos? In the words of one former Harvard and Nixon administration colleague, a policy of "benign neglect" is in order.

Response to such a policy might be a wave of righteous indignation at being closed off from the benefits of modern medical science. This uprising could have demonstrable consequences at the ballot box, perhaps even in growing support for militant groups and anti-Anglo violence. Alternatively, the "new" policy of benign neglect might go unnoticed since little is presently being done on behalf of ameliorating the Chicano's health problems.

In following Banfield's plan of (in)action, the policy maker's move to isolate the Chicano comes just when several forces are bringing Chicanos into more extensive interaction with Anglo society. Chicanos are increasingly moving to urban areas outside southern California and the southwest (as many as 250,000 Chicanos live in Chicago). Minority recruitment efforts such as Educational Opportunity Programs, Chicano studies departments, and MECHA and other student organizations are bringing dramatic increases in the numbers of Chicanos on college campuses. Migration, equal employment programs, and new educational opportunities, as well as the mechanization of agriculture, have brought thousands of Chicanos into factory, clerical, sales and service, and white-collar occupations. Cutting off outreach programs and reversing efforts to incorporate Chicanos in self-help, remedial, and community action projects, unless such action is part of a massive, comprehensive new isolate-and-hold-static effort by government and the Anglo society in general, would create confusion, recrimination, and a breakdown of communication.

Can Americans distinguish between class and race?

If the government decision makers take the position that the Chicano community is largely lower class and hence a threat to the culture and institutions of the dominant classes (as would be implicit in accepting Banfield's model as the basis for public policy), a drastic deterioration of Anglo/minority relations would result throughout the society. I do not share Banfield's optimism that Americans care to distinguish between human beings who are Chicanos and Chicanos who are lower class. To say, as Banfield does, that race is not *the* problem, that it is their style of life and not their color that makes many Chicanos unacceptable neighbors, is to ignore the extent to which race and class are seen as identical. It seems to me that in the United States, a Black or a Chicano (or Asian American or native American) is *assumed* to be, regardless of life-style, "an unacceptable neighbor." Let me take one example of the prevailing inability to distinguish fact from fiction when non-Anglo people are involved.

Every reputable study indicates that the overwhelming majority of the Japanese and Japanese Americans living in the United States before and immediately after 7 December 1941 neither gave nor intended to give aid to Japan's aggression against the U.S. But in 1942 *all* Japanese Americans living on the West Coast were rounded up and put into concentration camps. (In Hawaii, where Asians formed a majority of the population, Japanese Americans were not incarcerated.) The American public and its leaders did not have any difficulty distinguishing between subversive and nonsubversive German and Italian Americans; only the Japanese Americans were treated as an undifferentiated monolithic community; only the Japanese Americans aroused passions so frenzied as to drive them into camps. Race or behavior?

The possibility of making distinctions between race and class is further complicated by the fact that many Chicanos are not middle class—thus lending support to the notion that they are also "lower class" in the Banfield/Lewis sense. Perhaps unconsciously, observers generalize what is in fact a complex, class-divided population into a monolith. Note the number of authors who use the term "Spanish-speaking," "Black," or "Asian" when in fact they are referring to the members of a village, region or class, or to the particular customs or behavior of a segment of the overall community.

Consequences of doctrine
Middle-classification

There are two paramount issues raised by the Banfield/Lewis approaches to social policies that deserve serious contemplation. One is the notion that people should be brought to conform to the expectations of the dominant society. Lewis proposes social workers and psychiatrists; Banfield suggests that confinement may be necessary since government probably will not be able to take the children of the lower class from their parents before the younger generation is spoiled. Both writers imply that government, as an agent of the dominant society, should work to change attitudes and behavior that are seen as incompatible with the needs and expectations of existing institutions. Banfield cites and builds his argument on an array of unemployment, criminal, and other demographic data, while Lewis offers vignettes of the life-style of the poor; but when their accounts are stripped of normative interpretations, they portray differences only from middle-class norms. Yet these characterizations are used to support an assault on non–middle-class people— many of whom wish to enjoy social and economic justice but not the life-style, attitudes, and values of the middle class. The Banfield/Lewis approaches seek to change people; since we know that these "people" are largely non-Anglo minorities, these recommendations need sober analysis of their short-run ramifications for interracial relations as well as for their long-range impact on the degree of diversity of life-styles that will be tolerated in the United States.

Blaming the victim

The second major issue stems from the theorists' emphasis on the responsibility of the individual for his or her own plight. Banfield is the most emphatic in placing the blame for the lower class's situation squarely on the class itself: it is the lower class's culture that is the cause, not the result, of poverty. Lewis places the origins of the culture of poverty on the economic and social system, but his focus on the individual and the family directs our attention from existing institutions and suggests the conclusion that the individual must be changed. The effect is to absolve schools, labor unions, corporate industries, hospitals, and similar institutions of responsibility for the poor's plight.

This propensity to look inward rather than at the community's external environment is reflected in the literature on Chicano health problems. While attitudes, beliefs, and folk medicine are the principle foci of scholars, several investigations indicate that the procedures and organization of existing health care delivery systems repulse many Chicanos. For example, the points have been made that those Chicanos who are deeply imbued with traditions of self-diagnoses, or who believe in the magical origins of maladies, or personal modesty are sometimes ridiculed and scorned by scientific providers; many Chicanos are suspicious of hospitals and are unwilling to be hospitalized, perhaps because they are shut off from their families, perhaps because of their inability to communicate with English-only medical personnel; and health care costs, or the fee system itself, constitute an irritant and a hardship for low income Chicanos.[12]

Bureaucratic medicine

It is interesting to note that these areas of friction between the Chicano consumers and the prevailing health care system are essentially the criticisms made by poor and middle-class *Anglos.* Could it be that both Anglos and

Chicanos have a difficult time with the health care industry but that the Chicano's problems are largely ascribed to folk culture when lack of facilities, high costs, and similar situational variables affect the poorer, less mobile, less self-confident, and more inexperienced Chicanos to a greater degree than their Anglo neighbors?

Clearly, the bureaucratic style of modern health systems is a principal variable in the delivery of services, a variable that is ignored by Banfield/ Lewis cultural determinism. For instance, Grebler and his associates, after a major review of the Chicano's relations with existing institutions, conclude that "even if their programs were designed for a minimum of *cultural* friction, their effectiveness in 'reaching' Mexican Americans would depend on their effectiveness of changing their operations so as to reduce the actual exercise of coercive power."[13] Here the emphasis is on the style or quality of the interaction, a condition that, unfortunately, is largely independent of ethnicity: Spanish-speaking health workers can be and often are just as coercive with their clients as Anglos.

The acceptance of either model results in the implicit assumption that the individual will be best served through conforming to the needs and expectations of the provider. It follows, then, that improving health care is contingent upon integrating the Chicano into the routine of the provider. This line of reasoning is reflected in the effort being made by many public health facilities in the southwest to hire bilingual receptionists, paramedical, and professional personnel: these Spanish speakers, most of whom are Chicanos, are used to explain to the patient what is expected by the facility—where to go, what to do, and when to do it.

Policy makers reject community exchanges

Armed with an official doctrine of the causes and consequences of poverty that incorporates the assumptions and recommendations of either Oscar Lewis or Edward Banfield, the policy maker or program administrator is not prepared to accept the proferred resources of Chicanos and other disadvantaged communities, because the decision maker does not accept as valid the proposed utilizations of government's resources. Doctrine places the responsibility for poverty on the poor, not the social, economic, and political institutions of the dominant society. The poor and disadvantaged are to be changed to conform to the needs of these institutions; where remedial efforts have little prospect of short-run success, public resources should not be "wasted." However, programs aimed at changing the attitudes, values, and life-style of future generations, such as Head Start, Upward Bound, and English as a second language, are favorably regarded. Little attention is paid to the chronically unemployed, the elderly, and the unassimilated and unacculturated because individuals so characterized are unable or unwilling to be converted. Whether following Banfield, Lewis, or some combination, the decision maker is disposed to regarding the Anglicization and middle-classification of minorities, not the reform of institutions, as legitimate goals to which government should allocate its resources.

Conflicts of perception

Conditioned by official doctrine and lacking personal experiences that might correct the distortions of this perspective (very few former barrio dwellers or other disadvantaged minorities are found in middle and upper level government positions), most decision makers see the problems and solutions of poverty quite differently than do Chicano activists. For example, consumer participation in the planning, administration, and evaluation of health delivery programs, a demand of many reformers, is rejected by officials because they see consumer control as threatening the "quality" and "professional standards" of these programs.[14] Decision makers see little of value to be gained, either by the government or the local community, from redistributing power from the health professionals to the consumers. Instead, plans are made to expand regional medical centers, prepaid health maintenance organizations operating through outpatient clinics, and educational programs to alert school children to the dangers of traditional (that is, nonAnglo) culture. Activists reject these "solutions" as only further expanding Anglo-dominated bureaucratic control and Anglo-oriented cultural imperialism at the expense of self-determination and cultural heritage.

Doctrine creates blinders

Because both the decision maker and the reformer see little of value to be gained from the resources that they can obtain through an exchange, there is little meaningful bargaining. Since government's resources are far more vital to the Chicano community than vice versa, the community pays a dreadful price in sickness, disease, incapacity, and death.

The possession of resources is a prerequisite for political exchange, but it is only the *potential* to control, to obtain a desired allocation from government. An exchange is made when each party agrees that the proferred deal is acceptable within their respective decision rules. It is my central hypothesis that the decision rules of the United States government, as represented in official antipoverty doctrine, represent a major obstacle to progressive reform leading to social justice. While I have centered my discussion on the government's inability to react effectively to the health care needs of millions of Chicanos, similar situations exist in education, law enforcement, employment opportunities, and other social policy areas, and for all minority communities as well. My conclusion is that a precondition to alleviating the gross disadvantages that the minorities suffer is the changing of prevailing doctrine. Only when this occurs will decision makers be able to comprehend and appreciate the merit and value of the demands for reform both to the disadvantaged and to government.

Moving toward community self-determination

In order to change prevailing doctrine, people must take action on several fronts. Obviously, the election and appointment to decision-making posts of increased numbers of Chicanos will bring experience and knowledge to replace ignorance and distortion. But even if Chicanos are able to win something close to parity in the decision-making cadre of government, a prospect that is almost utopian given the present number of Chicano decision makers, there simply will not be Chicanos in most of the strategic political and administrative positions. This is not cause for abandoning the organization and mobilization of the community for electoral political action; such activity is required to strengthen the overall bargaining position of the community. Greater electoral strength and more victories have important effects on local situations and on community morale, but electoral politics can be expected to have little impact on prevailing doctrine.

Since most antipoverty doctrine emanates from academic institutions, Chicanos can avail themselves of Chicano studies programs, foundations, and government grants to develop new information and to present valid data about the community. In this manner both the Chicano and academic communities will be served, the former by greater exposure of its positive as well as negative dimensions, the latter by the evolution of scholarship to higher levels of comprehensiveness and accuracy.

More Chicanos should be encouraged to enter the social sciences since scholars and intellectuals generate the materials that form the foundations of official doctrine. The merit in expanding the number of Chicano social scientists is revealed in the answer to the question of who is more likely to interpret correctly the problems and realities of the Chicano community—a middle-class Anglo sociologist or a Chicano sociologist who has been reared in a barrio and received a first-class social science education. Many young Chicanos feel that they can best serve their people through a career in law or medicine. And undoubtedly such careers can make important contributions. If the foregoing analysis is correct, however, the long-run problems of the barrio that the lawyer or physician treats can be corrected only by political action. To this end, identifying the strengths and problems of the barrio through research and publication may well perform a greater service and make a more profound change in the allocation patterns involving the barrio than can be won by a hundredfold increase in lawyers or physicians.

If the preceding assessment of the nature of the forces confronting those committed to reforming the barrio and eliminating the disadvantages of the Chicano community is correct, the optimal strategy for those seeking change is a partnership of activists and progressive intellectuals. Without the former, the community will be in no position to bargain; without the latter, the government decision makers will be unreceptive to demands for basic changes.

Notes

1. A discussion of resource exchange is presented in Warren P. Ilchman and Norman Thomas Uphoff, *The Political Economy of Change* (Berkeley: University of California Press, 1970), p. 58 and *passim*. For a more detailed presentation of the exchange theory presented in this chapter, see Jerry L. Weaver, *Conflict and Control in Health Care Administration* (Beverly Hills, Calif.: Sage Publications, Inc., 1975).
2. A. Taher Moustafa and Gertrud Weiss, *Health Status and Practices of Mexican Americans. Mexican-American Study Project, Advanced Report II* (Los Angeles: Graduate School of Business Administration, UCLA, 1968).
3. Paul M. Sheldon, "Community Participation and the Emerging Middle Class," in Julian

Samora (editor), *La Raza: Forgotten Americans* (Notre Dame: University of Notre Dame Press, 1966), pp. 125-157.

4. See the discussion in Chapter 4.

5. John Kenneth Galbraith, *American Capitalism: The Concept of Countervailing Power* (Boston: Houghton Mifflin Co., 1956).

6. Compare with Barbara Ehrenreich and John Ehrenreich, *The American Health Empire: Power, Profits, and Politics* (New York: Vintage Books, 1971); Medical Committee for Human Rights, *Billions for Band-Aids: An Analysis of the U.S. Health Care System and of Proposals for its Reform* (San Francisco: Medical Committee for Human Rights, 1972).

7. Based on the Introduction to Oscar Lewis, *La Vida: A Puerto Rican Family in the Culture of Poverty—San Juan and New York* (New York: Random House, 1965); also see *The Study of Slum Culture: Background for "La Vida"* (New York: Random House, Inc., 1968); and "The Culture of Poverty," in John J. Tepaske and S. B. Fischer (editors), *Explosive Forces in Latin America* (Columbus: Ohio State University Press, 1964), pp. 149-173.

8. Resolution of the Board of Supervisors of Orange County, Calif., 26 Jan. 1971.

9. The local medical lobby, the Orange County Medical Association, is allotted four seats on the Council (and the overall provider-community, including representatives from the nursing and hospital associations, were given 4 of the 14 seats on the Executive Board), but the Medical Association refused to participate on the grounds that the Council is "too political" and has "too many consumers as members." See the Santa Ana, Calif. *Register*, 21 July 1971.

10. Several authors have argued that Chicano parents are responsible for the poor health and social and economic failures of their children. See Frank C. Nall and Joseph Speilberg, "Social and Cultural Factors in the Responses of Mexican-Americans to Medical Treatment," *Journal of Health and Human Behavior* 8 (Dec. 1967), pp. 299-308; Celia S. Heller, *Mexican American Youth: Forgotten Youth at the Crossroads* (New York: Random House, Inc., 1966); Ari Kiev, *Curanderismo: Mexican-American Folk Psychiatry* (New York: The Free Press, 1968). See the rejoinder by Miguel Monteil, "The Social Science Myth of the Mexican-American Family," *El Grito* 3 (Summer 1970), pp. 56-63.

11. Edward C. Banfield, *The Unheavenly City: The Nature and Future of Our Urban Crisis* (Boston: Little, Brown and Co., 1968), p. 47. Page numbers in brackets refer to this edition.

12. Arthur J. Rubel, *Across the Tracks: Mexican-Americans in a Texas City* (Austin: University of Texas Press, 1966); William Madsen, *Mexican-Americans of Texas* (New York: Holt, Rinehart and Winston, Inc., 1964); Marvin Karno and Robert B. Edgerton, "Perception of Mental Illness in a Mexican-American Community," *Archives of General Psychiatry* 20 (Feb. 1969), pp. 233-238; Margaret Clark, *Health in the Mexican-American Culture* (Berkeley: University of California, 1959); Jerry L. Weaver, "Health Care Costs as a Political Issue: Comparative Responses of Chicanos and Anglos," *Social Science Quarterly* 53 (March 1973), pp. 846-854.

13. Leo Grebler, Joan W. Moore, and Ralph C. Guzman, *The Mexican American People: The Nation's Second Largest Minority* (New York: The Free Press, 1970), p. 529.

14. For example, the observation of the director of a major medical center: "A few misguided individuals . . . have already assured the community that it does in fact have all the requisite competence to manage its health needs. For them it can only be said that their least offense is lying, their worst a demeaning attempt to endear themselves to their own personal constituency." From Leonard W. Cronkhite, Jr., "What are the Conflicts Involved in Community Control?" in John C. Norman (editor), *Medicine in the Ghetto* (New York: Appleton-Century-Crofts, 1969), p. 284.

CHAPTER 10 Common bases of health care problems

In the preceding chapters I have used the notion of *community* to organize and convey the discussion of health care behavior, attitudes, and problems. The strategy of conceptualizing American society in terms of communities rather than strata or classes reflects the belief that many important differences as well as similarities within and among racial and ethnic groups are distorted or ignored as a result of using the more conventional analytical devices. The significance of the way we conceptualize and think about problems was demonstrated in Chapter 9 where we saw that theoretical abstractions such as the "culture of poverty" and the "lower-class culture" actually predispose policy makers to accept some and reject other policy alternatives. By thinking in terms of community, I feel that it may be possible to recognize issues and problems not otherwise likely to emerge. As we have seen, racial, ethnic, age, and gender characteristics, quite apart from other demographic factors, are associated with important health care characteristics.

In this final chapter I shall draw together several threads that run through my reviews of the different communities. This is not a final effort to gloss over the idiosyncratic needs and preferences that I have labored so long in developing; rather, it is an attempt to illustrate that while apparent differences have been identified, they often stem from common roots. For instance, we have observed that many Japanese travel great distances to obtain treatment from fellow community members while many Blacks obtain their health care from outpatient clinics and emergency rooms of public hospitals. Yet this quite distinct behavior may reflect the shortage of "suitable" providers. Working out what "suitable" providers are may again lead to divergence with the Japanese community definition of suitable being a Japanese and the Black community a Black. But this in turn leads to the "common" conclusion that the federal government, through both pressure for affirmative action and allocations of revenues to medical schools, *could* play a major role in correcting these apparently different problems.

I shall examine four general issues that emerge from the preceding analysis and that connect the health industry, the political system, and the minority communities. They are conceptualized as characteristics of the delivery system, consumer information, social network, and alienation.

Characteristics of the delivery system

While I have avoided a detailed analysis of the structural features of the personal health care industry, it is clear from the foregoing that several features of the organization and delivery of services are at the root of many health care problems. Three of these problem areas that the foregoing analysis points to as especially significant for minority communities are costs, availability, and bureaucratic style.

Costs

It is apparent that the general public is concerned about the steadily rising spiral of health costs. In good measure, the "politics of health," both in Congress and the mass media, is a reflection of the awareness by those who are themselves little inconvenienced by these rising costs about which the public is (or should be) concerned. While its advocates argue that national health insurance will lead to lower annual increases or perhaps a steadying of costs, it is not clear—judging from the impact of Medicare—that the fee schedule of health services will be controlled by enactment of NHI. Yet as prices rise, there can be expected to be more and more concern and growing clamor for relief.

There is a strong but not conclusive case to be made for the proposition that cost is the principal barrier to preventive care and timely remediation. An equally strong case can be made for the argument that available income in a population is a determinant of providers' decisions on where to locate their practice. Thus, efforts to attack costs either by providing greater funds for buying services or through regulating charges (or both) might overcome a major barrier to utilization. It must be noted, however, that it has not been demonstrated that cost equally affects decisions to seek care for different health problems. That is, available financial resources may not carry equal weight in deciding whether or not to obtain dental care, prenatal examinations, preventive checkups, elective surgery, treatment of chronic but nonthreatening complaints, and so forth. Nor is it clear that costs affect equally the health behavior of members of the various communities. Much more work needs to be done on the significance of economic factors in decisions to seek or refrain from care.

Availability of providers

We have seen a substantial body of literature calling attention to the unavailability of private practitioners, hospital beds, and health and hospital insurance. However, geographic proximity and accessibility is only one dimension of availability. Without information, potential patients cannot utilize providers. Without transportation, even a mile or two may render a provider inaccessible. (We saw that the frequency of contacting a provider decreases the further elderly Seattle Pilipinos had to travel to obtain care.) And because of language barriers or personal preferences, members of ethnic communities are often unable to locate or visit "acceptable" providers.

Potentially, there are several responses open to government. Perhaps the least financially costly and quickest to produce an increase in the number of providers would be changing licensing requirements to make foreign trained personnel more easily certified. Or, new categories of primary care providers could be created, such as nurse practitioners or physician extenders who could handle a wide range of curative and prescriptive services, thereby freeing the physician for procedures requiring greater training and sophistication. However, any reform, such as the return of midwifery, aside from simply increasing the pool of available providers, has far-reaching social and psychological implications.

It is the presence of these social and psychological implications, as well as the political and economic power and preference of major provider interest groups such as the AMA, that make governmental responses to demands for more providers so difficult. Would minority communities utilize providers who are not "full doctors"? Would not the creation of more categories of providers merely create additional layers of bureaucracy and further fragmentation, delay, and confusion for the consumer? More facilities are called for, but what kinds of facilities should be constructed—neighborhood clinics, major medical centers, 60- to 200-bed voluntary hospitals? Do we concentrate equipment and expertise in prepaid medical plans, or in health maintenance organizations? Or do we provide incentives to providers to establish practices in underdoctored areas, or disincentives for locating or joining specialities where there is a surplus of providers? Can we expect providers to go where they are needed if fee-for-service is allowed to operate as a means of determining supply and utilization?

Bureaucratic style

In coping with demands for more providers and facilities, we must keep in mind that we have seen a great deal of both direct and inferential evidence that it is the style of services obtained by minorities that contributes to their dissatisfaction and, perhaps, their lower rates of utilization. Bureaucratic style is encountered throughout the medical delivery industry-from the huge hospital that paints different colored lines on its floor from the reception desk down into a maze of corridors and expects hurt, frightened, and uninitiated people to follow summary instructions to a prescribed destination, on one hand, to the impersonalism and lack of understanding revealed in the physician's examining room, on the other. A classic example of the thoughtless ethnocentrism of the "bureaucratic provider" was reported by a south Texas Chicano; after a physician had laughed at the Chicano's diagnosis that his wife's complaint was the result of witchcraft, the physician ordered the lady to undress. "This I could not stand, that my wife should be naked with this man. We never returned, of course, and my wife was treated by a [folk healer]. Maybe Anglos let doctors stare at their wives' bodies and fool with them but not me. And the fool did not even know about *susto* [magically induced "fright"]. He is lucky I did not reduce his arrogance right there."[1]

It is this lack of understanding of the need for dignity, compassion, and respect for the values of its clients that is at the bottom of many complaints about bureaucratic medicine. How much of the bureaucratic style is a consequence of the organization of health care delivery in large hierarchically structured, task-specific facilities? Or is it a consequence of the middle-class cultural bias in the education and recruitment of providers and the dominance of the industry by the upper middle-class, highly educated male physician? What would be the results for the style of delivery of placing consumers in positions of planning, administrating, and evaluating delivery facilities?

Government bears a large part of the responsibility for these characteristics of the delivery system.[2] Through various construction programs, research funding, tax incentives, and educational subsidies, its policies have stimulated the growth of regional medical centers, research and teaching hospitals, and group health plans. Attempts to "rationalize" the industry through regional planning have reinforced the concentration of services: it is widely held that centralization removes duplication, strengthens research, makes supportive technology and services more readily available to both provider and consumer, and allows facilities to benefit from "efficiencies of scale" in negotiating contracts with suppliers, buying utilities, and scheduling procedures in high overhead units.

Bigness also facilitates capital formation, which, in turn, stimulates equipment manufacturers to develop ever more elaborate new technology. It is arguable that massive technology has made very little contribution to the nation's collective well being and that capital invested elsewhere would produce a greater savings in costs to individuals and the society arising from illness. It is also arguable that size brings inefficiencies in the form of highly specialized programs or equipment that rarely if ever is used at optimal workload. Open-heart surgery units may be an example.

Critics claim that government shares much of the responsiblility for rising health costs because little is done to control charges, to outlaw price fixing, or to restrict indirect costs, such as advertising, research and development, and exclusive patents, that find their way into the consumer's bills. Physicians, for example, are not free in most states to post prices or to advertise their services. The operation of the health insurance system, whereby insurance companies accept increased charges from providers and simply pass along increased premium costs to consumer, has been cited as a principal stimulant of health cost inflation. In this payment system, there is no incentive for the delivery industry to economize and no leverage in the hands of consumers to generate competitive pricing, because as individuals they directly pay only a small portion of the provider's charges. Efforts by government to "rationalize" the industry through planning, insurance, construction and research grants, and welfare programs for the medically indigent apparently result in strengthening those institutions that are least vulnerable to consumer demands for better service and moderate costs: medical centers, giant insurance companies, pharmaceutical houses, and medical technology producers.[3]

Consumer information

For all of its recent notoriety, "freedom of information" is little practiced in the policy-making arenas of government. Only a few nonofficials know the procedures and personalities that determine health policies. And, judging from the case of national health insurance, I believe that little effort is being made to enlighten the general public or to permit new actors such as representatives of minority communities (which, given our definition of "minority," includes consumers as a group) into the decision process.

On another level, although there is considerable evidence that some environmental pollutants, food additives, occupational procedures, and diets may be related to cancers, heart disease, chronic disabilities, and other health threats, to date the federal government has done little to alert the public, stimulate consumer education, or fund potentially conclusive research. More aggressive public interest educational programs on the part of the Food and Drug Administration, the National Institutes of Health, the Environmental Protection Agency, and similar organizations could produce information very useful to consumers and policy makers alike.

The review of how information about health providers is disseminated through ethnic communities reveals that there is a significant degree of difference in the utilization of printed material and the mass media. These differences, however, merely reflect the basic differences in communications' networks among the several communities. As noted in Chapter 2, health educators must take the particularities of the populations into account. Using visible leaders and spokespersons, national organizations, and community media would be an effective means of reaching almost all sectors of the Japanese community because of its complex integration through multiple institutions. But relying on the equivalent means would produce little communication or education throughout other more loosely tied communities such as the Pilipino or the Black.

It seems one of the imperatives of improved health care that much closer attention be given to the ramifications for health behavior and attitudes of social networks—especially in light of the evident dissimilarities that characterize the various communities within the national population. I think it a fair operational hypothesis that much if not most of the educational efforts presently aimed at minority communities are largely wasted because they fail to be properly introduced to the rank and file of the populations. Both cultural anthropologists and sociologists could make major contributions in developing ways to use social structures in the fight against disease and disability.

Social network

A concomitant of using community to organize the analysis is the emergence of social network as a major explainer of behavior and attitudes. Social network refers to the interaction of structural and psychological relations within a particular population.[4] It implies more than just social or economic intercourse; it implies binding ties. For example, while Japanese may confine much of the commercial, recreational, and cultural activities to the community, it is the *strength* of the community as a reference group, a source of values and criteria for evaluating and controlling their behavior, that provides the durability and continuity conceptualized as social network. As was noted in the discussion of women as an emerging community, it is the set of interactions and supporting attitudes and values that is as yet only vaguely developed and limited to only a small portion of the gender group. When the responses of the elderly and feminists to their particular collective health care problems are compared, the extent and vitality of their individual social networks appear to be powerful factors in explaining the present and future impact of public policy.

Social network also directs us to two related phenomena that have a major bearing on health care behavior and attitudes: acculturation and assimilation.

Acculturation

Acculturation refers to the taking on and internalization of a particular set of beliefs, values, practices, symbols, and attitudes. Acculturation is expressed in life-style—language, diet, interpersonal behavior, choice of leisure activities, and so forth. When social scientists speak of subcultures or folk cultures, they are indicating that the subject of the discussion manifests a life-style distinct from that that they consider normal. "Normal" is determined by the life-style of the dominant (majority) element of the society.

Where communal social networks are strong, members may be acculturated into one, two, or more sets of values and attitudes. This is the case for most Nisei: while they were instructed in Japanese customs during their early childhood, most also received, largely through the public schools, an overlay of "American" culture. The children of the Nisei, the Sansei, however, although they are racially different from the Anglo, share almost none of the Japanese norms of their grandparents.[5] Thus, racial or demographic characteristics often are not good clues to an individual's life-style.

While it is often difficult to predict the extent and substance of acculturation, this in no way reduces its significance. Acculturation is the social mechanism through which much of the distinctiveness that has been documented above is imparted and reinforced.

Assimilation

While acculturation is an important determinant of health care behavior and attitudes, we must bear in mind that groups that appear "Americanized" in cultural practices may still demonstrate little integration into or appreciation of the institutions of the dominant society. The case of the elderly is illustrative: in spite of decades of Anglo acculturation, more and more elderly persons are found to be almost completely contained within a social subsystem composed of fellow elderly individuals. The same subsystem containment is true for the vast majority of Blacks.

This social separation, quite apart from any cultural distinctiveness of the population under discussion, may be said to reflect an unwillingness or inability to join (or in the case of the elderly, to remain) with the dominant society. Assimilation, then, refers to the extent to which primary and secondary social relations are integrated with the processes and institutions of the dominant society. Racial and ethnic groups are often acculturated but not assimilated. Aside from the communities dealt with here, see the vast research on "white ethnics" such as the Italians, Irish, Poles, Jews, and Greeks.[6]

The importance for health policy makers of the content and extentiveness of acculturation is self-evident: ethnic communities require special consideration because of language, diet, value, interpersonal style, and other cultural particularities. Institutions of the dominant society such as schools, corporations, unions, and, of course, hospitals and other health delivery facilities can hardly be expected to complete effective, efficient interactions with non-Anglos if cultural differences remain unrecognized.

But how are they to react to cultural differences? By hiring bicultural personnel? Requiring staff to attend sensitivity-type instruction? By bringing community members into the organization? Or by simply ignoring cultural factors and demanding as a price of admission and treatment that the consumer adapt to the needs of the institution?

An equally complex, and perhaps even more baffling, problem is presented by the unassimilated. The "melting pot" thesis mentioned in Chapter 1 is so pervasive that many decision makers fail to recognize that millions of Americans operate with a complex independent set of imperatives that keep them largely separate from the dominant society's values and institutions. Sometimes decision makers, perhaps raising Americanization to a normative prescription, refuse to accept unassimilation as legitimate. Either or both positions are likely to frustrate the ability of community representatives to secure popularly desired enactments.

Parenti argues that despite a wide degree of second and third generation "Americanization," (1) residual ethnic cultural valuations and attitudes persist; acculturation is far from complete; (2) the vast pluralistic parallel systems of ethnic social and institutional life show impressive viability; structural assimilation seems neither inevitable nor imminent; and (3) psychological feelings of minority group identity, both of the positive enjoyment and negative defensive varieties, are still deeply internalized. The evidence he adduces for these conclusions include the following. First, increases in education have not necessarily led to a diminished ethnic consciousness. Surely this is the case for the Japanese and for the Black intellectuals and college students who popularized "Black is Beautiful" and other manifestations of racial pride and cultural distinctiveness. Second, increases in income and adaptation to middle-class styles have not noticeably diminished the viability and frequency of ethnic formal and informal structural associations. Third, geographical dispersion, like occupational and class mobility, has been greatly overestimated. And even without geographic contiguity, socially and psychologically contiguous ethnic communities persist. Finally, intergroup contacts that may occur do not necessarily lead to a lessened ethnic awareness; they may serve to activate a new and positive appreciation of personal ethnic identity. Or intergroup contacts may often be abrasive and therefore conducive to ethnic defensiveness and compensatory in-group militancy.[7] (We need but substitute "minority" for "ethnic" to broaden this analysis to cover women and the elderly.)

With the present proliferation of life-styles and concern for individuality plus a continuation of identity-asserting demands by an ever growing number of groups within the society, the problems that diverse acculturation possesses for the health industry are multiplied manyfold. Working out a resolution of the apparent conflict between the demands of organizations for conformity, uniformity, efficiency and effectiveness, and control over their environments, on the one side, and the demands from consumers for humane, technologically expert, financially reasonable, speedy care, on the other, presents in microcosm one of the central dilemmas of postindustrial society: the individual's preference versus organizational "rationality." Moreover, not even an outline of a solution to this conflict has as yet emerged. It is a problem worthy of the society's best minds and most sincere determination.

Alienation

The great contribution of the concept social network is its linking together the social and psychological aspects of the individual's existence. Social network directs us not only to the structural aspects of interactions but also to their cognitive and normative consequences.

Alienation, like social network, is a potentially powerful analytical tool. After an intensive review of the literature dealing with health care utilization, McKinlay concluded that "the concept of alienation could make a considerable contribution to the explanation of utilization behavior. . . ."[8] The power of alienation arises from its use to link situational factors to motivation.

Marx placed alienation in the center of his scheme of class conflict and gave it a principal motivational role. For him, alienation refers to the phenomenon that arises when people are estranged from the products of their mental, physical, and social activity. Alienation arises from the organization of the means of production, in particular, from capitalism. But Marx failed to take the notion of alienation beyond the narrow question of economic alienation or, for that matter, to suggest alienation as it might arise out of forms of production other than capitalism (such as socialism).[9]

Other analysts, however, have recognized the potential utility of a concept that relates situational and motivational factors. The result has been a series of theories that describe alienation as a condition of "socially induced neurosis."[10] Characteristics of this neurosis include the ideas of powerlessness, meaninglessness, normlessness, value isolation, and self-estrangement. In part, the interest social scientists have shown in alienation as a correlant of social position derives from its prominence in the works of such leading theorists as Weber, Durkheim, Tönnies, and Mannheim. And in part, as Seeman and Evans point out, conceptualization of alienation in terms of powerlessness, normlessness, and so forth, when turned about, represents a powerful array of humanistic values: mastery and autonomy, insight and understanding, order and trust, consensus and commitment, integrity and involvement.[11]

While in the medical sociology literature assertions abound that one or another group of people (usually low income and /or ethnic minority) avoid health care facilities because of their alienation from the institutions of the dominant society, there is little empirical investigation of this hypothesized relationship. Nevertheless, attempts have been made to relate alienation to health care behavior through studies of patients in hospital wards,[12] utilization of well-child programs,[13] acceptance of polio vaccine,[14] family planning,[15] participation in prenatal care,[16] and use of preventive health care services.[17]

The results of these investigations are inconclusive, in part because of methodological shortcomings in sampling.[18] Moreover, it appears that not all operational indices of alienation (such as powerlessness and social isolation) produce consistently high intercorrelations, thus suggesting that scale items may be measuring different personality and attitudinal dimensions.[19] But even with these limitations in mind, preliminary findings suggest that a great deal of further attention should be given to alienation.

For instance, Morris, Hatch, and Chipman report that alienation is inversely associated with the number of immunizations that mothers obtain for their infants. Bullough found alienation to be strongly associated with family-planning behavior and, to a lesser degree, with dental care and with maternal and well-baby care. Moody and Gray discovered that "the higher the subjects' alienation scores, the lower their oral polio immunization participation when controlling for both measures of socioeconomic status and social participation."[20]

The speculation I offered about the greater willingness of non-Anglos to support reforms of health industry reflecting their greater overall dissatisfaction with or even alienation from institutions of the dominant society is indirectly supported by findings from two studies that compared the alienation profiles of low income Anglos and Blacks. Both Bullough and Morris, Hatch, and Chipman report higher alienation scores for Blacks. In the former study, Chicano profiles also ranked above Anglos'. Thus, utilization patterns as well as attitudes toward the industry among minority communities to a great degree may be affected by alienation.

Lest we draw the conclusion that little or nothing can be done to change this behavior since alienation is an "untreatable chronic condition," Dean cautions that it is perfectly reasonable to speculate that alienation is not at all a personality trait, but a situation-relevant variable. It is plausible, he suggests, that an individual might have a high alienation coefficient in regard to political activity, but a low one in regard to religion. From this conjecture we can hypothesize that the style of delivery, personnel encountered, price, or any number of other factors may be related to high alienation from health care among minority communities. If this is the case, then it follows that lower alienation and, therefore, higher utilization could be achieved by procedural and structural reforms of the delivery system. Contrary to the recommendations reviewed in Chapter 9, it may not be necessary to middle-classify minorities to increase their participation.

Be this as it may, the existing research using alienation as a major tool is sufficiently suggestive to warrant further work.

Conclusion

Responding creatively and constructively to the diversity and complexity of the needs and demands of minority communities requires effort by community leaders, the health industry, and policy makers alike. They must carefully select their own priorities, marshall their resources, and initiate and carry out their programs and projects. But for any real improvement in the quantity and quality of health care to be seen, the efforts of these three actors must be integrated and coordinated. To a very large degree, the present state of inefficiency, confusion, and criticism that characterizes the American health industry reflects the inability or unwillingness of community, industry, and government to work together.

But herein lies a dilemma: whose priorities, resources, and efforts are to take precedence? Can the demands of the communities be met without subordinating industry and government to community control? Many have answered yes. Their response is to stress-increased productivity through "rationalizing" the delivery of health care as the solution to present short-comings. They recommend greater reliance on planning, health education, and structural reforms such as prepaid plans, health maintenance organizations national health insurance, and other measures that shift economic burdens and increase cost-effectiveness through managerial control. No mutually exclusive or irreconcilable interests are seen among community, industry, and government. The argument concludes that incremental, piecemeal changes will produce results satisfactory to the three parties involved.
parties involved.

Alternatively, it is argued that the defects in the performance of the health industry "are duplicated in many other areas of American society, and that the roots of these defects lie deep in the structure of a class society and create great difficulties for the effective articulation of social needs as political demands and their translation into legislation and subsequent administrative implementation."[21] This view holds that both the industry and government reflect the interests, values, and power of the dominant economic elements of the society. And the long-run self-interest of this element, called by Domhoff the "ruling classes"[22] and Mills the "power elite,"[23] are not consonant with the basic redefinition of relationships of power, status, and wealth, which is a prerequisite to improving the lot of the minority communities and other elements of the mass society. Here the assumption is that no meaningful improvement of the "second-class" health industry is possible, because those who control it serve and reflect the preferences not of the masses but of those who enjoy economic and political privileges. Turning to government for assistance in carrying out needed reforms, so this argument runs, will prove ineffective since politicians, planners, policy makers, and bureaucrats serve their elite masters, not the masses. At the very best, community interests will be tolerated only as long as they pose no threat to the social and economic institutions of the dominant society. Beyond this point government will not go.[24]

As Alford points out, "Successes in bringing about health insurance, health maintenance organizations, and comprehensive prepaid care—valid and valuable though they are—do not rule out a more comprehensive attempt to change health institutions in ways which will fundamentally alter the pervasive tendency to reproduce continously the same problems and defects, year after year, despite reforms."[25] Are these changes possible? Are they likely to be forthcoming? It may be that the most important result of studying minority communities is the light that it sheds on answering the question: Can social justice in the form of equal access to quality health care be realized within the constraints of America's prevailing social and economic institutions? In the year of our Bicentennial the answer is surely negative. Perhaps 1984 offers an appropriate point for another critical assessment.

Notes

1. Quoted in William Madsen, *Mexican-Americans of South Texas* (New York: Holt, Rinehart and Winston, Inc., 1964), p. 92.

2. James F. Blumstein and Michael Zubkoff, "Perspectives on Government Policy in the Health Sector," *Milbank Memorial Fund Quarterly* 51 (Summer 1973), pp. 395-431; Howard A. Palley, "Policy Formulation in Health: Some Considerations of Governmental Constraints on Pricing in the Health Delivery System," *American Behavioral Scientists* 17 (March/April 1974), pp. 572-584; Anne R. Somers, "Regulation of Hospitals," *Annals of the American Academy of Political and Social Sciences* 400 (March 1972), pp. 69-81; Barbara Ehrenreich and John Ehrenreich, *The American Health Empire: Power, Profits, and Politics* (New York: Vintage Books, 1971).

3. For two critiques of government's role, one polemical, the other "scholarly," see Elizabeth Harding, Tom Bodenheimer, and Steve Cummings (editors), *Billions for Band-Aids: An Analysis of the U.S. Health Care System and of Proposals for its Reform* (San Francisco: Medical Committee for Human Rights, 1972); Roger M. Battistella, "Rationalization of Health Services: Political and Social Assumptions," *International Journal of Health Services* 2 (1972), pp. 331-348. Also see Harry Schwartz, "Health Care in America: A Heretical Diagnosis," *Saturday Review* (14 Aug. 1971), pp. 14-15, 55; Robert R. Alford, "The Political Economy of Health Care: Dynamics Without Change, *Politics and Society* 2 (Winter 1972), pp. 127-164; Milton I. Roemer, "Nationalized Medicine for America," *Trans-Action* 8 (Sept. 1971), pp. 31-36; Eliot Friedson, *Profession of Medicine* (New York: Dodd, Mead & Co., 1970).

4. See John B. McKinlay, "Some Approaches and Problems in the Study of the Use of Services—An Overview," *Journal of Health and Social Behavior* 13 (June 1972), p. 131.

5. Acculturation has been widely used in analyzing the Japanese American community. See Minaka Kurokawa, "Acculturation and Childhood Accidents Among Chinese and Japanese Americans," *Genetic Psychology Monographs* 79 (1969), pp. 89-159; Kiyoshi Nagata, "A Statistical Approach to the Study of Acculturation of an Ethnic Group Based on Communication-Oriented Variables: The Case of the Japanese-Americans in Chicago," (Ph. D. dissertation, University of Illinois, Urbana, 1969); F. K. Gerrien, Abe Arkoff, and Shinkuro Iwahara, "Generation Difference in Values: Americans, Japanese-Americans, and Japanese," *Journal of Social Psychology* 71 (April 1967), pp. 169-175; Harumi Befu, "Contrastive Acculturation of California Japanese Comparative Approach to the Study of Immigrants," *Human Organization* 24 (Fall 1965), pp. 209-216; William Peterson, *Japanese Americans: Oppression and Success* (New York: Random House, Inc., 1971); Harry H. L. Kitano, *Japanese Americans: The Evolution of a Subculture* (Englewood Cliffs, N.J.: Prentice-Hall, Inc., 1969).

6. Milton M. Gordon, *Assimilation in American Life* (New York: Oxford University Press, 1964); Erich Rosenthal, "Acculturation Without Assimilation?" *American Journal of Sociology* 66 (Nov. 1960), pp. 275-288.

7. Michael Parenti, "Ethnic Politics and the Persistence of Ethnic Identification," *American Political Science Review* 61 (Sept. 1967), p. 724.

8. McKinlay, "Some Approaches," p. 125.

9. See John O'Neill, *Sociology as a Skin Trade: Essays Towards a Reflexive Sociology* (New York: Torchbooks, 1972), pp. 113-136.

10. *Ibid.,* p. 131.

11. Melvin Seeman and John W. Evans, "Alienation and Learning in a Hospital Setting," *American Sociological Review* 27 (Dec. 1962), p. 772.

12. *Ibid.,* p. 772.

13. Naomi M. Morris, Martha H. Hatch, and Sidney S. Chipman, "Alienation as a Deterrent to Well-Child Supervision," *American Journal of Public Health* 56 (Nov. 1966), pp. 1874-1882.

14. Philip M. Moody and Robert M. Gray, "Social Class, Social Intergration, and the Use of Preventive Health Services," in E. Gartly Jaco (editor), *Patients, Physicians and Illness*, ed. 2 (New York: The Free Press, 1972), pp. 250-261.

15. H. T. Groat and A. G. Neal, "Social Psychological Correlates of Urban Fertility," *American Sociological Review* 32 (Dec. 1967), pp. 945-959; A. G. Neal and H. T. Groat, "Alienation Correlates of Catholic Fertility," *American Journal of Sociology* 76 (Nov. 1970), pp. 460-473.

16. A. Yankauer and others, "An Evaluation of Prenatal Care and Its Relationship to Social

Class and Social Disorganization," *American Journal of Public Health* 43 (Aug. 1953), pp. 1001-1010.

17. Bonnie Bullough, "Poverty, Ethnic Identity and Preventive Health Care," *Journal of Health and Social Behavior* 13 (Dec. 1972), pp. 347-359.

18. Morris, Hatch, and Chipman, "Alienation," have a "southern, lower class, semirural largely Negro clinic population . . ." p. 1874; Seeman and Evans, "Alienation and Learning," a white male sample.

19. See Dwight G. Dean, "Alienation: Its Meaning and Measurement," *American Sociological Review* 26 (Oct. 1961), pp. 753-758.

20. Moody and Gray, "Social Class," p. 260.

21. Robert R. Alford, *Health Care Politics: Ideological and Interest Group Barriers to Reform* (Chicago: University of Chicago Press, 1975), p. 263.

22. G. William Domhoff, *Who Rules America?* (Englewood Cliffs, N.J.: Prentice-Hall, Inc., 1967).

23. C. Wright Mills, *The Power Elite* (New York: Oxford University Press, 1956).

24. There is a vast amount of literature arguing the composition, span of control, recruitment and socialization, and access by the mass to the political elite. The present analysis reflects the views and research of Gerhard Lenski, *Power and Privilege: A Theory of Social Stratification* (New York: McGraw-Hill Book Co., 1966); Paul Baran and Paul Sweezy, *Monopoly Capital* (New York: Monthly Review Press, 1966); and Michael Parenti, *Democracy for the Few* (New York: St. Martin's Press, Inc., 1974). For a comprehensive survey of community power (that is, subnational politics) research, see John Walton, "The Bearing of Social Science Research on Public Issues: Floyd Hunter and the Study of Power," in John Walton and Donald E. Carns (editors), *Cities in Change: Studies on the Urban Condition* (Boston: Allyn & Bacon, Inc., 1973), pp. 318-332.

25. Alford, *Health Care Politics*, p. 266.